PENGUIN BOOKS
ISLAND OF BLOOD

Anita Pratap has worked for leading Indian and American newspapers and magazines, including *Sunday*, *Indian Express*, *India Today* and *Time*. Until 1999, she was the New Delhi Bureau Chief for CNN, reporting news from South Asia.

She has won several Indian and international awards, including the prestigious George Polk award for her coverage of the Taliban takeover of Afghanistan in 1996. In 1998 she was awarded the Chameli Devi Jain award for her 'sensitive portrayal of the human condition' and for her 'talent, dedication and courage as a reporter'.

She is currently freelancing, making television documentary films and writing columns for magazines.

Island of Blood is her first book.

www.anitapratap.com

Island of Blood

FRONTLINE REPORTS
FROM SRI LANKA, AFGHANISTAN
AND OTHER SOUTH ASIAN FLASHPOINTS

Anita Pratap

PENGUIN BOOKS

PENGUIN BOOKS
Published by the Penguin Group
Penguin Group (USA) Inc., 375 Hudson Street, New York, New York 10014, U.S.A.
Penguin Books Ltd, 80 Strand, London WC2R 0RL, England
Penguin Books Australia Ltd, 250 Camberwell Road,
Camberwell, Victoria 3124, Australia
Penguin Books Canada Ltd, 10 Alcorn Avenue, Toronto, Ontario, Canada M4V 3B2
Penguin Books India (P) Ltd, 11 Community Centre,
Panchsheel Park, New Delhi – 110 017, India
Penguin Books (N.Z.) Ltd, Cnr Rosedale and Airborne Roads,
Albany, Auckland, New Zealand
Penguin Books (South Africa) (Pty) Ltd, 24 Sturdee Avenue,
Rosebank, Johannesburg 2196, South Africa

Penguin Books Ltd, Registered Offices: 80 Strand, London WC2R 0RL, England

First published in India in Viking by Penguin Books India 2001
Published in Penguin Books by Penguin Books India 2002
Published in the United States of America in Penguin Books 2003

1 3 5 7 9 10 8 6 4 2

Copyright © Anita Pratap, 2001
All rights reserved

The cover photograph by Robert Nickelsberg shows a woman
in Lunuganwehera, Sri Lanka, whose husband was arrested for
interrogation during the JVP insurrection in 1989.
She knows she will never see him alive again.

LIBRARY OF CONGRESS CATALOGING IN PUBLICATION DATA
Pratap, Anita.
Island of blood : frontline reports from Sri Lanka, Afghanistan
and other South Asian flashpoints / Anita Pratap.
p cm.
ISBN 0 14 20.0366 2
1. Political violence—South Asia. 2. Terrorism—South Asia. 3. Sri Lanka—
Politics and government—1978-   4. Afghanistan—Politics and government—2001-
5. Ayodhya (Faizabad, India)—Politics and government. I. Title.
HN670.3.Z9V57 2003
303.6'25'0954—dc21   2003051199

Printed in the United States of America
Set in Bembo

For

Zubin
You helped me touch the sky,
for you are the wind beneath my wings,
thank God, thank God for you;

my parents K.J. Simon and Nancy,
for giving me the foundation to fly;

and

my husband Arne,
for helping me fly in new directions.

CONTENTS

ACKNOWLEDGEMENTS

Many thanks to my mother for plying me with endless cups of strong decoction coffee and glasses of curry-leaf flavoured buttermilk as I wrote into the night.

My father's encouragement, Zubin's wit and humour...

Cyber Saviour Markus who enthusiastically fixed the never-ending computer glitches and safeguarded my files even though during the writing of this book we were hit by so many viruses—Love Bug, Code Red, Code Red C etc., and Arne, who carefully read all the chapters and offered invaluable suggestions. Alas, a few could not be incorporated. He felt I was stingy with adjectives and suggested in the eighth chapter, I could mention that the towel was draped around his 'magnificently athletic, breathtakingly chiselled body, bronzed by the sun.' I had to remind him this book is not fiction.

My Rakhi brother Sudhir Varma, for always coming to my rescue and especially for re-sending my notes when they were offloaded from the plane.

My friend Ram Jethmalani, buddy Ravi Shankar, soul sister Nina Pillai, pal Ashish Saraf, cousin Jose Cyriac and childhood classmate Achala Narayan for their love and logistical support.

The late Karsten Prager, managing editor of *Time*, who urged me a decade ago to write about my experiences and who tried hard, but in vain, to get me to do it in his lifetime.

Deepak Puri and Meenakshi Ganguly, my colleagues at *Time* who still are like family to me.

Researcher Vaani Arora for her patience and diligence, photographer Dominic Sansoni, Sandy Ciric, my friends Sonny and Livleen Sharma, Harish Samtani, Binita Mohanty, Bindu Dalmia, Gautam and Prita Mukgerjee for all their help.

No words of thanks would be sufficient for my publisher and friend-of-decades, David Davidar, the first person who asked me to write a book—and that was in 1987. He sculpted this book.

And to V.K. Karthika, Penguin's senior editor, who started getting grey hairs in the final days when we had to work closely and intensely. I must give her some of my smelly coconut oil, spiced with curry leaves.

And last, but certainly not least, deep-felt thanks to my friend and *Time* photographer Robert Nickelsberg for sifting through his extensive files and giving me the perfect cover picture—the one picture that captures the spirit of this book. So now in these troubled times of inflation and television, we have to revise our estimates and say a picture is worth a hundred thousand words.

AUTHOR'S NOTE

When people asked Paul Theroux what they should do to become writers, he advised: First leave home... 'enlightenment will always involve the poetry of departures.' How true! This is a book that has been lying curled inside my head for over a decade. For one reason or the other, it just remained there. It took my departure from India to Norway in the winter of 1999 to get me started on it. Perhaps, I needed the distance and the isolation for it to uncoil.

And yet, to complete the book, I had to return home, back to India, back to my parents, back to my roots in Kerala. I would add to Theroux: 'And then return... appreciation will always involve the poetry of homecomings.'

Sri Lanka

A RAVAGED NATION

MOTHERS AND SONS

I have often been asked to define my happiest moment. What people expect to hear is about the time I got a prestigious international award, or a fancy job, or cracked a story. But my answer is probably the same many women would give: the birth of my firstborn.

What a cliché! But like all clichés, how true!

Zubin, my son, is the only child I have borne. So I don't know whether women experience the same joy at childbirth when they deliver their second, third, or tenth child. But his birth was for me the most beautiful moment. I experienced the miracle of life unfold from within my body. No experience before or after has measured up to that instant of pure joy.

Perhaps the moment was so special because I witnessed Zubin's birth. I saw him being born, without any of the accompanying labour pains that young mothers often find unendurable. I was twenty-two years old, and what allowed me to enjoy this magic moment was that he was a Caesarian baby. I had a lumbar puncture, which meant I was benumbed waist down but was fully conscious and alert above the waist. For the three preceding months, I had been vomiting for no apparent reason and had become thin and weak. The doctor decided it was no longer safe for the baby to remain inside.

'With you as mother, how could I possibly be safer outside?' Zubin would wisecrack much later.

I watched my gynaecologist, Lalitha Kumari, directing her team of doctors, nurses, anaesthetist, as they cut open my belly. I, of course, couldn't feel a thing. A green sheet covered my waist and I kept trying to raise myself on my elbows to take a better look at the infant lying curled up inside, upside down.

'The baby is perfectly positioned,' I heard my gynaecologist murmur. Even before he was born, Zubin was responsible, did things just right.

As I peered down to have a better look at my belly, the doctor whacked my arm and pushed me flat, warning me not to get up again.

'You have such big eyes, I am surprised you have to raise yourself to see the baby. If you get up once more, I will give you full anaesthesia,' she threatened.

'But why can't I see my baby? I'm not afraid of blood and gore,' I said.

'You will be when you realize the blood and gore is your own,' she said, pushing me back and ordering the nurses to keep me pinned down.

I rolled my big eyes pleadingly at the nurses, but they looked like carvings on Mt. Rushmore. I lay back in resignation, glaring evilly at my gynaecologist. I could see her smile behind the mask.

Then I realized I could see my baby after all—in the reflection in the doctor's spectacles. I stared intently at my split-open belly and saw my baby, inverted, knees raised, head down. Then Lalitha Kumari's arms blocked my vision. She was lifting my baby out.

'You have a fine baby,' she said.

'Is he okay, is he normal, does he have all ten fingers,

does he have toes?' I asked in rising panic.

I had known all along that my baby would be a boy. Not that I had tested for his gender, and not that it mattered to me either way, but I just knew. So I didn't need the doctor to tell me that. But it was so important to know that he was normal—a fear that plagues all mothers-to-be. 'Is he okay, is he normal, does he have all ten fingers?' I asked again.

'Yes, yes, he is absolutely normal,' assured the doctor.

'Does he have all ten fingers? Does he have toes? Does he have fingernails? Does he have both eyes? Are his nose and mouth in their proper place?' I could think of a million things that could go wrong. So many things had to be put together and in the right place. One small mistake, one careless oversight by God, and my baby would be deformed for life.

'Of course they are. Relax,' she said patiently. 'Now be quiet.'

She held my baby by his ankles to whack the breath of life into him. The whole world stood still. I stopped breathing. It was the longest moment of my life. Every nerve, every pore, every cell extended expectantly out of my body like a zillion quivering antennae to catch the very first decibel of sound from the planet's youngest being. My son!

Then he let out a wail. Strong, loud, full-throated. The tension in the room eased visibly, and I heard sighs of relief.

'You are the mother of a handsome baby boy. Believe it or not, he is absolutely normal. The most perfectly shaped nails I have ever seen—though I must admit I have never looked at a newborn's fingernails before. They're already a bit long, so you'll have to clip them soon. But I will say this: he is one of the most beautiful babies I have helped deliver,' she said, holding up my baby for me to see.

It was the ugliest thing I had ever seen in my life!

His face was pink and furrowed, his eyes shut tight and his toothless mouth wide open as he protested his exit from the womb. Then I realized it was MY SON, and he became the most beautiful creature I had ever seen. I couldn't believe it. My son! I had delivered a baby. And he was normal, healthy and beautiful—well, at least the gynaecologist thought so, and she had a million babies to compare him with.

Watching his screwed-up face, hearing him cry, was such a tender moment. I felt tears well up in my eyes. Before I knew it, I was crying. Tears of joy that I've never wept, before or after.

And then nothing. I lost consciousness.

That was flashback, twenty years ago. In the present: Zubin driving his car, and me sitting beside him on the front seat. We are driving down from Bangalore where he is studying law, to vacation with my parents who live in Kochi in Kerala. It's actually a ten-hour drive, but Zubin and I have decided to take three days, meandering through the hills and forests and beaches of south India.

'Rediscovering my roots,' I tell Zubin.

'Oh, then we will wind up in Africa,' laughs Zubin, who says I look like a cross between Michael Jackson and pop star Des'ree. Cross, not as in combination, but separately. Meaning, I look like Michael Jackson when I've washed my hair—it gets curly like his in that song 'Remember the time'.

I agree. I mean, I do resemble the new Michael Jackson, not the darker, rougher Jackson who bears no semblance to the fairer, smoother version. And Zubin claims I look like Des'ree when I am lipsticked and dressed up to go out. I don't agree. I think I am better looking. My mouth is big, but not that big.

'Very funny,' I say mockingly, but can't suppress my giggles. Zubin makes me laugh. I find him extremely funny. Two people in the world find all of Zubin's jokes funny— Zubin and me. He pretends he doesn't—that's part of his cultivated cynical image. And he has a scathing tongue. Most of the time I am his victim. He makes fun of my clothes, my hair, my work, my reactions, my sermons. In short, he pokes fun at everything.

'I really enjoyed reading Edward De Bono's article in this morning's newspaper,' I say. I am a great fan of De Bono and gave his book on lateral thinking to Zubin on his thirteenth birthday. 'De Bono says people should learn to think "holistically". Most people tend to look at a problem from only one plane—either emotionally, or financially, or whatever. He says you should think holistically, meaning think logically, think emotionally, think psychologically.'

'Think regularly,' quips Zubin. 'Solves most problems.'

'The problem now is, where do we halt for the night? Let's think holistically—logistically, geographically, financially, security-wise,' I tell Zubin.

'We don't want to be kidnapped by Veerappan, we don't want to spend a fortune, it has to be somewhere in south India and a place we can reach by car,' says Zubin. 'I am thinking holistically, but we have a hundred choices to wade through. Or maybe we should pull over and sleep in the car, then wait for tomorrow's newspaper and read De Bono's second instalment to give us more ideas on how to solve a problem.'

'Very funny. To solve a problem, it's more important to find out what you want, rather than what you don't want,' I say. 'It should be some place we can access in about three hours—we have to reach before sundown. The landscape should be beautiful. We don't want to sleep in some crummy lodge facing a parking lot. We are on holiday, so the price is negotiable. I don't mind paying more if it's worth it. Wynad is beautiful and close by. Let's head there.'

'Why do you bother to read Edward De Bono? You have your own way of solving problems. Mom, why don't you write a "how to think" book? You'll make lots of money, and you'll get paid for doing the two things you love most —travelling and lecturing,' says Zubin, cackling.

'Shut up and drive, Zub,' I say threateningly.

'In case you didn't notice, I am driving. Unlike some people I know, I can do two things at a time—I can talk and drive at the same time,' chuckles Zubin. He knows I have difficulty doing two things simultaneously. I can't listen to someone speak and think of something entirely different at the same time. When my mind wanders, it is evident on my face, and Zubin will interrupt his own speech to ask, 'What did I just say?' and I am stumped. But when I catch him doing the same thing and ask him what I had just said, he does a quick recap without batting an eyelid. In fact, when I am concentrating on reading or writing, I often don't breathe properly. I hold my breath for long periods until Zubin reminds me gently: 'Mom, take a breath.'

We reach Wynad and after bumping along on a stony road in blinding rain, manage to reach the Vythiri jungle resort, which is located in absolutely the most stunning surroundings. The resort is expensive but well worth it. The rustic cottages, designed in terracotta, are set on a hill alongside a waterfall. We are surrounded by dense, virgin forest. The mountains are thick with trees. Vines overhang our veranda, rich, green and luscious. The monsoon has made the foliage even more luxuriant than usual. The sound of pouring rain blends with the gushing waterfall. We are in the midst of a constant, thunderous roar.

When there is a break in the rain, Zubin and I go for a walk up the hill. Little do we know that danger lurks ahead.

As we set off, we are completely overwhelmed by the beauty of the surroundings. It's like walking through an unexplored part of the Amazonian forest. I have travelled a great deal, but nowhere have I seen such wild, luxuriant growth. Tall trees packed together, entangled moss-covered boughs heavy with leaves as big as salvers, glistening with the moisture of freshly-fallen rain. It is riotous fertility. We walk on the wet, narrow, winding mountain road, even walk through clouds. It's like being on another planet. We could have walked forever, but it is getting dark, so we return to our resort.

We still have an hour to while away before dinner. So we order hot chocolate. I am sitting on the sofa and reading, while Zubin is sprawled on the bed, doing two things as usual—reading and listening to his MD player.

Half an hour later, a piercing yell shatters my eardrums. 'Leeches,' screams Zubin. 'I have leeches on my feet.'

Like a good mother, I jump away from him in horror. And then gingerly edge closer to discover splotches of blood on the white bed sheet and three blood spots on Zubin's right foot. From these hang three blood-swollen leeches. I scream. My screams are even louder than Zubin's.

Initial reaction over, Anita the Combatant takes over. I grab the telephone and thunder at the operator: 'My son is being bitten by leeches. Please send someone over immediately. I want someone here right now!'

The operator calmly assures me that help is on its way— right now.

I turn back to Zubin, who is staring with morbid

fascination at the three leeches on his foot. 'Do we have to set your foot on fire to get them off?' I ask.

'I think that would be a bit drastic. Let's just try a simple technique like pulling them off,' replies Zubin.

'How can you touch those slimy things? I think we'd better wait for the hotel guys. They'll know what to do. They obviously live with them.'

Zubin is peering at his bed. 'Mom, my bed is full of leeches,' he says, pointing to his blood-stained sheet. It takes me a few seconds to notice the leeches—they are tiny, about a centimetre long, and as thin and elastic as a rubber band. We spot about ten of them.

'Are you sure they are leeches? Aren't leeches supposed to be bigger?' I ask.

'They become much bigger when swollen with blood. But before they become Draculas they can be pretty small,' says Zubin the wise one. Sometimes I think he cooks up answers because in any case I am none the wiser. We both stare at the bed in total absorption, watching the leeches do their strange moonwalk. I look up at the ceiling. They must be falling from the roof. We look at the floor then, and to our horror discover many more moonwalking leeches. Now I am hysterical.

No hotel guy has landed up yet. That aggravates my hysteria. I grab the telephone and yell at the operator, 'How long does it take for you guys to get here? Our room is crawling with leeches. Three leeches are sucking my son's blood. I haven't given birth to my son to watch him bleed to death. What nonsense is this?'

'Madam, somebody will be knocking on your door within seconds. Please don't worry. There is nothing to be scared of. You can look upon this as a tropical experience.'

I explode. 'Tropical experience be damned! My son

looks like St. Sebastian with blood oozing from his wounds, he is bleeding to death, and you say enjoy the tropical experience! Are you mad? This room is full of leeches. The bed is crawling with leeches, the floor is crawling with leeches, and you have the audacity to say enjoy the tropical experience. What is the matter with you people? You go and build a resort in some leech-infested jungle and joke about tropical experience! How can we sleep on these beds? How can we walk on the floor? And you charge five thousand rupees for this! How dare you? Bunch of Draculas sucking money while leeches suck our blood. I can't get a refund on my son's lost blood, but I am damned if I don't get my money refunded from you. And you talk of tropical experience! If you think getting bitten by leeches is a wonderful tropical experience, you should be building a lunatic asylum, not a resort in this jungle. I can't believe it. You people...'

'Mom, take a breath.'

I stop for breath and in that instant hear a knock on the door. I drop the telephone and run to the door. A short, dark attendant with a moustache stands smiling, with a bottle of white liquid in his hand.

I am so relieved to see him, I could have hugged him. He comes in and dabs the liquid on Zubin's foot. The leeches fall off like overripe fruit.

I feel an itch on my foot and look down to see a leech about to drain my blood. I shriek. The attendant smiles and begins dabbing my foot.

'Quickly, quickly, get it off. Look carefully to see if there are any more,' I say, my words coming out in another torrential gush of panic. 'I am anaemic as it is. I can't afford to lose blood. I'll turn white.'

'Then you will look even more like Michael Jackson,'

murmurs Zubin, back to normal now that his leeches have been removed.

'Zub, I am not in the mood for your stupid jokes. This is serious. I can't sleep in this room. It's full of leeches. What if a leech crawls inside my ear? It will suck blood, and become so big my ear will explode. Ugh, ugh, ugh! God, why did we ever come here? They will probably give us another room, but that will also be full of leeches. This whole jungle is crawling with them. It's so late, and we are so far from civilization and a decent hotel, where on earth can we go now to find a safe place?' My hysteria is rising again.

The attendant looks at me, amazed. A broad smile lights up his face. He says in Malayalam: 'There is nothing to worry about. The room is not full of leeches. You both went for a walk in the jungle, didn't you? You brought back the leeches in your shoes. During the monsoon, the jungle is infested with leeches. But don't be afraid. We'll get rid of the leeches, put fresh bed sheets, and you will be fine. Believe me, you will have a good night's rest.'

'Yeah, if I fall unconscious,' I say. But sarcasm is wasted on the attendant, who is clearly enjoying the spectacle I am making of myself.

Zubin and I trail behind him as he heads towards our shoes. A den of leeches. He is right. We had brought them back in our shoes and as we walked on the floor, they had fallen off. Quietly and efficiently, he dabs the shoes and the entire floor with his white antiseptic liquid, and within half an hour life returns to normal.

'Leeches are not dangerous. They suck a little blood, and then they fall off. In fact, there are treatments in which they use leeches to suck out impure blood. A few leeches once in a while are actually good for you,' says the attendant.

'Next time I want leech treatment I'll check into a hospital,' I say. But the sight of leeches succumbing so easily to the white liquid calms me down. They no longer seem evil and dangerous. They are just one of God's million creatures that you don't normally come across. Frightening at first, but actually quite a fascinating and unforgettable tropical experience in the final analysis.

'Mom, how come you are so terrified of leeches? Didn't you encounter them during your travels in Sri Lanka?' asks Zubin.

'It's strange, but I've never seen a leech until today. Not even in Sri Lanka, although I've travelled in the jungle during the monsoons,' I reply. 'Come to think of it, it's odd that I didn't encounter them, especially during that November trip of mine in 1987, when Shyam and I spent six days in the jungle trying to reach Jaffna.'

That trip was one of the most memorable adventures I have had in Sri Lanka: it was horrible. It was November 1987, a month after the India–Sri Lanka accord had disintegrated into a vicious war between the Indian army and the LTTE (Liberation Tigers of Tamil Eelam). I was then working for *India Today* and wanted to get an interview with LTTE chief V. Pirabhakaran. I telephoned my international Tiger contacts, and they got back to me saying if I reached Jaffna, an interview could be arranged. The Indian authorities had banned journalists from visiting the Tiger stronghold of Jaffna, so there wasn't a straightforward way of accessing the town. The plan was to reach Vavuniya, a Tamil town that borders the Sinhalese areas. In Vavuniya, I was to establish contact with Dinesh, the LTTE's area commander who would arrange for me and photographer Shyam Tekwani to be taken to Jaffna via the jungle route.

We reached Vavuniya and managed to meet up with

Dinesh. But it took a great deal of persuasion to get him to arrange our trip. He said it was too dangerous. 'The Indian army is all over the place. They have closed all entry and exit points. All roads into Jaffna have been sealed. All the jetty points are heavily guarded,' he said in Tamil.

'But your guys in London suggested we take the jungle route,' I said.

'It's not as easy as it sounds. But if you are prepared, we will take you. We'll have to keep stopping and moving according to the movement of the Indian patrols. It will be time-consuming and very risky,' warned Dinesh.

'We are prepared to take that risk, so long as you don't send us on a suicide mission,' I said.

Dinesh smiled and said, 'Since you insist on going, let's hope for the best. It takes a full day to reach Jaffna by the jungle route normally, but we may take twice the time because we'll have to be extra cautious and take a more circuitous route.'

'Good idea. We have time,' I said. If we got an interview with Pirabhakaran, it mattered little if we didn't make it in time for this edition. It would still be a grand scoop for the next one. In any case, I was confident no one else could wangle an interview with Pirabhakaran, now or a fortnight or even a month later.

We idled away the time while Dinesh and his associates worked out a route for us. By the straight road, it takes just a couple of hours from Vavuniya to Jaffna. But as it turned out, it took us six harrowing days to reach our destination.

Dinesh saw us into a tractor-trailer and waved goodbye. Inside the vehicle were seven LTTE guerrillas huddled together, armed to their teeth: AK 47s, sub-machine guns, grenades. From then on, for six days, it was a treacherous relay race, as one group of LTTE cadres handed us over to the next. I lost count of the number of groups and vehicles we changed—we went by van, car, jeep, trailer, cart, bicycle, and even on foot.

We travelled on asphalted roads that gave way to hard gravelly paths that gave way to mud tracks. Soon, we left Vavuniya behind us to enter a luxuriant jungle. It was beautiful—a lighter shade of green, and not as thick and wild as the jungles of Kerala. It was more tame, more remote, more calm. There were small clearings of green grass and little lakes with black stumps of trees sticking out like primordial relics, around which swirled brightly plumaged birds. The jungle was serene, not dark and forbidding. There was no point thinking of the danger lurking around us in the form of uniformed Indian soldiers. It was best to sit back and enjoy the scenery—which I did.

But not for long. Local villagers warned us that a huge contingent of the IPKF (Indian Peace Keeping Force) had arrived to clear the jungle, to secure routes and block LTTE movement. There followed a nightmarish three to four hours, when we had to take sudden turns—sometimes, where none existed—to avoid running into oncoming IPKF patrols. It was like a bizarre cops-and-robbers routine. The real danger was that we were with the so-called bad guys. If we bumped into a patrol, the soldiers would shoot first and question later. Even after we were dead, they would assume Shyam and I were Tigers. Not in their wildest dreams would they expect to run into a reporter and photographer deep in these jungles. Only on checking our bags would they realize we were journalists. By then, it would be too late. Not only would we be dead, we'd probably be buried as well.

As we hurtled through the jungle growth we came

across some villagers who warned us not to go any further because a group of Indian soldiers were just ahead of us. 'The jungle is crawling with IPKF soldiers. It's very unsafe,' they warned.

Bad news. Trust the Indians to launch a major operation to rid the jungles of the Tigers just when we were skulking about. By now the rain had become a thick, noisy curtain around us. We were drenched to the bone. The downpour was so furious, it hurt to keep our eyes open. But we pressed on for another hour until we came to a rather large clearing.

We must have been halfway through the clearing, when suddenly a foot patrol of the IPKF came out of the jungle into our line of vision to the right. We chugged along as if nothing was amiss. The soldiers waved their arms and shouted, obviously ordering us to stop. We sensed rather than heard them shouting because of the crashing rain. We knew that if we stopped we would be killed, because they would lift the tarpaulin to discover the weapons in the trailer. If we pushed on, there was perhaps a fifty-fifty chance we would make it. The tractor-trailer lurched forward, and we saw the soldiers breaking into a run behind us.

Shyam and I lay down flat in the trailer, and I can't quite recall what happened next. I didn't see anything because my eyes were pressed shut. I don't know if a gun-battle broke out. I can't say for sure I heard the sound of bullets. The Tigers were hyperactive and chattering away excitedly to each other in rapid-fire Tamil. They were like a pack of monkeys, the way they squawked and scurried about in the narrow trailer. I don't know how long it was before one of them tapped me on my shoulder and said we were safe and that we could sit up. Shyam and I heaved huge sighs of relief.

I don't know what saved us—was it our Tiger

bodyguards who fired at the advancing soldiers to keep them at bay, or was it the blinding rain? Whatever it was, we were safe—drenched and trembling, but safe.

The rain began to ease and then finally stopped, though the sky remained grey. We had reached a part of the jungle that was thick with trees and bushes. Here, there weren't even mud tracks; we had to burrow through brambles. Thin narrow slashes became slivers of red as thorns cut into the skin on my face and arms to raise blood.

The ground became slushier and we, sitting in the open trailer behind, were showered with the wet earth gouged and thrown up by the front tyres. In no time, Shyam and I were brown blobs, covered from head to waist in muck. The cuts on my face and arms began to sting as the slush mingled with my blood.

I looked at my arm, and my arm looked back at me. Two bulging, bulbous eyes of an insect or reptile glared at me from my arm. I screamed in terror, flailing my muddy arms in panic that exploded from the depths of my being. But the eyes still remained, clinging to my arm, its owner frozen with terror that probably exploded from the depths of *its* being. One of the Tigers caught my arm and shook the thing off. They found the whole episode hilarious, laughing and cackling as they watched me shuddering in revulsion long after the eyes had been flung away.

It took a while for my world to calm down, my eyes to focus, my breathing to become normal, my trembling to cease. I kept looking at the spot on my arm where the creature had been…I almost expected to see its little babies rise and stare back at me. I kept scratching the spot as if to erase the memory. Gradually, my panic subsided, and I became normal. I started laughing foolishly, provoking the Tigers into another round of giggles.

I could now look at all the worms and insects crawling on my muck-covered skin with total composure. I couldn't help thinking how fertile the wet earth was—what seemed like just mud to us was home to a million different organisms. Of course, it would have been much nicer if they didn't make a home of my skin, but that couldn't be helped in the circumstances.

Where we were, it was not only yucky, it was also very uncomfortable. We had to keep our mouths pressed shut, or we would be having Sushi meals of a whole new variety of creepy-crawlies. We had to keep wiping our noses so that we didn't inhale and choke on the mud. Though we kept our eyes closed, little specks got in and stung like crazy. I could feel slimy creatures biting my face and arms. Wet earth had coated my hair a clammy brown, and I could feel a zillion organisms slithering all over my scalp.

And then we sank into the earth. The tractor-trailer was well and truly stuck in the slush. The Tigers clambered out and fished out wooden planks and thick iron chains, which they placed near the tyres to provide friction. After much whirring and grinding, the vehicle lurched out of the mud. We were on our way again.

Night fell early, and it was about seven o'clock when we stopped. We had reached an LTTE safehouse deep in the jungle. About half a dozen Tigers lived there. The house was small and dark-tiled, with a shed in the yard, a well, and a garden that had some fruit trees and vegetable shrubs. The house comprised two rooms, one small and one large. In the small one were mounds of rice, some onions, and a few other provisions. The large room had one broad bed in dark wood, several rolled up mats, and two ropes tied across the room like a clothes-line, from which hung several checked lungis. A single tube-light powered by a lorry battery lit the room dimly.

'You can take the bed. We will sleep on the floor,' said the leader of the Tigers. It really is an advantage being a woman. 'We will start cooking dinner now, but it will take about an hour. Do you need anything?' he asked in Tamil.

'I need to take a bath. I am dying to get all this filth off me,' I replied.

'You can go to the well and have a bath,' he said.

It would have been absurd to expect a jungle safehouse to come with attached bathrooms. Still, I was unnerved at the prospect of bathing outside, in the dark. There could be snakes. But there was no choice. I went down to the well with my towel, soap, shampoo and a change of clothes. A Tiger guerrilla drew two iron pails of water for me, and then he left. I realized to my dismay that there was no enclosure, not even a thatched screen to protect me from prying eyes while I bathed. I knew the Tigers had renounced sex, but how could I bathe in the nude before twenty young men? Nor could I bathe with all my dirty clothes on—how could I get clean that way?

I was annoyed, frustrated and helpless. The Tigers had bigger things to worry about, and it seemed ridiculous to bother them with my bathing problem. But there was no other way out. I went up to the leader and presented my dilemma. He wasn't irritated. He thought for a moment, then summoned two of his boys. He had a simple solution. The boys would hold up a sarong like a screen, to shield me from anyone who might look out from the safehouse window while I bathed.

As I undressed, I glanced sideways at the boys to check whether they were stealing glances in my direction. I needn't have worried. Standing about five feet apart from each other, they were holding up the two ends of the sarong, which hung down like a perfect screen. One was looking north, the other south, and they were chatting as if I didn't exist, as if this was something they did every day. Reassured, I undressed fully and poured a mug of water on myself...and screamed. I hadn't realized the well-water was ice-cold. I heard the boys giggle and bit my lip to stop further screams as I poured some more water on myself. After a few mugs, my body adjusted to the cold, and I started breathing normally. I scrubbed myself all over with soap and reached for more water, only to find that both pails were empty. There were only two options: either I could draw water myself, or ask the boys to draw water for me. But then, where could I hide?

.I decided to draw water myself. I had done it as a child in my ancestral home in Varapetty in Kerala, when we went down to spend summer vacations with my grandparents. I would accompany our maid Mary, who taught me how to pull and tug like a pro. So there I stood, drawing water, possibly exactly like my great-great-grandmother. I was educated, had a job, lived in an apartment in a city, drove a car, was a single parent, spoke fluent English, intrerracted with presidents and prime ministers, travelled abroad, and yet for all that, some things, it seemed, never change.

I shampooed my hair four times, stopping only when I realized that it felt dry and stiff like straw. I dried myself, sprinkled on talcum powder and got into fresh clothes, feeling magnificently refreshed and sparkling clean. I was also hungry enough to eat a horse.

I thanked the Tigers, gathered my belongings, and began strolling back to the safehouse. I looked around and breathed deeply. The air was so pure. The night sky was lit by a million brilliant twinkling stars. A pale moon glowed, distant and mysterious. All around me I could see the silhouettes of trees and bushes. And then I stopped and stared. About fifteen metres away, something dangled from a tree, something that gleamed white in the moonlight.

'What's that?' I asked the Tigers who were a few steps ahead. They stopped and looked in the direction in which I was pointing.

'Dinner,' one of them replied.

I didn't understand what he meant, so I peered at the thing again. 'What do you mean, dinner?' I asked.

'That's a peacock being skinned. We are having rice and peacock for dinner tonight.'

I peered again, and realized to my horror that it was true. Dangling from the tree was a peacock whose feathers had all been plucked. The freshly shot bird had been tied to a low branch of the tree so that it hung down, making it easier for the Tiger chef to pluck the feathers and skin it. In the pale moonlight, I could now clearly make out the peacock's long neck, its swollen stomach, its long, skinny legs.

In about an hour, the peacock was on our plate—little brown cubes of tough meat. I put one cube into my mouth and kept chewing for several minutes. If the meat was so hard to chew, it would be impossible to digest. I kept it aside. But the wild rice was tasty, and I ate a big mound with the gravy of the peacock curry. The Tigers may be great guerrillas, but they are lousy cooks.

We slept almost immediately after dinner. As I lay on the broad bed, I felt like a queen with my minions sleeping below. I was in a room with twenty young men, but not for a second did I feel unsafe or threatened as a woman. Pirabhakaran rose in my esteem—that he could inculcate such discipline in his boys was truly remarkable. I have felt more vulnerable in the cocktail circuits of New Delhi, and visually stripped on its streets. But here, there was no lewdness or lechery in the Tigers' behaviour, in their gestures, or even in their eyes. In fact, what was most reassuring was that they did not look at me as if I was a woman. I was another object in the room, and they looked at me with the same expression as when they glanced at the clothes-line or the lorry battery.

I slept soundly that night. Truly, hunger is the best spice, exhaustion the best sedative.

Day two. We woke up to a bright, beautiful morning—a brilliant blue sky, vast and cloudless, energetic birds chirping and singing, the air pure and flower-scented, the leaves fresh and glistening. Nature was a riot of colours—blue sky, green trees, red earth. It was all so pristine, so serene, so wonderful. I felt as though I had stumbled upon a lost world. It was impossible to imagine we were in the nerve centre of a war.

Actually, we were way off course to Jaffna. The leader came to us and broke the bad news. It would take us at least two days more to get to Jaffna, he said.

So once again we climbed into our tractor-trailer and bumped along for a while before transferring to a pick-up van. We had travelled out from the heart to the periphery of the jungle. There were more people and dwellings to be seen. But we seemed to be going around in circles.

One LTTE boy was driving, and another by his side was scanning the countryside. Shyam and I were alone in the open section behind. The other LTTE cadres had melted away. A few had gone ahead on bicycles and the remaining were following, also on bicycles. Each bicycle carried two LTTE guerrillas—one pedalling and the other sitting in front, side-saddle.

Dusk had fallen. We were near Killinochi. Suddenly the

van came to a halt. The Tigers whispered to each other. They seemed excited. Shyam and I exchanged nervous glances. We didn't have a clue what was happening. Then the Tiger sentinel who was in the passenger seat came to us and whispered in Tamil: 'We have come to the last major army camp. This is the mother camp from where patrols go out into the jungles. Up ahead, the road will turn to the left. On the right side you will see barbed wire which runs for about a kilometre—that's the army camp. Keep your head down and don't make a sound. If we are spotted, we'll be killed.' He went back to his seat.

All the LTTE guerrillas on bicycles had assembled near our van. One by one, they disarmed and quietly placed their AK 47s by our feet and covered them with the tarpaulin. Then they vanished, and we started moving forward slowly. The headlights were switched off, so were the engines. About four of the LTTE boys who had been sitting side-saddle began pushing the van. Soundlessly and stealthily, we inched forward on the moonlit path. Then, slowly, we turned left.

From the corner of my eyes, I saw the barbed wire. I lifted my head slightly to get a better look. In the distance I could see lights. A fully inhabited army camp. My heart stopped. This was danger zone. I prayed to St. Teresa, Jesus Christ, Mother Mary. I tried sending telepathic messages to my mother to light her specially blessed holy candles from Rome, as she does every time she knows I am in Sri Lanka. I started saying Hail Marys.

I don't know how long it took us to cross the army camp. Fifteen minutes, half an hour, a full hour. I don't know. It seemed an eternity. My heart was pounding and my head was hurting. My neck was stiff because of the odd angle at which I was holding my head. My feet had gone to sleep. I was dying to cough, scratch, sneeze. There seemed a million things I needed to do but couldn't because it was too dangerous.

Then I heard the driver start the engine. In the stillness of the night, it sounded like a rocket. I was sure the soldiers would hear the roar and come running after us. The engine settled to a steady thrum, and the driver switched on the headlights. The four boys clambered into the van. In the dark I could see their white teeth. They were grinning at us. They had enjoyed themselves thoroughly, and our fear only increased their merriment. 'The danger is over—for now. We have crossed our first obstacle,' one of the boys said with a chuckle. The van picked up speed and trundled into the beckoning darkness ahead.

Without further mishap, we drove on for another hour, then stopped. We were asked to get down and walk. It was pitch dark. A thick black curtain seemed to hang over the horizon. I could see the red dirt road snaking into the darkness. On either side were heavily foliaged trees. The night was alive with the sounds of the tropics—cicadas, crickets, and many other insects that I didn't particularly care to know about.

We walked for about a mile and then reached our night halt: a long, low thatched hut amidst thick trees, near Paranthan. It was too dark to make out the surroundings. We had a meal of rice and vegetables and were shown into the hut, where two mats rolled out on the floor awaited us. One was for Shyam. The other one, near the door, was for me. I guess the Tigers figured I could run out easily, should the need arise. The door was left open to let in fresh air—and maybe for the Tigers to keep an eye on us.

We were given cotton sheets to cover ourselves with because it could get cold early in the morning. I lay there with only a mat to protect me from the hardness of the floor, with a sheet that I didn't need because it was so humid, and without a pillow that I am accustomed to. But I was too tired to care and drifted off to sleep, only to wake up with a start.

I could have sworn I'd heard fighter planes—the sharp whine of jets as they roared down from the skies to drop bombs on unsuspecting targets. I pricked up my ears to listen and was at once both relieved and dismayed.

The sound came not from fighter jets but from a squadron of mosquitoes. Their angry whine pierced my head like a dentist's drilling machine—insistent, relentless, painful. I jumped up because I could feel a million bites. My arms were covered with blood-heavy mosquitoes. I swotted them and some flew away, while others just keeled over, no longer aerodynamic with all that blood inside them. Shyam was sitting in his dark corner, whacking himself like some crazed, self-flagellating monk.

We didn't have any mosquito repellants. We were tired, we had another tough day ahead of us, we really needed our sleep. But the mosquitoes wouldn't let us.

'I think the best thing to do is to pull the sheet over and cover yourself tightly,' I said.

'But it's too hot to do that. I'll suffocate to death,' protested Shyam, cursing and slapping himself.

'It's better to sweat than to die of malaria,' I said, pulling the sheet over me. Soon, I fell off to sleep and was refreshed and wide-eyed when woken at the crack of dawn by a Tiger guerrilla.

Poor Shyam was a mess. His eyes were bloodshot, his stubble spiky, and his bushy moustache all askew. He had sat up all night flapping at the mosquitoes, without much success. His face and arms were a blotchy red mass of mosquito bites. That night was disastrous for Shyam. Three weeks later, he came down with malaria, and it recurred several times, affecting his liver.

Day three. We were back on a tractor-trailer and heading towards Elephant Pass, the major camp at the base of the Jaffna peninsula, the chicken neck or the choke point that was the entry into Jaffna. A causeway connected the Elephant Pass to the tear-drop shaped mainland.

It was getting hot and steamy. Gradually the landscape changed. We were leaving the jungle behind and coming to more open countryside. The red earth was changing to white. We were nearing the coast.

By midday it was burning hot. The sun was beating down on us, and I could feel my skin char. Eventually, the tractor-trailer stopped, and we were told to get down and walk. Shyam and I walked side by side, led by one Tiger in the front and one behind.

We must have walked for about a kilometre when the Tiger who was leading us announced that we had reached Elephant Pass. We had approached it from the eastern side. We had to now cross the causeway, go on to the west side and walk along the coconut groves. About fifty yards from the point where we crossed the causeway was the checkpost to the heavily guarded Elephant Pass. I could see the Indian soldiers manning the barricade and checking the identity cards of Tamils who were crossing into the peninsula. The Tigers' plan was for us to cross the causeway on foot into the coconut grove and walk on as if we were a refugee family. The primary task of the IPKF soldiers was to detect and prevent movement of Tiger cadres, so they did not usually pay much attention to those who appeared to be displaced Tamils. Nevertheless, if we were stopped, Shyam and I were to surrender. The Tigers would run, risking getting shot. If they were captured, they would swallow their cyanide. The trick, the Tigers told us, was to walk slowly with heads hanging down in a gesture of submission and despair.

We did a faithful imitation. It was tense, especially the few minutes it took us to cross the causeway. I could hear the soldiers questioning and barking orders at the hapless Tamil civilians. Sweat was pouring down our faces—as much from the steamy heat as from fear. Luck was on our side. The soldiers who were checking the group of civilians didn't care, or were too busy, to notice us. We slipped by and reached the coconut grove. The shade of the coconut trees was soothing, and we walked on for a few hours with the shore of a lagoon on our left. Our Tiger escorts told us to sit down while they did a recce of the area and established contact with their local comrades.

Half an hour later they returned, saying we could not go any further as Indian troops had set up barricades all over the place. They had failed to contact their local unit. The best option was for us to spend the night in a fisherman's hut, while the Tigers tried to touch base next day with the local cadre to hand us over.

The fisherman's thatched hut was small, with a single room. There were two soot-blackened pots. The cleaner one stored water. There was a wooden ladle, a few black and dented aluminium plates and two glasses. This was the kitchen section. In one corner, rolled up mats lay on the floor. This was the bedroom. The clothes-line strung across the hut was the cupboard. From it hung some old, tattered clothes.

In this hut, the impoverished fisherman lived with his wife and two small children. The whole family was thin and wiry. They greeted us with genuine smiles of welcome, apologizing profusely for the poverty of their home. We apologized for our intrusion. We chatted a bit, and I asked how life was, now that the Indian troops were here. The fisherman got worked up. A string of complaints followed. They had always been poor, but now they were afraid as well. Earlier, they at least slept safely. Now they were terrified to go out. If they ran into a patrol or a barricade, they were harassed. The Indian army suspected all villagers to be Tiger sympathizers and treated them harshly. The result was that even those who had nothing to do with the Tigers, those who actually disapproved of the Tigers, began secretly supporting them. They and their homeland were better off without the Indian soldiers, the fisherman said.

Besides, they were poorer because of the Indian soldiers. Earlier they could go out fishing for a few miles into the lagoon. The Indians had banned that to block LTTE movement. They couldn't distinguish the local fishermen from the Tigers, so their solution was to forbid all activity and movement. Fishermen like our host were deprived of their livelihood and daily food.

The Indian soldiers also stole things.

'Like what?' I asked, astounded. I had no difficulty believing Indian soldiers harassed, raped and shot civilians. But stealing from the poor seemed somehow even more preposterous.

'They stole our two goats. Those turbaned soldiers are the worst,' said the fisherman. The situation was tragic, but I couldn't help smiling. I could imagine the big, burly, hungry turbaned men of the Sikh Light Infantry, sick of eating dry rations and suffering withdrawal symptoms from their chicken tandoori and lassi, gleefully pouncing on village goats. Gosht for dinner. Impossible to resist such a temptation.

We talked some more and then bidding us to be comfortable, the husband and wife went outside the hut to confer. As we would figure out later, they were wondering what to serve us for dinner. The fisherman walked away and came back in about half an hour with a small package wrapped in leaves. He had walked into the lagoon and managed to catch two small fish, each about three inches long. He had also washed and cleaned them.

The wife took the packet gratefully and began frying the fish—actually roasting, because there was no cooking oil in the house. She placed the fish on a blackened pan on the stove till it smoked. Then she replaced the pan with a pot in which she cooked rice. There was not enough fish to go around—how could six people eat two small fish? So she did the next best thing—she dropped the smoked fish into the cooking rice, so that instead of plain rice, we could eat fish-flavoured rice.

She poured some of the kanji into two plates for us. We insisted she feed her children first, but husband and wife wouldn't hear of it. We ate our meal, and then I watched the wife pour out the rice for her husband and two children. Silently she watched her family eat. Then she picked up the plates and went out to wash them. I went over to the pot and saw that there was nothing left. Because of us, she had to go hungry.

I felt tears sting my eyes. How simple and uncomplaining this woman was. So poor and yet so generous. We—the middle class and the rich—tend to be so selfish and acquisitive. If guests dropped in suddenly, most of us would pack them off with a cup of tea and some cookies, at best. We would grumble about visitors and their irritating habit of dropping in unannounced. Most of us wouldn't even share a meal. But here was a woman who not only shared her food, but sacrificed her own meal so that her uninvited guests would not sleep hungry. I have noticed this again and again—the poor are so much more generous and giving than the middle class and the rich, who as a rule tend to be selfish and hoard things for themselves. The ability to share often decreases with rising wealth.

My head felt heavy, so I went out of the hut. It was dark now, and the stars were up and twinkling. But I was in no mood to appreciate nature's beauty. I was angry at the unfairness of life, overwhelmed by the generosity of the woman, the poverty of the family, the cruelty of the world, the injustice of it all.

Day four. Both Shyam and I woke up tired. But the worst was yet to come. We set off on foot once again at the crack of dawn, accompanied by two Tigers. I am reasonably good at navigation, and I realized that instead of going up north to Jaffna we were going sideways, criss-crossing the peninsula from west to east and back. The Tigers said we had to take a really long, roundabout route to circumvent IPKF checkposts.

After walking for several hours, we reached a place close to Palaly. Here at last the Tigers were able to connect with their local corps. They said we would have to henceforth travel on bicycles. One of the Tigers asked if I knew how to ride a bicycle.

Of course I did. When I was fourteen years old, my cousin Joe had spent hours holding onto the bicycle with all his might as I swerved madly to gain my balance. I am sure Joe never reached his full height because of the number of times the cycle and I crashed on to him in the gravel-strewn paths of his garden in Kottayam. When after three days of coaching and crashing, I finally pedalled out of the garden, out of the gates into the big wide world, Joe was even more thrilled than I was—and infinitely more relieved.

The Tigers whispered among themselves and we set off again, eventually coming to a halt at a wayside shop. They asked us to wait, while two of them sauntered away. They returned a short while later with bicycles. Now our rate of progress was much faster. We criss-crossed the peninsula more rapidly, but we still didn't seem to be heading north.

Many times we saw IPKF soldiers patrolling up ahead, or in the next street. Each time, we changed course quickly, but not so abruptly as to arouse suspicion. I was thoroughly enjoying this cat-and-mouse game. Even danger can be enjoyable in daylight. We never took the tarred lanes—they were infested with IPKF patrols. Instead we took the bleached, sandy country roads. The landscape was picturesque—palm and cashew-nut trees on either side of white paths that snaked through green fields, fringed by blue lagoons. Very tropical. I started humming film songs. Shyam joined in, and I quickly shut up. Unlike me, he could really sing well— a talent I wasn't aware of until then. He sang those beautiful, sentimental songs from the old Hindi film *Guide*. Even today, when I hear songs from *Guide*, I remember us pedalling through the scenic countryside, choosing to enjoy the surroundings and the adventure rather than allow ourselves to be bogged down by fear and anxiety.

There was plenty to worry about. For instance, there was one stretch, a long alley, which we had to pedal through, with the Indian army camp on one side and the Sri Lankan camp on the other. Eventually, we reached a small concrete house for the night halt, somewhere between Palaly and Chavakacheri. This was a middle-class home, with its little garden of hibiscus bushes in the front and coconut trees swaying on the side and rear. The house was red-tiled and quite bereft of furniture, but for a few wooden chairs in the living room and two beds in the bedroom. There were a few steel and plastic utensils in the kitchen. The owner was a woman who looked about forty years old. I gathered she was a widow and her son was 'in the movement'— meaning he was a Tiger. She lived with her seven-year-old daughter.

The Tigers must have asked her to prepare something nice because she served us hot rice and spicy prawns. It was delicious, but so hot, the senses rioted. My eyes were watering, my ears smoking, my skin sweating, and my tongue lolling to cool the fiery aftertaste. When I think of that meal, even now my mouth waters. Tired and heavy with the rice meal, I slept soundly—as usual.

Day five. 27 November 1987. In the morning, one of the Tiger guerrillas, a young boy called Vincent, told us that our trip was getting difficult and dangerous. There were too many patrols in the area. I was arousing suspicion, dressed the way I was in faded army green trousers and a long shirt. The only way we could hope to reach Jaffna was by sneaking in as local villagers. It would be advisable for me to wear a sari.

I agreed, but there was a problem. I didn't have one. I had brought with me two jeans and four shirts. So the Tigers asked the lady of the house if she could spare a sari and blouse. She readily agreed, enjoying her role in our adventure. We were about the same size, so the green blouse she gave me fitted reasonably well, except that it was slightly loose around the arms. She gave me a printed green nylon sari. It was ugly as sin, but this was not exactly the moment to get finicky. I thanked her profusely and wore the sari quickly, pinned it securely in several places with rusty safety pins, and stepped out.

Shyam burst out laughing. 'You look like a typical Tamil village woman,' he said, 'except for your shoes.'

I was still wearing jogging shoes, which did look ridiculous with the sari. The lady volunteered her rubber slippers and with some regret I left behind the shoes that had served me so well. I had bought the pair in Colombo during my first trip to Sri Lanka several years earlier. I guess it was its destiny to remain in the country of its origin.

Like his colleagues before him, Vincent too instructed us that if we got caught, we should surrender. The Tigers would flee. We nodded our heads in agreement. Our clothes were in a bag that one of the Tigers carried on his shoulder. I took out my passport, asked Shyam to give me his as well, and put them along with all our money into a little bag that I hung around my neck. Then we set off.

We pedalled for a couple of hours and realized the sari had been a wise move. We looked like a bunch of villagers and were able to slip past the patrols without arousing suspicion. Tamil women riding bicycles is a common enough sight. But it was too good to last.

The six of us were pedalling along on a straight road that was like an embankment. There were coconut trees on the left, a lagoon to the right, and not a soul around. Suddenly, a vehicle came hurtling towards us. It was an Indian army jeep.

The Tiger guerillas reacted with instant reflexes. They shouted at one another, slammed the brakes, jumped off their bicycles, threw them on the kerb and ran away into the fields. Shyam and I looked at each other for a split second and then instinctively followed suit. We threw our bikes down and ran as fast as we could behind the Tigers. The guerrilla who was carrying our bag threw it away to enable him to run faster. They jumped into the waist-deep lagoon and waded like ducks with bullets in their backside. I don't know why they didn't swim. We imitated them unquestioningly. I lost my slippers along the way, but sprinted through the water, holding aloft the little bag with our passports and money. Shyam's camera bag dipped in the water as he ran, and all his cameras and accessories were ruined.

Never have I run for my life the way I did that day. As we neared the bank, I turned around to see that the jeep had stopped on the road and three or four soldiers were running after us. They were shouting, ordering us to stop. They fired a few warning shots in the air. Even as I ran, I wondered why they didn't fire at us. Clearly we were guilty of something, the way we were running.

I discovered much later the reason why they didn't shoot us. The Tiger leadership and the Indian soldiers had agreed to a two-day ceasefire, and this was the second day. Maybe the ceasefire had something to do with the fact that 26 November is Pirabhakaran's birthday. Whatever the reason, Shyam and I are alive today only because there was a ceasefire which the Indian troops honoured, even though they knew they had stumbled upon a group of Tigers.

We were out of the lagoon and running on the narrow earthen ridge that criss-crossed the paddy fields. It was then that I experienced the power of the survival instinct. I cannot walk barefoot, even on polished floors. My feet are so absurdly sensitive that if I walk on the ground, even tiny stones pierce my feet like arrows. But here I was running barefoot on a path that was full of thorns and stones, with my sari hitched up to my knees.

We reached a village called Sarasalai. People watched us run past in amazement. The Tigers yelled at them that we were being pursued by Indian soldiers and that they should mislead them. We ran through the village lanes and eventually reached its outskirts. A six-foot high barbed wire fence loomed in front of us. Without even breaking their stride, the Tigers leaped over like monkeys. I ran and stopped short, not knowing what to do. There was no way I could climb over the fence. Shyam managed to cross over. Everybody urged me to jump, but I couldn't. I didn't know how to.

The sound of barking dogs behind us indicated the IPKF soldiers were gaining on us. Realizing it was futile to coax me to jump, two Tigers climbed back over the barbed wire. They cupped their hands for me to step on, so they could heave me over. I tucked my sari in as best as I could, and then holding the two Tigers by their shoulders for support, stepped onto their cupped hands. They heaved, I jumped, and I felt myself flying in the air and landing on the other side—right on top of Vincent who had tried to catch me to break my fall. So there was Vincent lying flat on the ground, me lying on top of him, with parts of my sari ripped and caught in the barbed wire.

I have never been so embarrassed. Had my skin not been blackened by the sun, I would have turned a beetroot red. I pulled myself away from him and as I tried to disengage my sari from the barbed wire fence, stole a glance at Vincent, who was still lying on the ground. He was making the sign of the cross!

I burst out laughing. He was silently praying to God and to Pirabhakaran to forgive him!

The sound of barking dogs was closer now. Vincent scrambled to his feet, and we began running through the fields again. Eventually, we reached a house. It belonged to Vincent's father, Kangatharam, a school teacher. His youngest daughter, Ambi, lived with him. But it was unsafe for us to remain there. The Indian soldiers would ask around, and someone could lead them to Vincent's house. So Ambi took us over to her friend's house, about a kilometre away, for the night halt.

Ambi's friend, Sumathi, was twenty-five, unmarried, and lived with her father, who was old and nearly blind. Sumathi's two brothers had been in the movement. Both were dead. Her mother had died long ago.

Sumathi served us a humble meal of rice and some odd-tasting vegetable. We didn't talk much. There was something wearily gloomy and defeated about the dimly lit room and its occupants. There weren't any curtains or even a tablecloth to relieve the dreariness of the room. The lamp flickered, casting dismal shadows on the blackened walls, and in its light I caught Sumathi casting long, yearning glances at Shyam. With most young men either dead, or in the movement and abjuring sex, poor Sumathi didn't have much of an outlet for her hormones. Bridegrooms were the rarest commodity in Jaffna those days. Shyam must have been aware of her glances because he did not look up from his plate. From his pile of uneaten vegetables, it was evident that he found the taste even more odd than I did.

Just as we finished our meal, Vincent came in, accompanied by two others. He said we should sleep in the outhouse—should there be an army raid, Sumathi and her father would not be compromised. If we were found, we were to admit that we were two journalists on our way to Jaffna and had taken shelter at night in the outhouse. Vincent left, saying he would come to fetch us at 9 a.m. the next day.

Shyam and I went to the outhouse, which was a thatched shed in the extreme corner of the backyard. The slanting roof came low to the ground and was held up by wooden poles. There were no walls. There were a few planks and a wooden bench. We slept as best as we could.

Day six. Early in the morning, Sumathi came to tell us tea was ready. We went in, had the tea, washed ourselves and went back to the outhouse to wait for Vincent. Minutes ticked by slowly and eventually he strode in—to tell us the bad news. The Tigers were abandoning us. It was impossible to go a step further. The Indian army had tightened the noose around the village—all because they had come to the wrong conclusion.

The soldiers had questioned the villagers who had confirmed they had seen a group of Tigers running past. But they also revealed that with the Tigers were two strangers they had not seen before in these parts—a young woman and a man with a thick moustache. The Indian soldiers put two and two together to make five. They concluded that the fleeing couple was Pirabhakaran and his wife. (Those were the days when the most striking feature of Pirabhkaran's face was his moustache.)They knew the couple was holed up somewhere close by, so they decided to seal the area and do a house-to-house search.

According to Vincent, thousands of troops had reached Sarasalai. They had counted as many as seventy-two Shaktimans, that behemoth of an army vehicle, rumbling into the area to seal it tight. We were on our own from now on, and it was best to surrender, advised Vincent. He was sorry the mission had failed. We hadn't even reached Jaffna, let alone met Pirabhakaran, but it couldn't be helped.

He bid us farewell and left—for his tryst with death, as I learned much later from his father, who corresponded with me. Apparently, that morning Vincent walked out of the outhouse right into an army patrol. His associate managed to escape, but Vincent got caught. He swallowed

cyanide and hours later, the Indian soldiers fetched his father
to identify his body. Kangatharam was very proud of his
son, though years ago he had been dismayed when he
discovered two grenades in the drawer of his son's wooden
study-table (which he showed me when I visited him on
one of my subsequent trips to Jaffna). That was the day he
realized Vincent had 'joined the movement'. That was the
day he knew his son would die young.

    Shyam and I sat on the wooden bench in the outhouse,
wondering what to do. We were surrounded. The noose
had tightened. From where we sat hunched inside the
thatched shed, we could see the boots of soldiers marching
by. They seemed to be coming and going in all directions.
Rather than sit there and be discovered by the soldiers, I
felt it was better to walk out and surrender. It would be
less dangerous for Sumathi and her father, and it was better
to do something rather than just sit there and wait for the
soldiers.

    So we walked out, a sad and bedraggled pair, dirty and
tired. Shyam's stubble had grown into a wild beard. I was a
mess. My sari was torn in several places, and the bottom of
it was mud-stained and jagged. My arms were tanned black,
and I was barefoot.

    We saw a group of soldiers approaching. So this was it.
Six days of effort, all for nothing. I had never experienced
failure in any of my journalistic ventures. Despite seemingly
insurmountable odds, I had eventually triumphed if only
because, like a bulldog, I just never gave up. But now our
game was up. What a sad ending, what a futile trip.

    The soldiers cast a cursory glance at us and walked on.
They didn't even accost us, let alone arrest us. So we moved
on and on, past many groups of soldiers who didn't seem
at all interested in us. We figured out the reason much later.

They were looking for Pirabhakaran and his wife, and the last thing the LTTE chief and his wife would have done was wander about in the streets. Obviously they would be hiding somewhere. Besides, we didn't look poor; we looked like beggars.

We reached the main tarred road of the Jaffna peninsula, the road that connects Jaffna to Vavuniya. Jaffna was still several kilometres away. We sat on a roadside concrete bench, waiting to be arrested. A jeep full of soldiers came by, and Shyam rose to flag it down. I stopped him. Somehow, I still didn't want to give up. I had no alternative plans, but why hasten our surrender, I reasoned. Let them come and find us. Why should we go to them? The jeep went past us without stopping.

We must have been sitting there for about fifteen minutes when two young Tamil boys on bicycles approached us and struck up a conversation. Jaffna was about twenty kilometres further up, they informed us. As we chatted, an idea formed in my head. I started talking to them about their bicycles. It didn't take long to persuade them to sell the bikes to us for Rs 2,500 each. A tidy sum, so they agreed.

I told Shyam we would pedal towards Jaffna. If we were stopped and arrested, so be it. But if we could slip past so many soldiers, we might be lucky enough to slip past some more. We had to get to Jaffna before 5 p.m. when the curfew was enforced. We were so close, it would be a shame to abandon our mission now. Even if we didn't get an interview with Pirabhakaran, we could do a 'Life in Jaffna' piece, which would be a good exclusive story because Jaffna was out of bounds to journalists.

Shyam was game, so we rode off. We imitated the local villagers. Several yards before a barricade, they would meekly dismount from their bicycles and walk past.

Sometimes the soldiers would ask for identification papers. The locals had them ready in their hands. The chances of slipping past unnoticed would be better if we were part of a group. So, well before we reached a barricade we would dismount and walk slowly, waiting for some villagers to join us. Then we walked along with them. The disguise was not just in our dirty, shredded clothes but in our demeanour—we were meek, submissive, heads hung low, never looking the soldiers in the eye. We went through eighteen checkposts without incident.

Our luck ran out at the nineteenth barricade, at Navatkuli. It was nearly 4 p.m., and Jaffna was still about three kilometres away. There was nobody else around, so we finally had to approach the barricade on our own.

The guard on duty asked us for papers. There was no point pretending to be local villagers. I spoke to the guard in Hindi, telling him I was a nurse and that we were headed for the Jaffna hospital.

The guard let out a whoop of joy. 'You can speak Hindi! You can speak *Hindi*! My God, we haven't spoken Hindi to anyone here. We haven't spoken Hindi to any civilian for three weeks,' he exclaimed, with the broadest grin imaginable on his face. He insisted we have tea.

I just wanted to get the hell out of his friendly clutches. I said we would love to, but we had to reach Jaffna before five, and we were cutting it fine. I promised we would come back in a day or two and definitely have tea with him. But he wouldn't take no for an answer and insisted we come in and meet the other guards on duty. Making a dash for it would have been stupid, so we dispiritedly accompanied him to the bunker. All the other guards gathered around us, chattering away in Hindi. They told us they were fed up, they were dying to get out of this wretched place, the people were hostile, there were too many mosquitoes...

One soldier began making tea. I tried my best to protest. I wanted to get out fast because I knew I could fool them, but if a senior officer came by, he would see through my foolish story and catch on quickly to the fact that we were not hospital staff. Nurses and doctors travel to Jaffna by boat. They don't go cycling up the trunk road. And they certainly don't dress like us. Every minute inside the Indian army bunker increased our chances of capture.

As there was no way of preventing them from giving us tea, I decided the best thing was to get over with the ritual as quickly as possible. They served us tea which was so sugary it made me feel sick. Just as we were gulping it down, I heard the screech of tyres outside. My heart sank.

A tall officer strode in and the Indian sentries rushed to tell him the good news—an Indian nurse and attendant had arrived from India. They could speak Hindi!

The officer was immediately suspicious. He was young, smart and rather handsome in his combat fatigues. His name was stitched on the breast-pocket of his uniform. It said 'Dubey'. He scanned us carefully.

'Show me your passport,' he ordered.

Shyam showed his, and the officer studied it carefully and returned it.

'Sir, can we go please? The curfew begins at 5 p.m., and we don't have much time left,' I said, hoping to hurry him.

'Can I see your passport?' he said coolly, ignoring my desperate plea.

I handed over my passport. He looked at the first page, looked at me and then back again. He pulled up a chair and sat down. Then he looked me up and down again, slowly taking in every detail.

'You are Anita Pratap?'

'Yes, sir.'

'Anita Pratap, the journalist?'

My heart sank to the soles of my bare feet. What cursed luck, to be recognized by some middle-ranking Indian army officer who actually read magazines instead of playing volleyball or whatever.

Suddenly, the officer burst out laughing. I was stunned by his reaction. I had expected him to get angry with me for flouting rules or dutifully start arranging my deportation, but being laughed at was not a reaction I could have anticipated.

'I can't believe you are Anita Pratap.'

I didn't say anything.

'You really are Anita Pratap?' he questioned in wonder. He was still laughing.

'Yes,' I said miserably.

'But you are so ugly!' he said, convulsing with laughter. 'Look at you. You look like a churail,' he said, now literally doubled up with laughter.

I was miffed. I mean, I don't have fancy notions about my beauty, but nobody had called me a witch before. But there was so much mirth in the man, I couldn't take offence, even though I wasn't particularly pleased.

I waited with as lofty an expression as I could muster, for his mirth to subside.

'By the way, I am Major Ravi Dubey,' he said, extending his hand to me. 'Really nice to meet you, but why do you look like this?' he asked, wiping the tears from his eyes that still scanned me from head to foot for the umpteenth time.

'We are trying to get to Jaffna. It's not been easy. We had to run through jungles and wade through lagoons,' I said.

'You mean to say you are doing all this for the sake of an article?' he asked in amazement. He stopped rubbing his eyes and gaped at me.

'Well, there was no other way to get to Jaffna,' I pointed out.

Major Dubey sat down, shaking his head in wonder and laughing at the same time. 'You may not be as good-looking as people say, but you certainly are tougher. It would be wrong to send you back. So you carry on to Jaffna while I look the other way. We have never met, okay?'

I was so overjoyed, I could have hugged him.

'Thanks so much. I owe you one on this. You won't regret it. Your gesture has made the Indian army rise in my esteem. Truly.' My gratitude made me flatter him shamelessly, though I meant every word I said. 'I hope we can meet some day in better circumstances, and I can assure you that I normally look better than this. We've got to rush now because there is barely half an hour left for curfew, and we still have a few kilometres to pedal to Jaffna. Thanks for everything and really nice not meeting you,' I gushed with a big smile.

'Can I have your card?' asked Dubey, then pocketed it with a smile. 'I will be in touch.' I have never met him since, but we corresponded for a while, exchanging bits of gossip and news. Then, as with so many acquaintances, we lost touch.

Shyam and I pedalled furiously like chimpanzees in a circus and reached Jaffna virtually on the dot. We checked into Gnanam hotel, whose owners I knew to be sympathizers of the LTTE. The first thing I did on reaching my room was to look at the mirror. Not out of vanity, but out of curiosity. I hadn't looked at myself in a mirror for six days. And well, nobody had called me a churail before.

I stared at the mirror in horror. I could barely recognize the face that looked back at me. Ugly was an understatement. I had become so dark, there was no difference between the colour of my hair and skin. The whites of my eyes and teeth stood out in startling contrast. My lips looked more pink than normal. My over-shampooed hair stood out wild and rough like a haystack. I looked like the gollywog in the Noddy books I had read as a child. I looked down at myself—my sari was torn and dirty, my feet were cracked with dirt. I was a real sight. Major Dubey had had reason to laugh.

But horror at my appearance did not ruin my appetite. I ate heartily, slept soundly and woke up, refreshed and eager to discover life in Jaffna.

Earlier in the year, before the Indians arrived, Sri Lankan air force planes had carpet-bombed important Tamil towns in the Jaffna peninsula, like Velvettithurai (Pirabhakaran's home town), Point Pedro, Vasivilan and Urupiddy, and reduced them to ghost towns. The main streets looked like disused sets from a World War II film. Ruined hulks of buildings with collapsed ceilings and façades riddled with bullet holes were mute testimony to a brutal war. Artillery shells had left behind craters on the potholed roads. There was not a soul in sight—no human beings, no dogs, no birds. Nothing but eerie silence. It was as if one had stumbled upon a lost, ruined and forgotten civilization. A year ago, these had been bustling towns, selling onions and combs and saris. But now the Tamils were trying to piece together their lives from the debris of the past. Most were living with relatives or in refugee camps, having been forced to flee their devastated towns and villages.

There is something spooky about a war-ravaged town. You see buildings that had once been built with so much pride and care, now ruined and abandoned, moving symbols of the futility of war.

For the inhabitants of this area, there will never again be the sweet, warm, nostalgic homecoming that so many of us are fortunate to experience in our lives. The joy we experience when we see the house we played in as children, the trees we climbed, the swing we fell from, the cowshed where we watched the birth of a calf for the first time, the river we bathed in, the dales we picnicked in. A sweet and ordinary pleasure, but so warm and enriching that only those who have experienced it know its value.

Most of the residents of the destroyed towns fled to Jaffna. There they got hit by the Indian troops a few months later. Indian helicopter gunships now strafed the densely populated areas. 'Heli, heli!' became a frequently heard cry on the narrow streets, as people frantically ducked for cover whenever they heard a drone in the sky. It became a land of shortages, gun battles, artillery duels, malnutrition and diarrhoea. No other place seemed as cursed as Jaffna, once a proud city and the citadel of Tamil learning and culture.

In the lone functioning Jaffna hospital, equipment was rudimentary. Sandbags were used as weights for traction. Entire wards were closed because doctors and specialists had fled. At least hundred people died every month, mostly for lack of antibiotics. Rabies, spread by roving, ravenous dogs, killed even more people, because vaccine was not available. Her voice heavy with despair, Dr N. Kanagarathnam, the director of the hospital, once said to me, 'This war has reduced us to a nation of stray people and stray dogs.'

And stray bullets that could make even the most ordinary errand a fatal venture. We were driving around in a battered Morris Minor taxi, when we found ourselves right in the middle of a gun battle between the LTTE and the Indian soldiers. Our driver screeched to a halt. We jumped out and hid by the side of the car. Bullets zipped back and forth for a few minutes and then everything became silent. Minutes ticked by, but our taxi driver told us to stay put. 'We must not move for at least half an hour,' he whispered to us.

Fifteen minutes passed. Nothing happened. Then an old man came along on a bicycle. A long stalk of ripe yellow bananas was tied to his saddle at the back. He was very old and scrawny. His age made pedalling an effort. He must have been a mere six metres away from us when the gun battle erupted again. Before he could react, a bullet hit him on the chest, and he crashed, bicycle, bananas and all onto the road. He was dead even before his head hit the ground.

How many people have died here. How many homes have been wrecked, how many families torn apart. How many Jaffna mothers have suffered the fate of Mother Mary, holding their dying sons in their arms.

Jayamani Marianayagam was a broken woman when I met her in Jaffna. Her seventeen-year-old son had been rehearsing 'You are my rock, oh Jesus' on the organ in Jaffna's St. Mary's church when a gun battle flared between the LTTE and a rival Tamil group in the grounds outside. A wounded Tiger stumbled into the church, his enemies in pursuit. They couldn't catch the Tiger, so they grabbed Jayamani's son. Later that night, the boy's body was dumped near the church: his legs broken, his fingernails missing, half his head blown away. Holding the remains of her son, Jayamani cried the night away. 'No mother should have to face the tragedy of seeing her son like that,' she sobbed. She lived in mortal dread that her two younger sons, aged fifteen and thirteen, would become victims too, or join the

LTTE to take revenge on the rival group. She wanted to flee Jaffna with her sons. Her husband worked as a waiter in a West German hotel, and the only way she could guarantee her sons' lives was by joining him. But the previous year, a travel agency had cheated her out of the family savings, and she was left without the means to travel.

Despite, or maybe because of life's cruel and unceasing challenges, the people of Jaffna excelled in the art of survival. Years of adversity had honed their ingenuity. There was a total embargo on fuel, yet Jaffnaites managed to concoct their own fuel to run cars and motorbikes and even generators. They mixed vegetable oil with kerosene as a substitute for diesel. They made detergents out of palmyra, a type of palm oil, and paper out of straw and waste. Contraband goods from Colombo were craftily smuggled in: batteries in hollowed-out bars of soap, antibiotics in sanitary napkins, diesel fuel in coconuts.

Satisfied with our reporting, Shyam and I struck a deal with a truck owner who was transporting onions to Colombo to give us a ride back. Dressed in the same torn, dirty clothes, we travelled back, seated at the rear of the truck. We reached by nightfall and walked to Hotel Lanka Oberoi, our regular haunt, where our luggage was kept in storage.

Shyam managed to get in, but the doorman stopped me. He tried to shoo me away, mistaking me for a beggar. I told him I stayed in the hotel and that annoyed him. The temerity of the beggar! Shyam tried to defend me, but the doorman got even more agitated. So I requested Shyam to call the guest relations officer (GRO). All the receptionists and staff at the hotel knew me well. I would be able to convince them of my identity.

The young GRO strode up to me, stopped and stared in

pure shock.

'Yes, I am Anita. Would you please ask the doorman to let me in?'

Her jaw dropped in amazement as she took in my dishevelled hair, my wretched appearance, my tattered sari, my bare feet. 'Anita, what has happened to you?'

'It's a long story. I'll tell you later,' I said as I walked past the stunned doorman. Neither the GRO nor I wanted to hang about in the lobby—it wouldn't do the hotel's reputation, or mine, any good. I was hustled to a beautiful sea-facing room on the fifth floor, and by the time I finished speaking to Zubin and my office, my suitcase had arrived.

Never had a five-star hotel seemed more luxurious. Sinking into the foamy bathtub, I knew I was in heaven. An hour later I emerged, refreshed and squeaky clean. Then I ordered the biggest meal I have ever ordered for myself — fried rice, lobster, devilled prawns, a strawberry milk shake and a chocolate sundae for dessert.

After dinner, with my belly swollen like that of a python that had just swallowed a goat, I flopped on the bed. It was divine. Soft, clean and cushiony. Almost immediately I drifted off to sleep and woke up well past noon the next day with the feeling that the world was a marvellous place. One needs a harrowing experience to realize how wonderful life usually is. Normality is such a blessing—a blessing we don't count until tragedy strikes.

God knows Sri Lanka has suffered more than its share of tragedies. The very first tragedy that I reported was the burning down of the Jaffna Public Library in 1981, which I covered from Madras. Since then, I have been on innumerable reporting missions to Sri Lanka, a tropical paradise where the beauty of nature co-exists with the savagery of man—mass murders, bomb explosions, assassinations, civil war, prison massacres, riots, death-squad murders, bombs on Christian churches, attacks on Buddhist temples, curfews, kidnappings, aerial strafing, landmines, ambushes, car bombs, suicide bombings.

'Mom, don't look so serious,' Zubin's voice cuts through my thoughts. 'You look so stern, not at all like yourself.'

'At least then I don't look like Michael Jackson,' I banter, grateful to come back to my safe little world with its simple pleasures. We are on day three of our odyssey to Kochi. How different from day three to Jaffna. And this time, I know I will reach my destination as scheduled.

DESTINY

Sri Lanka is part of my destiny—both professional and personal.

My first trip to Sri Lanka was in February 1983, a time when the island nation had not yet attained its bloody reputation, though occasional violence erupted in Jaffna. Colombo was an exotic destination, and my ex-husband and I had a wonderful holiday. While there, I realized how little we Indians knew about our beautiful neighbour. I got some information on the nation's history, culture and economy. I also asked for an interview with President J.R. Jayewardene and was thrilled when it came through. After the interview was over, the state public relations department took photographs of the president and me greeting each other. A picture was published in the Sri Lankan papers the next day. It was my first brush with fame. I felt gloriously important. I was twenty-four years old.

A few months later, in July, news flashed that island-wide riots had broken out in Sri Lanka. Sinhalese mobs were butchering Tamils. It came to be described as the 'July 1983 racial holocaust'. Violence was spreading and even Indians were being attacked. I was then working for *Sunday* magazine and its newly launched sister publication, the *Telegraph*, headquartered in Calcutta. I called up editor M.J. Akbar from Madras, where I was based, wanting to go down to Sri Lanka to report. Akbar was reluctant, for reasons of security. This was 1983, few women reported politics, even fewer went into conflict zones. The situation was particularly dangerous because mobs were targeting Indians as well. Besides, this was a foreign country where an Indian magazine wouldn't have much clout if I got into trouble or danger. And I was so young. But I insisted, and eventually Akbar relented.

It was the story that made my career. Akbar provided the ballast for my launch. As I flew down to the burning island, Akbar published a highlighted item on the front page every day which ran:

Next week in
The Telegraph

On July 26, the violence against Indians and local Tamils reached a frenzy in Sri Lanka. Tamils were massacred. Our High Commission was attacked. Indians who happened to be there did not dare leave their hotel rooms, some even went without food. Because they could not trust the Sinhalese bearers.

On July 28, with Colombo still in flames and anti-Indian violence still taking its toll, on the day when all the Indians were coming back to India however they could, our correspondent Anita Pratap took a flight in the other direction. Despite the obvious personal risk, she flew to Colombo on Thursday to cover the worst case of anti-Indian violence ever known in a foreign country.

Her first-hand reports of the terror in Sri Lanka will appear in The Telegraph next week.

Akbar had planted the seeds of my reputation as a daring, fearless journalist. I didn't know this at the time because I was already in Colombo, and perhaps it was just as well— I had enough problems to cope with, without the added burden of living up to his expectations.

That Sri Lankan experience shattered me. It was a turning point in my life. Both at the personal and professional level, life for me has since been defined as before and after the 1983 riots.

I had lived in a cocooned world—loving parents, a sweet kid sister, a witty husband and an adorable son. God had blessed me with so much: I had good health, sufficient wealth, and happiness in abundance. Friends used to say I lived a charmed life—things came easy to me, people took to me instantly, I smiled and laughed my way through life. I had never seen human cruelty, savagery and vengeful hatred.

But the Sri Lankan experience helped me grow up, made me realize that another world of violence, horror, injustice and brutality exists. It prepared me for life, especially for the personal challenges that were soon to come hurtling my way.

When I landed in Colombo, it was in flames. Clouds of smoke rose like poisonous black mushrooms into the sky. In my hurry to leave Madras, I hadn't even booked a hotel room. So there I was stranded at Colombo's Katunayake airport, without a hotel reservation and without transport into the curfew-bound city. It was BBC Radio's Mark Tully who came to my rescue. He gave me a lift into the city and also helped me get a room in the Galle Face Hotel, where he was a regular customer.

The following day, my top priority was to get a curfew pass. It took forty-five minutes of argument and persuasion before the police inspector reluctantly handed me one. He argued that it was far too dangerous for me to go around in the city because I was a woman and an Indian. The average Sinhalese saw all Tamils as Indians and therefore all Indians were Tamils too. I tried to reason with the inspector—'all oranges are fruits, but all fruits are not oranges'. The inspector asked me how I would find the time to explain the difference between fruits and oranges when mobs were attacking. I'll take the chance, I told him, I have to because I am here to do a job.

With my curfew pass tucked away safely, I set off on foot. Everywhere, I could see proof of carnage: burnt-out hulks of buildings, burning bonfires of cars, motorcycles and furniture belonging to the Tamils. It didn't take an Einstein to figure out the attacks on the Tamils were systematic, pre-planned and well organized. The Sinhalese mobs seemed to be targeting the economic base of the Tamil community—textile and other factories owned by the Tamils were all completely gutted. Armed with voters' lists, the gangs came in empty trucks in which they carried away the goods looted from Tamil homes—television sets, radios, refrigerators, music systems, jewellery, clocks, clothes. They not only knew where the Tamils lived but seemed to have a list of their belongings as well. As one Tamil resident said, the marauders had come to his compound and, after setting fire to his vehicles and furniture, demanded to know where his Matador van was.

With my Kodak instamatic camera, I took pictures of ruined buildings, burnt shops, deserted streets, burning furniture, piled-up garbage. Taking pictures was highly risky because the government had imposed a full censorship. Photography was strictly banned. I would walk along the curfew-deserted streets, look around for the police, quickly take a few shots, shove the camera into my trouser pocket and then saunter along pretending to be an eager, curious tourist.

Two days later, when I was wandering on the streets taking pictures, my luck ran out. I was aiming to shoot a mound of garbage that symbolized how the nation had ground to a halt. Just as I was about to click, two rifle-toting policemen turned a corner and walked right into me and the frame of my camera. I hastily brought my camera down as the policemen instinctively aimed their rifles at me. They shouted, I stuttered. They seized my camera and asked me to come to the police station. I knew I was sunk if they found out I was a journalist.

'Why are you taking pictures out here? Don't you know photography is banned? Don't you know there is curfew and you are supposed to stay indoors?' one of them barked at me.

'I am sorry, but I happened to be in the island when the violence broke out. I am taking pictures of buildings because I am a student of architecture. Colombo has some really beautiful buildings. But I won't take any more,' I promised, hoping that if the pleading tone didn't do the trick, flattery would. Most citizens preen when they hear a foreigner praise their country. One of the policemen softened, but the other remained tough and sceptical. 'Why are you roaming around when you know there is curfew? We have to arrest you. Show me your bag,' he ordered.

Mercifully, the three exposed rolls of film were in my pocket. My bag contained notebooks, passport, money, hairbrush, lipstick, and a million other things that a woman's bag necessarily contains. Then I spotted the one thing that saved the day. I was carrying the picture of President Jayewardene and myself greeting each other with folded hands, taken on my previous trip to Colombo.

I whisked it out and said in an excited gush of words, 'See, I am a guest of the president. I know him very well. See this picture.'

That stopped the sceptical policeman in his tracks. He examined the photograph carefully and then handed it back to me. 'You are still violating the law. Don't take any more pictures,' he warned, giving me back the camera after removing the film. I was sorry to see that film go, it had pictures taken in the refugee camps and some pictures of injured Indians, but I was glad they hadn't discovered the other rolls in my pocket.

The Indians who had been injured in the riots were in a state of shock. Mohan Chandran worked in the passport section of the Indian High Commission. On the evening of 26 July, his wife, Omana, heard the window panes of their living room shatter. She ran to the front and saw half a dozen men pelting stones at their house. As she watched, they stormed in, armed with sticks, knives and iron rods. They ordered her to get out and began plundering and slashing furniture. Carrying her five-month-old infant and dragging her crying five-year-old daughter, Omana ran out of the house and into the neighbour's home. They were Sinhalese, but they let them in.

The Chandrans had finished their three-year tenure and were to return to India a month later. As foreign goods were not sold in India, they had used all their savings to buy household items. Everything was looted—a scooter, refrigerator, washing machine, television set, music system, watches, food processor, clothes, toys. 'We have nothing. We are beggars now,' Omana sobbed.

Another Indian, Mrs Trilok Singh, had a horrible story to narrate. She and her husband lived in a first-floor apartment. When the riots started, she heard people breaking into the apartment below and moving furniture noisily. There was only a sixty-year-old Tamil woman living there—she was raped. The attackers stormed into the house next-door, where too a Tamil family lived. They cut off the man's hand. He died the next day.

It was so dangerous to remain indoors that the Trilok Singhs ran out. A fleeing Tamil couple thrust their son on the Singhs. When I met them, the seven-year-old Tamil child, Sudarshan Ratnaraja, was still with them, happy and wide-eyed at the rapid turn of events in his life. He was being looked after well, but I couldn't help thinking how his parents must worry. I met many such parents in the refugee camps where rich, middle-class and poor Tamils were now huddled. Anguished mothers recounted how they had lost their children in the mad melee as they fled their homes. In other camps, lost children cried out for their mothers.

Almost two eventful decades have gone by, but the memory of the agony etched on the face of an elderly man, a Tamil named Sachithanandan, as he narrated his horrifying story to me, has not faded. Now I know it never will—and may probably be one of the flashback images that flits through my mind moments before I die. Sachithanandan was about sixty years old, dark and wizened with worry and hard work. His face was small and gaunt, and the white stubble on his dark skin gave him an unkempt, grizzly look. His eyes were small and glazed with pain. He recounted how the mob had invaded his first-floor apartment. They looted the goods and set the house on fire. He and his family ran out of the house. His son and he were the last to leave. Then one attacker caught him and held him in a hammerlock, while three others did the same to his son.

They were held on the veranda of his apartment. Below, his black Morris Minor car was in flames. Then the scene that I cannot rid my mind of, was enacted. The attackers threw his son into the burning car. Sachithanandan was forced to watch his son being roasted alive. He struggled to break free, to run to his screaming son, but he was held fast and forced to watch. 'I couldn't do anything, I had to watch my son burn to death. Why didn't they throw me instead, why didn't God make me die,' he sobbed.

I felt tears roll down my cheeks. How could God allow such wickedness? These were not men looting and burning and murdering on the streets of Colombo. They were demons escaped from some infernal region of hell. Most of them were drunk. It's not possible for human beings in their senses to commit such ghoulish crimes.

Another Tamil, K.C. Sinanathan, had fractured both his legs when he jumped off the fourth floor of a burning building. Gangrene had set in because he, like several other Tamils, was turned away from the Colombo General Hospital. Manian was another such patient. He had festering wounds all over his body. Five drunk men had beaten him with iron rods. Half a bottle of pus had been removed from his head wound alone.

The conditions in the refugee camps were awful. For five days, there was no food. On the sixth day, thirty food packets arrived for a thousand starving people. The hygiene in the camps was deteriorating fast. There was no water, so the bathrooms were locked up. The refugees had to go to one corner of the compound to shit and urinate. In a few days, the whole place was stinking. The torpid heat converted the camp into a germ charnel. Flies feasted on the filth. They droned in different colours and shapes— ordinary grey houseflies, bulbous blue-bottomed ones, shiny bottle-green flies, tiny ones, swollen ones, flat and broad ones. Diseases spread. Refugees vomited, adding to the stink. Snot blocked noses, phlegm choked throats. Eyes became bloodshot with fever. Lips cracked with dehydration. Bottoms became sore with diarrhoea.

Crisis can sometimes transform the most unexpected people into heroes. Overnight, they become leaders and towers of strength for the frightened, broken, sick people around them. Mrs Mercy Merais, a twenty-nine-year-old law graduate, was one such person. Effortlessly she took charge, comforting the grief-stricken and administering to the sick. She met the district minister and succeeded in getting a supply of rations. She sat up all night, making a list of refugees in the camp for a foreign relief agency that had promised help.

Merais told me many stories about the atrocities perpetrated on the Tamil civilians. She was burning with righteous rage, her anger giving her more strength to fight for the victims. She had introduced herself to me as 'Mrs Mercy Merais'. After several hours in the camp, when we took a break, I made the mistake of asking where her husband was.

Suddenly, her whole body crumpled, her face sagged. All the strength seemed to ebb out of her. 'I don't know. I am told he has been shot,' she whispered, and started crying. It was as if all the pent-up grief over her personal tragedy and the tragedy of the countless Tamils she was tending to so bravely, was pouring out of her being. I tried to comfort her, but felt inadequate when confronted with such sorrow.

I went from one refugee camp to another. They were all hell-holes of misery and grief. The experiences of these refugees were so much more traumatic than my personal tales of fear and danger, of having security personnel jab their rifles at me as I tried to see the signs of carnage, of them threatening to shoot me if I didn't go away or turn back that very instant. Since that Sri Lanka trip, I have never experienced stress or fear or anxiety. When I am in the midst of a personal difficulty, I just remember the faces and the trauma of the Tamils and realize how trivial my problems are in comparison. Instead of railing against God for piling difficulties on my plate, I learnt to thank Him for giving me problems that were so ordinary, so mundane. It is this realization—that life could be a million times worse— that has kept me happy since then.

The night before I was to leave Colombo, I discovered that somebody had been through all my things in the hotel room. But only my notebooks were missing. Two gleaming Sri Lankan coins had been left on the study table from where my notes had been confiscated. I have never divined the significance of those coins.

There was heavy checking at the airport. Journalists were frisked more than the others. I knew my papers and film rolls would be confiscated. So on slips of paper I jotted down names of people and places and the bare details of a few incidents, and put them in my shoes. As for the rolls, I would have to find someone else who could smuggle them out for me. At the hotel's insistence, I shared a taxi to the airport with an American, William Stuart, as it was night and there was curfew. All along the route we were stopped, and each time the soldiers wanted to know my identity. They were not bothered about Stuart because he was a foreigner. Inside the airport, I scanned the Indian passengers who were all headed for Madras. I spotted a young couple with a baby. I had seen them at the Indian High Commission, and they too recognized me. I approached the husband and asked if he could take the rolls into the aircraft for me. He agreed, but I couldn't hand them over to him while the lounge was crawling with security personnel. So his wife and I went into the ladies' room and when no one was around, I handed them to her. She clutched her baby and the rolls and took them back to her husband.

The customs officers checked me thoroughly. They specifically asked if I was carrying photographs or film negatives. I said no, and still they checked. Fortunately, they didn't ask me to take off my shoes. Eventually they let me go. Once inside the aircraft, I took back the rolls. Only when we were airborne did I take a deep breath of relief and relax.

I reached home and went to work early next morning. It was a Sunday, but I felt I had to start writing or I would fall apart. I didn't realize I was trembling. Back in the safety of Madras, in the comfort of my home, the full horror of all that I had seen and heard hit me like a tornado. It would take three days for my trembling to cease.

Those were the days of typewriters, and I had my old faithful iron Halda machine. We used rough, yellowish newsprint paper as typing sheets. I sat in my office and typed away, pounding the keys with such ferocity that I punched little holes in the paper, especially when I typed the alphabet 'o'. I wasn't really writing, it was an outpouring—words were tumbling out in a torrent. I was crying too. Fortunately, I was all alone in the office.

The telephone rang. It was Akbar. He had arrived in town and wanted to meet me. I told him I would meet him in the evening. By then I would have finished all my reports.

'What, you've started writing already? You wait, I'd like to discuss how we should handle the coverage. I have some plans in mind,' he snapped. I could detect anger in his voice.

'I can't wait. I am writing as it comes. There is nothing

to discuss. I will see you at about 7 p.m.,' I snapped back and banged the phone down.

Akbar must have sensed something was amiss. I had never been rude or sharp-tongued with him. It was totally unlike me. He called back.

'Are you okay?' he asked.

'I am fine,' I said.

'I want you to know I am really proud of you,' he said.

I was close to sobbing. I didn't want to lose control now. His concern brought an added lump to the many lumps constricting my throat. I didn't want to talk any more.

'Thanks, I'll see you at seven. Bye,' I said and gently put the phone down.

I worked on, without water or food, and finished by about 5.30 p.m. I read my reports—they were very emotional, not the dispassionate dispatches of a professional reporter. I couldn't help it. If Akbar didn't like them, he could flush them down the toilet.

Clutching the papers, I walked into Akbar's hotel room. I gave him the rolls and said he could develop them in Calcutta. He asked me to sit down.

'I know you've had a tough time. But a reporter has to be a reporter, and an editor has to be an editor. I know you are a great reporter, and you would have done your best. But now comes the hard part—how we shape our coverage.'

I didn't know, and I was too tired to care.

'You are the only Indian journalist to have gone to Sri Lanka. We are the only ones to have this exclusive coverage. So I want to serialize the reports. Carry a front-page story for several days. I don't want just one consolidated report.'

In spite of myself, I was relieved. Without thinking, that was exactly what I had done. I fished out my reports from my bag and gave them to him.

He started reading them. One by one, all of them.

'Anita, this is fantastic. You've done a great job. This is good stuff,' he said excitedly.

I could feel those dratted tears again. Without really knowing why, I suddenly felt overwhelmed by the trauma and grief of all that I had seen and experienced over the past few days. I broke down. Akbar was alarmed to see one of his toughest reporters dissolve into tears. He didn't know quite what to do, so he fetched a glass of water for me.

I took it gratefully, but it slipped out of my hands and crashed to the floor.

He brought another glass. It slipped too. I was trembling, all that bottled-up fear and anguish seeping out of me.

Akbar was really alarmed now, but without saying anything, he fetched me a third glass of water. It slipped and fell too. With that I lost the last vestige of control and began sobbing uncontrollably.

Akbar just let me be. I sensed rather than saw the housekeeping boys clean the floor. Gradually, I regained control. Akbar handed me a fourth glass of water. I clutched it with both hands and drained it in one go. I handed the empty glass back to him and smiled.

Akbar was relieved. He began smiling too and started talking about which of the stories he would run first. Then he showed me the little item he had been front-paging about me every day. I had exceeded his expectations, he said. I marvelled at how he could have put his, mine, and the *Telegraph*'s reputation on the line like that. How could he have been so sure that I would return with good stuff? He said he knew me well enough to know I would.

Akbar flew back to Calcutta and ran the reports from the very next day, with an added highlighted box: 'Our correspondent Anita Pratap reports on the situation in Sri Lanka after a dangerous trip to that violence-ridden country. She was unable to file her reports from Colombo because of the heavy censorship, especially on Indian journalists. Even her notes were confiscated when she was on her way back from Colombo to Madras. A series of Anita Pratap's exclusive reports will be published in The Telegraph over the week.'

The public and government response to my dispatches in the *Telegraph* and the cover story in *Sunday* magazine was overwhelming. People wrote in innumerable letters, some of which were published—warm letters full of praise and admiration. Akbar devoted a whole page to my pictures in the *Telegraph*, and angry parliamentarians flashed the newspaper in the well of the House, demanding India's intervention in Sri Lanka. It was my first big story.

Prominent Moderate Sri Lankan Tamil parliamentarian, A. Amirthalingam, told me later that my reports were used by the Indian government to officially intervene in Sri Lanka on moral grounds. Prime Minister Indira Gandhi had appointed noted diplomat G. Parthasarathy as her special, envoy to Sri Lanka, and he apparently used my reports in his meeting with President Jayewardene to emphasize that India could not remain passive when Tamils were being treated so badly. India had to be mindful of the emotional repercussions and the wave of sympathy for Sri Lankan Tamils within India, especially in Tamil Nadu. Of course, India had already clandestinely intervened in Sri Lanka by arming the Tamil militant groups. But my reports gave the government the moral armour to intervene.

And India did, to the detriment of both countries. A chain of tragic events would follow over the next decade.

A chain of good and bad events would follow for me

too from this trip. Akbar moulded a new image for me. I liked reporting from the field, especially from conflict zones, and the image of an intrepid reporter was sustained and strengthened over the years. Much professional success came my way amidst a floundering marriage. Newspapers and magazines glorified my courage and fearless reporting. Divorce, reporting from war zones, facing the world and raising a child all alone, strengthened my image as a brave woman, both at the personal and professional level. After all, this was still the 1980s, when much of urban India was innocent and unspoilt by Western soap opera. It was still a time when divorce and war zones were unusual and unchartered territory for women. Public fascination with me also spawned all kinds of stories, some of them utterly untrue, and some that were amusing distortions of reality.

Almost a decade later, I heard a bizarre story from Meenakshi Ganguly, then a researcher in *Time* magazine. She said my temper was 'legendary'. (Actually, I have lost my temper only a few times in my whole life, whereas Akbar's temper was, and perhaps still is, legendary). She told me about a story she had heard as a cub reporter, about one of my famous tantrums with Akbar. I have never quarrelled with Akbar. I believe he is responsible for shaping my career, and I harbour nothing but gratitude and affection for him.

According to Meenakshi, I got into a massive fight with Akbar while we were sitting and drinking in a bar (something we have not done until today). As the story did the rounds, it got magnified and embellished, though the reason for the quarrel was lost in the process. But apparently I was so furious with him, I hurled at the mirror not one but three wine glasses!

It never fails to amaze me how what really happened—

dropping three glasses of water offered to me by Akbar—
got so twisted with each telling that the version that came
to stay bore absolutely no semblance to the truth. But then,
who wants pathetic reality when there is a spicy myth up
for grabs?

Some of the spiciest myths about me revolve around
LTTE leader V. Pirabhakaran—myths kept in circulation by
journalists, diplomats and politicians, both in India and Sri
Lanka.

FROM THAMBI TO ANNAI

The passage of time has not blurred the vivid images of my first meeting with Pirabhakaran. It was a sunny morning in a Tiger safehouse in Madras. The modest first-floor apartment faced the deep blue waters of the Bay of Bengal. Pirabhakaran was meeting a journalist for the first time in his life. For me, it was a big scoop, but before I finally met the elusive guerrilla leader, I had to wait for two hours in a room furnished with cushionless settees, a few cane chairs, and a Formica-topped dining table with six chairs.

Shortly after I was seated, taciturn Tiger guerrillas switched on a colour television set (a rare commodity in those days) and made me watch several video documentaries (even rarer commodities) on the LTTE and its leader. They were beautifully shot. The dance of sunlight and the angle of the camera made Pirabhakaran seem larger than life. He looked strong, tough and brave. The film depicted LTTE as the disciplined national army of a proud nation—Tamil Eelam.

And there was Pirabhakaran in combat fatigues, holding a machine gun, inspecting a guard of honour. He strode past neat rows of uniformed Tiger soldiers to unfurl the red flag of the LTTE. No speech, all action. As the patriotic music in the background reached a crescendo, Pirabhakaran gazed, clear-eyed and proud, at the Tiger emblem on his flag, fluttering against a sunlit horizon. Che Guevara seemed small and insignificant in comparison. Pirabhakaran was the idealistic macho man—revolutionary and romantic.

When I saw Pirabhakaran in flesh-and-blood for the first time, I was speechless with disappointment. Hypnotized by the handsome, six-foot tall warrior in the video, I didn't recognize the man who walked in: he was short, stocky and ordinary—indistinguishable from a million other Tamil men; he might have been just another businessman or government employee. I assumed he was a Tiger supporter and gave him a cursory nod, then gazed out of the window to pass time, while I waited for Pirabhakaran to turn up.

Several moments later, a soft voice said in Tamil: 'Naan thaan Pirabhakaran.'

I directed my gaze disbelievingly from the sea to the source of the voice, saying to myself, 'Yeah, and naan thaan Cleopatra.'

The man was smiling, almost apologetically. I scrutinized his face and realized with astonishment that it was indeed Pirabhakaran.

He was dressed in grey trousers and a sky-blue bush shirt that couldn't quite hide the first signs of an expanding waistline. Had he walked down the street, no one would have thrown him a second glance. Any resemblance between the powerful, confident, camouflage-uniformed guerrilla leader in the video and this mild-looking, self-effacing civilian was purely coincidental.

Now I realized why Pirabhakaran was silent in the video. Macho guerrilla had a soft voice that would have undermined the action-hero image. I struggled to camouflage my disbelief and disappointment, but I am a journalist, not an actress. I didn't succeed. Fortunately, it only amused Pirabhakaran. He smiled a boyish, lopsided smile. The best way to cover up my gaffe was to get down briskly to business and begin the interview—which I did. It lasted two hours, and at the end of that first meeting I realized that he was one of the most remarkable persons I had ever met, and was ever likely to meet, in the course of my life. Certainly, I was not surprised when within a decade he became a legendary guerrilla leader.

Pirabhakaran came across as ruthless, cunning and brutal, but he was also clearly a master tactician and a brilliant strategist. There were no cobwebs in his mind. It was sharp, clear, and incisive. No doubts, no fears, no worries clouded his vision. His foresight was amazing as well. He could see today what his opponents would do years later. He would have made a brilliant chess player.

In the course of our meeting, he told me, 'Eventually, I will have to battle India.' This was years before the Indian troops were sent to Sri Lanka, even before Rajiv Gandhi became prime minister. It was the time when RAW (Research and Analysis Wing), India's intelligence agency, was training, arming and funding the LTTE.

I was shocked and told him so. How could he bite the hand that fed him? Not only was it ungrateful, wouldn't it be suicidal?

'Even more than Sri Lanka, India will not allow us to create Tamil Eelam because of its own fifty-five million Tamils in Tamil Nadu state,' he replied.

Then why was he taking India's help? 'Right now I am small. I need India's help to grow.' And he grew and grew until he became a monster in India's eyes.

The other thing about Pirabhakaran that made a deep impression on me was his unwavering commitment to the cause of Eelam. It was a deep-rooted, non-negotiable conviction.

I have interviewed him many times. Over the years, there have been many changes in the man—he is older and heavier, and no longer sports a moustache. When I asked him during one of my interviews in the mid-1990s why he had shaved off his moustache, he confided it was because it had greyed. A white moustache didn't go with his image, and it was ridiculous—and difficult—to dye a moustache. So he shaved it off. But it was so much a part of his macho image, I joked that a Pirabhakaran without a moustache was like a tiger without stripes.

Pirabhakaran laughed, but pointed out that the tiger continued to spring like before. And that's true. Age may have induced a few physical changes, but it has not induced any softening or dilution in his commitment to his cause.

In one of her interviews, President Chandrika Kumaratunga said to me, 'Even the best of guerrillas must tire of fighting and war.' That was in 1994. But Pirabhakaran is better than the best. His energy and commitment to his cause show no signs of flagging. From a hit-and-run guerrilla fighter he has evolved into a mastermind of conventional battles, the commander of a national army that forced the world's third largest army to retreat, and now the main reason for Sri Lanka's huge defense budget. A few years ago, I asked him what he had learned over two decades as a guerrilla fighter. He answered, 'He who dares, wins.' That was also the headline given to my interview with him when it was published in *Time*.

Five months later, I happened to travel in Europe and the US and was amazed to see the number of Sri Lankan Tamils wearing T-shirts with that motto—Tamils shopping in malls, Tamils walking on the streets, Tamils working in airports. Pirabhakaran had spawned a world-wide legion.

Sometime during the course of that first meeting I

remarked that it was good to meet at last. Pirabhakaran replied, 'You are seeing me for the first time, but I have seen you before.'

I was not on television at the time, but my coverage of the anti-Tamil riots in Sri Lanka had won some measure of recognition in Tamil Nadu.

'You've seen me in Tamil magazines?' I inquired.

'No, I've seen you in flesh and blood,' answered Pirabhakaran.

'Where?' I asked, astounded. Pirabhakaran and I did not exactly move in the same social circles.

'Remember, three years ago you came to interview Nedumaran (a prominent Tamil Nadu politician) in his house? I was in a room upstairs. When you walked in through the front gate, I was watching from a window upstairs.'

That sounded creepy. I was glad I wasn't on his hit list.

In a way, Pirabhakaran and I hit it off much before we met. After the July 1983 riots in Sri Lanka, all the Tamil militant leaders were granted political asylum in Tamil Nadu. They all set up offices and had several cadres indulging in covert and overt operations. They launched a massive publicity drive and gave interviews to journalists freely. At that time there were five Tamil militant groups. I met all of them and interviewed their cadres and leaders frequently— except Pirabhakaran. It was impossible to meet him. LTTE guerrillas told me flatly that Pirabhakaran did not meet journalists.

This only sharpened my curiosity. My encounters with the LTTE guerrillas and their prodigious literature convinced me that Pirabhakaran was the man to watch out for. Compared to the other Tamil groups, the LTTE cadres were clearly superior. They exuded an aura of single-minded devotion to their cause. Their commitment was strong and genuine, symbolized by the cyanide vial that hung like a talisman on a black thread around their necks. They would rather die than be captured alive. I saw the LTTE guerrillas as the blue bloods of the Tamil Eelam struggle.

But they were also extremely secretive. They didn't leave any tracks, senior leaders never lolled about in their offices, and they were very careful on the telephone. Yet, they were publicity savvy. They had excellent documentation. They had plenty of well-produced literature on the history of the Tigers, and every military action of theirs was chronicled—in print, and later on video. Clearly, the Tigers had a sense of history and personal destiny— they believed that one day they would hold the key to peace in the Tamil homeland.

I shared the Tigers' vision of their destiny. I was sure Pirabhakaran's uncompromising commitment to Eelam would ensure his trajectory as the most powerful leader of the Sri Lankan Tamils. So I ignored the other groups and concentrated on the activities of the LTTE. Needless to say, this endeared me to the Tigers. They felt that I was the only one who understood their spirit, their superiority, and their inevitable pre-eminent role in the Sri Lankan ethnic conflict.

Just as I singled out Pirabhakaran for attention, he singled me out among the press corps for his attention. Much later, in one of our many interviews, he told me he admired my courage, especially the way I reported the 1983 riots in Colombo. He said to me, 'We are guerrilla fighters, we have chosen a path of danger, so it's normal for us to face such difficult situations. But you as a journalist didn't have to risk your life, or actually be in the conflict zone, for the sake of reporting the truth. It was your reports that internationalized the Tamil problem, and for that the Tamil people will always be grateful to you.'

Of course, I was flattered by his praise. A few months after the 1983 riots, Pirabhakaran gave me the first interview, and he continued to give me interviews at every single landmark in the history of the Tamil struggle. This despite the fact that along the way, I described him variously as ruthless, despotic and egotistic.

Fr. Singharasa, a Tamil priest whom I met in Jaffna and who at one time was close to the LTTE, told me years later that Pirabhakaran had told him that he respected me as a journalist and that there were two other reasons why he continued to meet me: because I never misquoted or misinterpreted what he said, and because I was gentle in my questioning. I did not harangue or grill him. My desire was not to put him in a spot but to understand what made him tick, what made him command such a powerful organization, what made his cadres die for him, what he would do in the future. Fr. Singharasa claimed Pirabhakaran gained confidence in talking to the media from his interactions with me. Not that he talked much to the media. He has given interviews only to a handful of journalists, and that too perhaps only twice to the same person.

Pirabhakaran has always been very secretive about personal details, about his family, his childhood, his upbringing. Once I asked him to tell me what in his personal life had convinced him that an armed struggle alone would deliver the Tamils from Sinhala domination. He recounted images from the 1958 anti-Tamil riots that had left a deep impression on him. He was only four years old then. 'The shocking events of the 1958 racial riots had a profound impact on me. I heard of horrifying incidents of how our people had been mercilessly and brutally put to death by

Sinhala racists. Once I met a widowed mother, a friend of my family, who related to me her agonizing personal experience of this racial holocaust. A Sinhala mob attacked her house in Colombo. The rioters set fire to the house and murdered her husband. She and her children escaped with severe burn injuries. I was deeply shocked when I saw the scars on her body. I also heard stories of how young babies were roasted alive in boiling tar. When I heard such stories of cruelty, I felt a deep sense of sympathy and love for my people. A great passion overwhelmed me, to redeem my people from this racist system. I strongly felt that an armed struggle was the only way to confront a system which employs armed might against unarmed and innocent people.'

Pirabhakaran was only seventeen years old when he, along with a small band of Tamil youths, started the TNT (Tamil New Tigers) in 1972 on the sandy shores of his hometown, Velvettithurai. He was known to be a radical socialist and a committed nationalist. Indian and Sri Lankan intelligence agencies believe he received training and assistance from the Palestine Liberation Organization. He also had the reputation of an excellent marksman. In 1975, from a distance of 200 feet, he shot a constable named Bastianpillai as he ran, right between the eyes. The legend of Pirabhakaran was born.

Everybody called him Thambi, which in Tamil means younger brother. He earned the nickname because he became a revolutionary when still in his teens. Soon, Thambi became part of common Tamil parlance. All through the 1980s, his colleagues, associates, supporters and even ordinary civilians who had never met him called him Thambi. People used the nickname with affection as well as admiration.

In 1976, Pirabhakaran renamed his group Liberation Tigers, and a few years later changed it to Liberation Tigers of Tamil Eelam. Asked why he had chosen the tiger as his symbol, Pirabhakaran said: 'I named the movement Liberation Tigers since the Tiger emblem has deep roots in the political history of the Tamils, symbolizing Tamil patriotic resurgence. The Tiger symbol also depicts the mode of our guerrilla warfare.' The symbol is borrowed from the imperial crest of the Chola dynasty, a line of aggressive Tamil conquerors from India, who in the eleventh century sought to extend their influence to the territories that now form northern India, Sri Lanka, Java and Sumatra. In his patience, cunning, stealth and ferocity, Pirabhakaran himself is like the forest tiger, and his opponents would do well to remember that he has a snarling tiger as his mascot.

In that first interview, Pirabhakaran refused to be drawn into specifics and preferred to answer questions philosophically. Asked who his friends, philosophers and guides were, Pirabhakaran replied: 'Nature is my friend, life my philosopher, and history my guide.' As I reflect on that answer today, more than a decade and a half later, I can see how accurate a clue it is to the personality of this elusive man, and I marvel at the truth of that carefully thought out statement. Asked how he combated loneliness, Pirabhakaran replied, 'I have never felt lonely at any point of time. Loneliness is only a problem with those who are buried in their own individual egos.'

That first interview made it to the cover of Sunday magazine. In those days, Sunday was India's leading newsmagazine—courageous, forthright and inexpensive. The cover displayed a colour photograph of a clear and wide-eyed Pirabhakaran in combat fatigues, sitting behind a desk, with a gun and a tape recorder by his side. Behind him were posters of slain Tiger guerrillas. The cover carried a blurb from the interview: 'If Jayewardene (the Sri Lankan president) was a true Buddhist, I would not be carrying a gun.'

By this time, Pirabhakaran had already assassinated more than thirty politicians and policemen, raided armouries, robbed banks and attacked several Sri Lankan army camps.

Since our first meeting, I have not had much trouble meeting Pirabhakaran. But the process of meeting him has been time-consuming and tortuous because of the thick security blanket that protects him. A short while before I met Pirabhakaran for the first time, I had met the Indian prime minister, Indira Gandhi. The security around her was weak. There were the usual checks, but they were all done cursorily. At that time, Pirabhakaran was only one of five Tamil militant leaders. He was only a guerrilla striving to liberate a tiny patch of land in a tiny country, yet the security around him was astounding. To make sure I was not being tailed by the Tamil Nadu police, I would be taken to three safehouses before the encounter finally took place. Invariably, I was seated in a safehouse with a large posse of LTTE bodyguards around me when he finally arrived on the scene. Except on one occasion—a meeting in the Wanni jungles of Sri Lanka in 1990—I had to wait for at least an hour before Pirabhakaran arrived. Only in Wanni was I taken to a safehouse where he was already present when I arrived.

Then his women cadres would frisk me thoroughly, each and every time. They trusted my credentials and knew for a fact that I was not on a clandestine mission to assassinate Pirabhakaran, but they didn't take any chances. Every inch of my body was searched. The contents of my cavernous bag were spread out on a table, and every single item was examined. If I shuffled my feet or grunted in impatience, the women ignored me. They didn't offer explanations or apologies either. Their body language conveyed the message—they had a job to do, and until it was done to their satisfaction, they would not be hurried. They played the tape recorder and then opened it up completely to ensure there was nothing concealed within. Even my pen was dissembled and the tiny cavities within scrutinized.

Once, in the mid-1980s in Madras, Pirabhakaran brought his wife and three-month-old son along for the interview. His marriage was the culmination of a sweet love story. A few young girl students were on a fast-unto-death to protest against the examination policy of the Sri Lankan government that discriminated against Tamil students. Under orders from Pirabhakaran, a group of Tiger guerrillas swooped down on the spot where the girls were fasting, abducted and forcibly fed them. Then Pirabhakaran married the prettiest of the fasting girls. No one in the LTTE spoke against him for breaking their cardinal rule of celibacy. As she sat by his side during the interview, Pirabhakaran's wife did not speak even once out of turn. She wore a printed wrinkle-free sari and a modest blouse. She seemed gentle and domesticated. At his request, she handed him their son. 'His name,' said Pirabhakaran looking down at his infant, 'is Charles Antony.'

I realized then that loyalty begets loyalty. The reason LTTE cadres are so loyal to Pirabhakaran is because his loyalty to them is legendary. Charles Antony had been Pirabhakaran's right-hand man, his trusted lieutenant and his oldest friend. He was a very good military strategist and had executed many successful ambushes. In early July 1983, Charles was killed in a military operation. When they realized who the dead man was and how important he was to Pirabhakaran, the Sri Lankan soldiers were ecstatic. They boasted that Antony's death would be a fatal blow to the LTTE and that it would weaken both the organization and its leader.

Like a wounded tiger, Pirabhakaran is most lethal when hurt. The Sri Lankan army's euphoria provoked him to plan and stage the infamous ambush of 13 July 1983 in Tinnevely in Jaffna peninsula, in which the Tigers killed thirteen soldiers. It was a vicious attack. The bodies of the soldiers were badly mutilated. It was as if Pirabhakaran had taken personal revenge for the loss of Charles Antony and was going out of his way to prove he was now more, not less dangerous. The coffins of the dead soldiers arrived in Colombo, and reports of the savaged bodies triggered the brutal July 1983 reprisals against the Tamils.

While Pirabhakaran named his firstborn after his loyal right-hand man, he named his daughter after his slain personal bodyguard and his younger son after his brother-in-law who was killed in an encounter with the IPKF. Pirabhakaran does not take the death of his cadres lightly. In 1987, several top LTTE commanders were arrested by Sri Lankan authorities and were to be taken to Colombo. India tried hard to set them free, but Sri Lankan National Security Minister Lalith Athulathmudali refused. Just before they were to be shifted to Colombo, the LTTE men swallowed cyanide and died. That incident lifted the pin off Pirabhakaran's fury. He launched his war against the Indian troops.

In November 1994, the Tigers had announced a unilateral cessation of hostilities with President Chandrika Kumaratunga's government. But there appears to have been a communication gap—the government said it didn't get to know about the LTTE decision till several days later. In the meantime, Sri Lankan soldiers ambushed an LTTE patrol and killed one of their leaders, Lt. Col. Amudan, also known as Malli. They decapitated him and took his head with them, but left the mutilated body behind. Pirabhakaran was furious. At that time, he was exchanging secret letters with Kumaratunga to set a peace process in motion. For Pirabhakaran, Amudan's death took precedence over the peace process. Before talking about peace any further, he wanted Amudan's head returned so that he could be given a decent burial. He also demanded an immediate investigation into the incident. Even the proposed cessation of hostilities had to be suspended as Pirabhakaran insisted on first getting details about Amudan's head from the Sri Lankan army.

Pirabhakaran's demand for an immediate inquiry was met quickly enough. In two days, Dy. Minister for Defence Col. Anurudha Ratwatte replied to Pirabhakaran's letter. Amudan's head, he said, 'had been in an advanced state of decomposition and as such was duly cremated.' He promised to hand over the ashes. He also informed him that a military court of inquiry had been set up to probe the incident. Only then was Pirabhakaran appeased enough to resume discussing modalities for the peace process.

My meeting with Pirabhakaran in the five-star Ashoka Hotel in New Delhi in July 1987 was a study in contrast to my usual encounters with him in the jungles or safehouses of Sri Lanka. The meeting took place on the eve of the signing of the India-Sri Lanka accord between Prime Minister Rajiv Gandhi and President Jayewardene, an accord that paved the way for the arrival of Indian troops in the Tamil areas of the island nation. This was Pirabhakaran's worst, most humiliating moment. He was a prisoner of India.

He was living in the comfort of a five-star hotel, but he was under house arrest, guarded by Indian troops. Unless escorted, he could not venture out. All incoming calls were monitored, and only government officials were allowed to speak to him.

Pirabhakaran had been persuaded to attend the New Delhi talks by Indian diplomats based in Colombo. He was lifted out of Jaffna by helicopter. Once inside the hotel, he realized he was a captive. Much later, he told me the Ashoka Hotel experience strengthened his animosity towards India. He felt tricked and helpless and vowed that he would never again allow himself to be at the mercy of the Indians. Most of all, he resented the attitude of supercilious Indian diplomats who treated him like a kid, a country bumpkin, a poor cousin, someone they could manipulate and push around. There was no respect, no appreciation of the fact that he was a leader of a group of people, he said.

I was then based in Bangalore, working for *India Today*. I flew to New Delhi to try to get an interview with him. Even before I took the plane to Delhi, my mind was working on a plan to outwit the security so I could meet him. I packed something I never take along on reporting assignments: a bunch of silk saris.

New Delhi was abuzz with the big story. Rajiv Gandhi had pulled off a major coup. He had engineered a peace deal in Sri Lanka, and Pirabhakaran had agreed to go along. There was euphoria in the air, Rajiv was the new star, and this triumph would steal the thunder from his critics who were booming louder than the Bofors gun. The scandal over India's purchase of the Swedish Bofors artillery guns had erupted a few months earlier and newspapers were on an overdrive, accusing Rajiv of taking a fifty million dollar kickback for clearing the deal. The scandal had severely undermined his image. But now, his aides calculated, the scandal would fade to the background with the news of this peace bombshell. His advisors started having visions of Rajiv receiving the Nobel Peace Prize for ending Sri Lanka's ethnic conflict.

Pirabhakaran was incarcerated on the fifth floor, and I checked in on the same floor but in a different wing. The government-run Ashoka Hotel is huge, with long, labyrinthine corridors. On my first day, I did not even try to meet Pirabhakaran. I wore a silk sari, and with a plastic folder tucked under my arm, walked along the fifth-floor corridor pretending to be a hotel employee. There were two guards at the entrance to one of the wings of the hotel. Clearly that was where Pirabhakaran was holed up. So I headed that way. The guards tried to stop me, but I said pleasantly, with a plastic smile, that I was from housekeeping. They let me in. On this occasion, I was doing a recce, just checking where Pirabhakaran's room was and what the security was like. I walked down the corridor and came to a turning to the right. Guarding the first room along this corridor were several cops in plain clothes. There was no doubt that this was Pirabhakaran's room. I didn't slow my pace, I kept striding along the corridor.

Further down the carpeted corridor, I pretended to check if the rooms were locked or open, as if this was part of my daily routine. I walked briskly and efficiently in my best imitation of the housekeeping girls, aware that the gaze of the cops was literally burning a hole in my back.

Fortune favours the brave. The door to one room was slightly ajar. I knocked, waited for a few seconds, then pushed it open and walked in confidently. Perfect—it was empty. I looked around and noticed a little ceramic flower vase with a wilted flower in it. I took it with me and held it prominently so that the watchful cops could see I was merely doing my duty, taking away an offensive flower. I walked back past the cops, gave them a practised, polite, plastic smile again in recognition and walked on.

Next day, I repeated the procedure. The two guards at the entrance of the corridor let me through without even raising their eyebrows. They had recognized the housekeeping girl. But this time, I walked on, turned right, and knocked on Pirabhakaran's door. The cops posted outside just watched me lazily. The door was opened by Thileepan, one of Pirabhakaran's trusted aides, who I had dealt with often in Madras. He was only twenty-five years old, soft-spoken, gentle and almost scholarly in speech and demeanour. A few months later he was dead—fasting unto death in Jaffna in a protest directed against India. He was one of the few LTTE members who, instead of swallowing a cyanide capsule, died in a Gandhian way.

It took Thileepan a few long moments to recognize me. He, like most others I meet in my professional life, had never seen me in a sari. I said 'housekeeping' loudly for the benefit of the cops behind me and winked at him. He stepped back, and I walked in. It was a small suite and Pirabhakaran was sitting in an inner room. He was shocked at first to see me and then, like Thileepan and the others around him, smiled broadly. I told him I would have to go out immediately so as not to raise the suspicion of the cops outside. I would return later at an appointed hour with a photographer and do an interview. I walked out with two unused ashtrays.

I went to do the interview later that day, this time accompanied by veteran *India Today* photographer, Pramod Pushkarna. If I am a trench reporter, Pramod is a trench photographer, always in the middle of action, always the first to reach bomb and assassination sites. When we reached Pirabhakaran's door, the guards stopped us. They were a different set of cops. This was a new shift. I told the sentry who stopped me that Pirabhakaran was expecting us. He wanted to know my name and where I was from. I replied in my most authoritative tone, 'My name is Anita Pratap, and he knows where I am from. I have to go back quickly, so please hurry.'

This was still the 1980s, when women reporters were not a common sight, certainly not in tricky areas and conflict zones. Cops never suspected I was a journalist, and that helped me sneak into many forbidden areas. Tearing off a slip of paper from my notepad, I wrote my name and gave it to the cop, directing him with a curt nod to take it inside. In moments of indecision, it always helps to take the lead firmly. The cop took the slip of paper in, and we were ushered in immediately.

I was completely taken aback by Pirabhakaran's tone. All of us had been to varying extents influenced by the optimism emanating from Rajiv Gandhi's office, but Pirabhakaran looked and sounded bleak. He didn't think the accord would settle the problem. He also said if the Indian troops that were to be sent down to keep peace in the Tamil areas did not protect the rights of the Tamils, he would fight them. Warning bells began clanging in my ears. The accord was not the end of the Tamil problem; it was only a chapter. It was a reaffirmation of one of Murphy's Laws that I had used in an earlier dispatch: 'Every time you think a solution has been reached in Sri Lanka, you are proved wrong. The situation gets worse. It is this blighted nation's curse that what seems to be the light at the end of the tunnel, is usually the headlamp of an oncoming train!'

Watching Pirabhakaran's face as he spoke, I had no doubt

that he would fight the Indians. He never made empty threats. I went back to the office to file my report and interview, which I ended with Pirabhakaran's gloomy prediction that 'the accord will not bring lasting peace.'

It ended violently in less than three months.

I met Pirabhakaran in Jaffna, about a month before the accord fell apart. Throughout the interview, Pirabhakaran lovingly stroked his leopard cub Sita, who was lying on the table. It was an adorable cub. A few months later it was dead, slaughtered by Indian soldiers. That was one time when the Indians came really close to capturing Pirabhakaran. Indian soldiers claimed they had surrounded Pirabhakaran's hideout, but he had managed to escape moments earlier. He was in such a hurry that he left his pet behind, and the Indians paraded photographs of the dead cub to prove they had got really close to Pirabhakaran.

The high point of this interview with Pirabhakaran in 1987 was a dramatic physical transformation that I witnessed in the guerrilla leader. Well-built with clean, regular features and a thick, dark crop of hair, Pirabhakaran is a man whose persona and aura grow bigger the more you interact with him. He is always relaxed and easy during an interview, which often lasts as long as four hours. I ask my questions in English, and they are translated into Tamil for Pirabhakaran, who answers in Tamil. Even though I understand Tamil, I insist on having it translated back to me in English because I want to be absolutely sure that I have understood all the nuances correctly. The four-way translation is time-consuming, but Pirabhakaran has always been patient.

Halfway through the interview, Puliendran, his area commander in Trincomallee, walked in. Puliendran was a strange looking man with small, slanting eyes. He looked a bit like a prowling tiger. There was something wild and intense and controlled about him. He whispered to Pirabhakaran in Tamil. I tried hard to eavesdrop, but I couldn't decipher what he was saying. Clearly, he was conveying bad news.

I have never seen anyone's face change so dramatically. When he began listening to Puliendran, Pirabhakaran's face was calm and relaxed. But as Puliendran continued with the details of his bad news, Pirabhakaran's face started changing. By the time Puliendran finished what he had to say—which must have taken all of five minutes—Pirabhakaran's face had become dark and ominous. His eyebrows furrowed and bristled and were raised at sixty-degree angles. His eyes slanted, his mouth pursed and his even, clean features seemed to dissipate. He is dark-complexioned, but like a chameleon, he turned colour before my astounded eyes. His face swelled and turned even darker, becoming almost the colour of his hair. I felt the hair on my arms rise. I was scared and yet mesmerized by the metamorphosis. He looked like a thundercloud about to erupt.

But he didn't. He sat motionless and spoke softly, the words escaping his mouth in a menacing hiss, 'Tell them, if one boy of mine is hurt, I will kill ten of theirs. And if our people are attacked again, we will return to arms. I mean it.'

It turned out there had been a few clashes in the eastern areas, and some Tamil civilians and a few Tigers had been injured. The threat Pirabhakaran issued was to the Indian soliders. His message was clear—if the Indians couldn't assure the safety of the Tamils, the Tigers would return to battle. And he would avenge the death or injury of every LTTE member.

The large room we sat in became dead silent. There was no sound except for Pirabhakaran's hiss. I suppressed an urge to scream. In Pirabhakaran's place, I saw a large king cobra, poised to strike. If there's one thing that terrifies me, it's snakes. It's an irrational fear, but extreme and paralysing. No matter how often Zubin or my friends tell me that snakes are harmless and don't strike unless struck, I am petrified of them and have a deep-rooted biblical conviction that they are evil.

When I was a child, somebody told me that because of my scanty eyelashes and my tendency to stare, I must have been a snake in my previous life. If I have scanty eyelashes, Pirabhakaran has none. In which case, he too must have been a snake in his past life. He looked like a snake in this life too, sitting motionless, with swollen head and hooded eyes. His eyes glowered unblinkingly in his dark face. He made low, dangerous sibilant sounds. He had gone taut, all coiled up and ready to spring.

I summoned all my strength to control myself and croaked with as much composure as I could muster, that it was time to go. My words broke the spell, and Pirabhakaran stirred and relaxed. His eyes, nose and mouth fell back into place. He leaned back in his chair and in a matter of seconds, he was himself again—soft-spoken, relaxed, smiling.

But in that instant I realized with a sinking feeling that the accord would collapse.

About a month after I met Pirabhakaran, additional Indian troops who were being dropped into Jaffna came under LTTE sniper attack. Thus began the bloodiest chapter in the history of this tragic nation, with the eruption of a war that killed and maimed thousands of civilians, a war that ravaged the land, a war that tarnished India's reputation, a war that battered the Tigers, a war that plunged the Tamils further into the abyss of fear and violence.

But Pirabhakaran survived, eventually emerging stronger than ever before, though he remained deep in hiding. Due to his foresight and strategic planning, he had built a mammoth subterannean war empire that could tide over months of shortage and siege. He had built massive, multistoried underground bunkers and gigantic tanks to store fuel. Slowly and steadily, he had masterminded a gigantic war effort, and every need, right down to importing camouflage cloth for Tiger uniforms, was taken care of.

I succeeded in meeting Pirabhakaran again only when the Indian troops left Sri Lanka. I had been in touch with him during the 1987–90 period when the IPKF was fighting him and had made one unsuccessful attempt to meet him. Through intermediaries, I did manage, however, to extract a promise from him: after the last Indian soldier left, he would give his first interview to me.

Along with Ranjan Wijeratne, a minister in the Sri Lankan cabinet, I was among the few Indians gathered on the pier to watch the last batch of 2000 Indian soldiers leave the shores of Trincomallee. It was a sad and humiliating exit—unwept and unsung, in stark contrast to their arrival, when thousands of Tamils had lined the streets to cheer and garland them. With 1500 Indian soldiers dead and many more maimed for life, on a mission that did not achieve any of its stated objectives, which instead of bringing peace resulted in the island nation's bloodiest chapter, the Sri Lankan intervention was India's biggest mistake. A day before the IPKF left, an Indian major general said, pointing to a copy of historian Barbara Tuchman's book *The March of Folly: From Troy to Vietnam*, 'We can add Sri Lanka to that.'

I sat on the pier and watched until the boat sailed out of

sight. The past slipped out of the horizon and I headed for the future—a rendezvous with Pirabhakaran. I managed to meet him three days later, on 26 March 1990, in the Wanni jungles in northern Sri Lanka. I was pushing to meet him on the twenty-fourth, latest the twenty-fifth, because I had to return to Colombo by the twenty-sixth to file my copy in time to catch that week's edition. But I was told Pirabhakaran would meet me only on the twenty-sixth. No amount of persuasion would get him to meet me earlier. Finally, when he realized my problem with the deadline—that his interview should accompany my article on the Indian pull-out from Sri Lanka and not appear a week later—he agreed to meet me shortly after midnight of the twenty-fifth, so that we could head back by daybreak and reach Colombo the same night. I would then be able to squeak past my deadline.

That was when I discovered that Pirabhakaran is superstitious. The number twenty-six has a special significance for him. He was born on 26 November, but he finds twenty-six and any number that adds up to eight unlucky for him. He never conducts a military operation on the twenty-sixth of a month. He prefers to do something non-military on those days, like giving an interview, because all other days are spent planning or executing military operations. The week of his birthday is celebrated as 'Heroes' Week' to honour dead LTTE guerrillas, and it is usually a time when Pirabhakaran ceases hostilities.

Having been picked up from a predetermined spot by the LTTE, *Time* photographer Robert Nickelsberg and I went into the Wanni jungles. Bob, as we call him, is the toughest and most intelligent photographer I've worked with. He knows the stories as well as the best reporters and his brain is as sharp as his eye. We were travelling in a tempo and with us were the chief spokesman of the LTTE, Anton Balasingham, and another senior LTTE member, Dileep Yogi. We were discussing the future, and I remarked that this was the best time for Pirabhakaran to settle for peace—a package that provided autonomy and security, but not a separate state.

This was a historic opportunity to wage peace because of the unique circumstances. The historical enemies—the LTTE and the Sri Lankan state, personified by President Ranasinghe Premadasa, had united to drive out their common enemy—the IPKF. For both, it had become a matter of survival to throw the Indians out. And so together they conspired and struck a secret deal. Premadasa supplied arms and ammunition to the Tigers to help them fight the Indians, who eventually evacuated. The vacuum left by the Indian soldiers was quickly filled by the Tigers as Premadasa continued to keep his army confined to their barracks. It seemed that Premadasa had virtually surrendered Eelam to Pirabhakaran. What more could he ask for?

We landed in a safehouse deep in the jungle, at 2 a.m. It took us a few minutes to straighten our weary limbs and pull all our accessories out of the van. Dressed in combat fatigues, Pirabhakaran was waiting on the veranda for us.

I know there are people who think that the elusive guerrilla broke his cordon of self-imposed seclusion to meet me so many times only because of an ongoing romance. The reality is that I have never been alone with him. Seeing me now, he smiled and said cheerily, 'Hi.' That is the only English word I have ever heard him utter off-the-record. During interviews, he has often used English words for technical terms or concepts—words like 'ideology' or 'engineering'.

He looked the same, no wear and tear, though the

preceding two and a half years must have been the most
harrowing of his life. His hair and moustache were still
dark and thick, his face still unlined, and his lashless eyes
were as clear and sharp as ever. His smile was as boyishly
lopsided as the first time I met him. The only difference
was that he had gained a few pounds.

That was surprising. You would expect a Tiger on the
run for two and half years from the world's third largest
army to lose, not gain weight. I said so to him.

'Actually, I haven't been on the run literally. I don't take
part in the attacks any more because my physical safety is
of paramount importance. So I usually remain in well-
fortified, underground bunkers directing the operations. I
am like a spider at the centre of the web,' said Pirabhakaran
with a laugh.

As usual, the interview lasted four hours, and he touched
upon a wide range of issues. More than anything else, I
wanted to know what gave him the courage to take on India.
It's always interesting to know how someone has triumphed
over seemingly impossible odds—the old David and Goliath
syndrome. Pirabhakaran's answer, born of the wisdom of
experience, had a universal message: 'Some of my top
colleagues cautioned me against it [taking on the Indian
army] and wondered how long the LTTE could hold out. I
gave them the Vietnam example—a small nation can fight a
superpower with determination and dedication. When I was
deciding to fight, the thought of winning or losing didn't
bother me. What you have to assess is whether you have
the will to fight. People cannot give up their cause, their
rights, for fear of defeat.'

Before and after the interview, I noticed the camaraderie
between Pirabhakaran and the other LTTE leaders. The
bonhomie was remarkable—they would giggle and whisper

among themselves like schoolboys in a locker room. I assumed war and the difficult two and a half years had helped them bond in a unique way. Pirabhakaran was one of the boys, chatting and joking in an endearingly affectionate way.

Three months after I met Pirabhakaran in the jungles, violence broke out in the Tamil areas. It was war again, Eelam War II, as everybody referred to it. Pirabhakaran's version is that the Sri Lankan army had moved out of the barracks and attacked the Tamils first. My investigation showed that a domestic quarrel was used by the Tigers to go on the offensive. In a well-planned assault, they simultaneously attacked several police stations, and laid seige to sixteen army camps and two naval bases. The Sri Lankan authorities were taken completely by surprise.

The Tigers are adept at inventing reasons to justify their actions, to give the impression that their assaults are always in self-defence. The real reason for the resumption of war I would glean from Pirabhakaran himself only a year later. This was after the Elephant Pass debacle.

Pirabhakaran's greatest strength was that he had created his organization as a guerrilla force. The LTTE excelled in hit-and-run ambushes. They hurt the Indian army with their lightning ambushes, booby traps and minefields. But 'defeating' the Indian army had a profound impact on Pirabhakaran. After 1990, his persona changed. From a guerrilla leader Pirabhakaran grew into a national leader. Video fantasy became a reality. He believed the LTTE had grown from a guerrilla group to become the standing national army of the Tamils. It was this belief that led him to stage the Elephant Pass battle.

The Elephant Pass garrison is located at the base of the Jaffna peninsula, the point where it connects to the mainland. The LTTE's attack on this Sri Lankan army camp was not a guerrilla ambush. Instead, it was a conventional battle, with two large forces confronting and attacking each other face-to-face. For the first time, the Tigers stood their ground and waged war, and they got clobbered.

The Sri Lankan army inducted the navy and then the air force to fend the attack. The Tigers were strong on infantry. Like waves hitting the seashore, squad after squad of Tiger guerrillas stormed the garrison, but they didn't have planes or naval vessels for cover. They were hit from all sides—from the front by besieged soldiers, from the flanks by sailors, and from above by aerial bombers. They took their worst beating to date: in three weeks of battle they lost nearly 600 guerrillas, whereas during the entire two-and-a-half-year period of conflict with the Indian troops they had lost about 800.

For a whole year, the Tigers had prepared for this attack under the cover of darkness. Surreptitiously, they dug trenches, inch by inch, right up to the barbed wire enclosure of the garrison. All around, they built bunkers from railway tracks ripped from nearby places, and they fortified these bunkers with sandbags to protect against artillery fire. It was a painstaking, meticulous operation, right down to the last detail, which even included fake outposts manned by uniformed dummies. The surrounding terrain was open and sandy, and the Tigers sorely needed tanks and armoured vehicles, which of course they did not possess. This was where Tiger ingenuity showed itself at its best. They converted bulldozers and tractors into armoured vehicles by covering them with iron chains and sheets of steel.

The Tigers launched the attack on 10 July and pounded away relentlessly for three weeks. Helicopters with troop reinforcements found it impossible to land inside the besieged army camp because they came under the angry fire of the Tigers' anti-aircraft guns, mortars and homemade rocket systems that could hurl a fifty-kilogram bomb over a distance of 1000 metres. Almost 3000 Tigers, including 500 women—or almost half the Tiger's fighting squad— were engaged in the battle. Government helicopters could not be brought in to drop fresh supplies and ammunition or evacuate the wounded in the Sri Lankan garrison. A Sinhalese sergeant major had to turn into a surgeon, amputating the limbs of injured troopers by following radioed instructions.

The Elephant Pass garrison seemed to be fighting a losing battle. But the tide turned when the government took a bold decision: to land 8000 fresh troops in an amphibious operation on a beachhead ten kilometres away. Under fire from the moment it landed on the beach, the relief column advanced barely half a kilometre a day as the Tigers tried to stop it by literally charging headlong, wave after wave. But with fighting breaking out on two fronts, the Tigers were spread thin. Still, it took twenty-four days for the relief column to reach the garrison and break the siege.

It was a crushing military blow to the LTTE. But Pirabhakaran's spirit was far from crushed by the debacle. It actually blossomed and crystallized into a new persona. Gone was the boyish guerrilla. Instead, there was a man who moved and behaved like the Big Boss. With me he was his usual courteous, polite, accessible, relaxed self. The change was noticeable in the way he now interacted with his colleagues and even more revealingly, in the way they interacted with him.

I noticed that nobody called him Thambi any more. Everybody now referred to him as Annai, or elder brother. LTTE leaders and cadres treated Pirabhakaran deferentially. The cordiality and bonhomie that I had seen only a year and a half earlier had been replaced by reverence and formality. Associates did not banter with him, they spoke only when spoken to. Everybody looked subdued. Nobody giggled any more.

Until a year ago, he was first among equals. Now he was the undisputed leader among unequals. The gulf between Pirabhakaran and his own second rung was huge. The only person who continued to share that warm, easy equation with him was Anton Balasingham, the chief spokesman and elder statesman of the LTTE. But even he had stopped calling him Thambi. Since he was about twenty-five years older than his leader it would have been odd for him to call Pirabhakaran Annai. He now referred to him as Mr Pirabhakaran. Thambi had grown up, had ceased to exist.

I couldn't help inquiring about Mahatiya.

Mahatiya had been Pirabhakaran's number two. He was like Pirabhakaran in many ways—strong, tough, macho. But he interacted much more with the people and the cadres and was very popular. He was the LTTE's military commander, and he had planned and executed some of the most daring attacks. But there were rumours that after 1990, he had fallen out with Pirabhakaran because Mahatiya had advocated peace. Others claimed Pirabhakaran suspected him of dallying with RAW. Rumours had it that he had been imprisoned, tortured and executed.

'Where is Mahatiya?' I asked Pirabhakaran as innocently as I could.

'Why do you ask?' asked Pirabhakaran as innocently as he could.

There was no point bullshitting. So I was direct. 'I am told that you both have fallen out, that you tortured and killed him for defying you.'

'What nonsense. You really mustn't believe all these

cock-and-bull stories. You know my enemies, especially RAW, keep putting out stories to malign me,' said Pirabhakaran in his calm, confident, relaxed manner.

'I didn't hear this from your enemies or RAW. I heard it from people here. It's the big rumour in Jaffna these days,' I said.

'Well, all I can tell you is, don't believe the rumours,' he said.

'Is he alive?'

'Of course he is,' retorted Pirabhakaran.

'Well then, can I see him? I have dealt with him a lot in the past. I would love to say hi to him,' I said.

'Sure,' he said, and instructed an aide to bring Mahatiya. I felt small for having suspected him of murdering his closest aide.

The interview began, and Pirabhakaran admitted he had failed to capture Elephant Pass because he could not move food and ammunition to the front due to heavy strafing by the helicopter gunships. 'We learned the logistical problems of conventional war,' he admitted. But the defeat had not dented his morale one bit. And it had not diminished his new self-image as leader of the Tamil National Army. Despite the defeat he gloated, 'We have shown the world that we have evolved from a guerrilla force to one that can fight a conventional war with a modern army.'

I asked Pirabhakaran the question that had been haunting me for a year and a half: Why hadn't he opted for peace when it was in his grasp? After all, Premadasa had virtually given Eelam to them on a platter. Pirabhakaran denied they had started the war and laboured the Tiger version of events, that the Sri Lankan army had violated their agreement and come out of their barracks. And anyway, he said, 'We don't want Eelam on a platter. We will fight and win Eelam.'

That then was the crux of the matter, the reason for the fresh violence. Pirabhakaran did not want anybody else's version of Eelam—he wanted his own, an Eelam that he liberated militarily. 'Thousands of my boys have laid down their lives for Eelam. Their death cannot be in vain. They have given their life for this cause, how can I betray them by opting for anything less than Eelam?' he asked.

He didn't see the conundrum he was in—by fighting for the dead he was engineering the death of the living. Unable to bury the past, he was digging a burial ground of a nation. I told him that at the rate he was going, it would not be Eelam but a graveyard he would create. If Eelam finally dawned, expatriate Tamils would rejoice but by then, most Tamils in their homeland would be six feet under. Pirabhakaran scoffed at the idea.

A young girl in combat fatigues sat in the room throughout the interview. This was unusual. Normally there were only Balasingham, Yogi and one or two other top aides. Pirabhakaran treated her like a badge of honour. She was an LTTE guerrilla who had returned from the Elephant Pass battle—alive, but without both arms. She had walked into a fusillade from the garrison and had taken cover behind a coconut tree. In the fire, both her arms were blown off, but the tree trunk protected her face and torso. She was present on Pirabhakaran's orders so that she could give me some first-hand accounts of the battle.

The interview over, I shut my notebook, switched off my tape recorder and chatted with Pirabhakaran and Balasingham. Lunch was being set out on the table in the dining hall below. As we chatted, a man walked into the room. I stared dumbfounded. It was Mahatiya. But it was not the Mahatiya I knew. This Mahatiya looked like a beaten dog. Gone was the swagger, the confidence, the muscular machismo. He had become a shadow of himself—in size and in spirit. His eyes were lowered. He stood like a supplicant serf, his palms held together—like a convict habituated to manacles, I thought. It looked as though he had been summoned from the dungeons, though as far as I could tell, his face and arms bore no signs of torture. But the sight of Mahatiya confirmed my worst suspicions.

I asked him how he was, trying to be as natural and effusive as I could. He mumbled that he was fine, nodded his head to most of my questions, answered others tersely. He didn't sit down, and he wasn't offered a seat either. I ran out of questions, and the atmosphere became noticeably awkward. He mumbled some excuse and walked out. I have never seen him again.

Rumour has it that Mahatiya was executed a few months later.

I met Pirabhakaran three years later, in the heady days of Chandrika Kumaratunga's ascendance to power. She had just become the president of Sri Lanka with a huge margin that was interpreted as a mandate for peace. Sri Lanka was euphoric with new hope. Kumaratunga's commitment to peace and her deep-seated desire to strike a peace deal was known to all, and everybody wished her success in her endeavours. Educated in France, Chandrika was a liberal. Her husband had had leftist sympathies. She herself was idealistic and young. More than anyone else, she personified Sri Lanka's tragic politics. Both her father and her husband had been assassinated by gunmen. She fervently wanted to end this tragic cycle of violence.

After my interview with Chandrika, I went up to Jaffna to meet Pirabhakaran in November 1994. I realized the hope-bug had bitten the much-betrayed Tamil people too.

There were signs of hope in the way shops remained open, in the way people moved without fear, in the way they talked. Above all, there was hope in their eyes. After a long time, Tamils were walking with their heads held up, like people do in peaceful areas. Normally, they walked on the streets with their heads hung low: dark, moving symbols of fear and despair.

Now the Tamils had placed their faith in Chandrika. She was very popular in Jaffna. Her portraits hung in public places, and posters were displayed on the streets. Saris named Chandrika were selling briskly.

I too was infected by the new atmosphere of peace, but meeting Pirabhakaran was like an antibiotic. He denied that the people of Jaffna were tiring of the war, he said the army would stymie peace and claimed that Chandrika's commitment to peace had waned. All my earlier suspicions were reinforced. The ceasefire would be temporary; peace talks, even if resumed, would lead nowhere, because Pirabhakaran remained as committed to Eelam as he was the day when I first met him.

Exactly as Pirabhakaran predicted, the much-publicized ceasefire lasted another four months. Eelam War III erupted in April 1995 and has been going on since. The LTTE and the Sri Lankan government have regressed to being 'historical enemies' again, and both have scored some successes and some failures. President Kumaratunga succeeded in wresting Jaffna in 1995 and almost lost it in 2000. Along the way, she almost lost her life as well. In one assassination attempt, she lost an eye. She is number one on the LTTE hit list and that makes her the most endangered woman in the world. At any given time, a dozen Black Tigers, the elite commandos of the LTTE's suicide squad, roam Colombo, looking for a chink in her security armour. A few of them have been caught by the police. But several remain, stalking her every move.

Pirabhakaran's true genius can be understood only by studying his followers. More than a thousand Tigers have consumed cyanide on capture—to avoid torture and more importantly, to ensure that they carried the secrets of their organization to the grave. Not that the LTTE cadres know much—they all function on a need-to-know basis.

Over the years, Pirabhakaran has created a band of followers who at his bidding will lay down their most precious asset—their life—for him or his cause. It can only be an extraordinary being who can wield such power. He commands the kind of unquestioning loyalty that makes his followers commit suicide, often brutally, with explosives strapped to their chest—just for him.

If there is something special about Pirabhakaran, there is something equally special about his guerrillas. They are reticent, disciplined and simple in their habits. They live austerely. Once recruited, cadres have to renounce their friends, their family, their home. The Tiger legion is their new family. They are not allowed to smoke, drink or have sex. Their prized possession is their weapon, usually an AK 47. They are taught to worship it. They are told that as many as ten Tigers may have lost their lives to acquire it. (This may have been true in the early days of the insurgency when Tigers got their weapons entirely by raiding Sri Lankan armouries, but in recent years, the LTTE has been acquiring boatloads from international arms suppliers. The myth, however, continues.)

The Tigers handle their weapons with adoration and reverence. They clean their guns lovingly and painstakingly, much like an ardent lover would stroke his beloved. Apart from their rifle and cyanide vial, their worldly possessions comprise a change of clothes and a pair of chappals. Indian and Sri Lankan policemen who have raided Tiger safehouses say that often, tens of thousands of rupees have been found— money given to buy supplies or conduct operations, be it an attack on security personnel or a suicide mission. Every expense is neatly documented in a book. Not a cent is taken by the Tiger guerrillas for personal use, not for a cool drink or a banana or a bar of chocolate.

Tiger thrift and honesty were exemplified by Kulaweerasingham Weerakumar, the twenty-four-year-old LTTE suicide bomber who detonated himself and President Premadasa in May 1993. He took two years to execute his mission. He came to Colombo with a large amount of cash, which he invested in a grocery business. Then he rented a room above his store, near Premadasa's private residence. The stocky, curly-haired man had no vices. He obviously had plenty of money, but he never lavished it on himself. He ate, dressed and lived simply. Slowly he began cultivating Premadasa's household staff—running the grocery store helped. He especially befriended Premadasa's valet, who was also a Tamil.

For two years, the suicide bomber stalked Premadasa. Then he struck. On May Day, as the president was greeting processionists at Armours Street Junction in the heart of Colombo, Weerakumar rode up to him on his bicycle, having managed to penetrate the security cordon. Eyewitnesses say that as he rode towards Premadasa, the valet suddenly sensed something was amiss and grabbed Weerakumar's bicycle. At that moment, Weerakumar detonated himself. So powerful was the explosion that arms and limbs were blown all over the area. It took more than two hours for the president's personal physician to identify what was left of Premadasa's body. The president's entire staff died. The explosion tore Weerakumar's body apart, but his severed head remained intact—as was the case with the assassins of Gamini Dissanayake and Rajiv Gandhi. They all used the same technique—detonating explosives strapped around the abdomen. Local newspapers published photographs of Weerakumar's severed head. His astonished business partner, with whom he had invested money to start the grocery store, identified him. His account revealed Weerakumar's patience, long-term planning and single-minded dedication to his task of killing Premadasa, the man who had helped the Tigers more than any other Sri Lankan politician. Nothing could deter Weerakumar from his goal. He was young, had plenty of money and could have broken free. Yet he functioned exactly like a programmed guided missile—nothing more, nothing less.

I once visited a Tiger hospital after a major battle. In one ward there were sixty young women, recuperating from serious wounds. Most had their arms or legs ripped off, some did not have a part of their face, some had craters where there should have been stomachs. But what was even more bizarre was the atmosphere in the ward—it was cheerful. Sixteen-year-old Sumathi, who had lost her right leg in battle, said, 'All I want is to get an artificial leg so that I can go back to the field. If I stay home, how will we get Eelam?'

This single-mindedness, this to-the-death determination is what has helped the LTTE to become so big and powerful, to remain intact and to take on superior and well-equipped armies, to command the loyalty of the people, to emerge as the sole representatives of the Tamil people.

But how is this single-minded devotion to Pirabhakaran and his cause instilled in these guerrillas? Fear explains the phenomenon to some extent. The LTTE is extraordinarily strict, and can be brutal in the way it deals with people who are seen as betrayers to the cause. In the early days of the struggle, it became notorious for its 'lamppost killings'. Informers and complainers were punished with a bullet in the head. Then the body of the victim was tied to a lamppost with a placard hanging from the neck: 'This is what happens to traitors'. Whenever Tiger recruiters visited Jaffna University, they asked students, 'Who does not want to become a member of the Tigers' student wing?' No hands went up. No one dared. The LTTE does not tolerate dissent. Its goal is to create a homogenous Tamil society, a land where everybody thinks along Tiger lines. More than ten years ago, a group of Jafffna University professors complained about the LTTE's heavy-handed tactics. One of the academics was shot dead; the others went into hiding in Colombo.

Tiger guerrillas who display anything other than implicit obedience are shown no mercy. Small infractions result in humiliating tongue lashings, usually in the presence of other Tigers. Serious offences like rape, murder or accepting bribes bring instant execution.

But more than the skilful and ruthless use of fear, it is discipline that is the Tigers' magic mantra. The discipline drilled into them during training keeps the Tigers obedient and on the narrow path of insurgency. It makes them shrug off familial ties and renounce worldly temptations.

Pirabhakaran himself identifies discipline as the key to success. As he said to me in one of his interviews, 'Commitment comes from strictly enforced discipline'. Firm resolve is instilled during the intense training, the most crucial phase in the moulding of a Tiger guerrilla.

Apart from physical endurance, use of weaponry and combat manouvres, a crucial aspect of the training is psychological indoctrination: moral, emotional and conceptual. The boys are instilled with the spirit of courage, revenge and sacrifice. Over and over again, recruits are told of atrocities by the Sri Lankan army, a point driven home by propagandists who display pictures of mutilated Tamil bodies and describe torture in horrifying detail. By the end, the recruits have developed a deep and abiding hatred for the Sri Lankan army.

The Tiger credo has two parts—to fight for Eelam and to be loyal to Pirabhakaran till the last breath. By the time the training is over, young Tiger recruits venerate Pirabhakaran. It is a carefully orchestrated indoctrination. There is Pirabhakaran the war hero fighting from the front. There is Pirabhakaran the incorruptible, who refuses to deviate from his goal of Eelam despite military pressure from India and Sri Lanka, and despite offers of money and power that had deflected the less resolute Tamil leaders. There is Pirabhakaran who loves and protects them. There is also the Pirabhakaran who embodies the spirit of a glorious Tamil past, a descendant of the Chola kings.

By the time they complete their training, the Tiger guerrillas are disciplined, committed, motivated and austere. Out of them, Pirabhakaran selects the best 200 to become Black Tigers. They are chosen for their discipline and loyalty to Pirabhakaran. A Tiger guerrilla greets this news with elation, even though he knows he will be dead within two years. This is the selection he has been striving and waiting for. This is the news that has made his decision to enroll in the LTTE, to renounce his family, to live a life of danger and rigour, worthwhile. It is the greatest honour that can be bestowed upon a guerilla by Pirabhakaran: to be made a part of the thin upper crust of the Tiger cult.

Many Tiger guerrillas do not even get to see Pirabhakaran in person until they are selected as Black

Tigers. That itself becomes their biggest reward. Once they become Black Tigers, recruits are further isolated. Their interaction with even ordinary Tigers is kept to a minimum. They are given additional training and indoctrination for about six months, and then off they go on their mission—to bomb a politician or conduct a suicide attack on a military installation. Just before setting off on their venture—from which they will not return alive—they are allowed the honour of dining with Pirabhakaran. There is also a ceremonial photo session with him.

After years of persuasion, Pirabhakaran finally allowed me to meet some Black Tigers in 1991. They are everything the ordinary Tigers are, but to a much higher degree. They are more reticent, more disciplined, more motivated, and utterly emotionless. I tried to get at least a flicker of emotion out of them—nostalgia, homesickness, regret. I talked about childhood memories, missing their mother, giving up life's pleasures, fear of imminent death. But I got nothing. No reaction at all. They sat, still and clear-eyed, answering calmly and dispassionately. It was disconcerting. They could have been lobotomized for all I knew. How could they not be afraid of death, especially violent death? But all the Black Tigers I interviewed said more or less the same thing: 'I feel honoured that my death will take our struggle one step closer to Eelam.'

The only time they showed some emotion was when they talked about Pirabhakaran, their Annai. A Black Tiger named Sunil said with something close to awe, 'For us, he is mother, father and God all rolled into one.' But I detected one fear in all of them: the fear that they might let Pirabhakaran down. They would die happily; their only hope was their death would inflict the kind of damage on the enemy that would make Pirabhakaran happy. Securing

Annai's happiness was all that mattered—then, they would not have lived and died in vain.

It is perhaps this desire that gives them superhuman strength and courage. Sri Lankan Brigadier Vijaya Wimalaratne, who was involved in the Elephant Pass battle, recounted an incident that provides a clue to the Tiger psyche. Sentinels reported an armoured bulldozer driving into the garrison. Soldiers opened fire to stop it. But unmindful of the fire, the bulldozer hurtled towards the garrison as if it were on autopilot. It crashed through the barricades and finally came to a halt. After waiting a while, the soldiers went to examine the armoured monstrosity that had been badly mutilated by the fire it had braved.

The autopilot turned out to be a Tigress. She was a bloodied mess. Both her arms had been blown away, bullets had ripped off her cheeks. Her shoulders were red pulp. With great difficulty, the soldiers extricated her from the bulldozer. According to Wimalaratne, she could not have been more than fifteen years old. She was still conscious, though life was ebbing out of her as rapidly as the blood. She did not scream, just moaned softly. Her eyes were bleary, her lips cracked and dry. Wimalaratne sent for some water, and tried to pour a few drops into her parched mouth. The dying girl reacted with ferocity. Recalling that moment, Wimalaratne said, 'I don't know where she got the strength.' Her eyes suddenly focused, and she spat out the drops. She was dying, her body was wracked by excruciating pain and fatal dehydration, but she would not take water from a Sri Lankan soldier!

Black Tiger Sunil was right when he said that for them, Pirabhakaran is mother, father and God all rolled into one. With her final breath, this fatally wounded Tigress called out, not to her mother, not to her father, not even to God, but to 'Annai, Annai!'

ISLAND OF BLOOD

Death chills. It chills the air, however sunny or balmy or humid it may be.

As I drove into Kandy in August 1989, I knew something was wrong because of the sudden chill in the air. I felt the hair rise on my arms. I instructed my taxi driver to slow down. He turned around to look at me, and I saw worry on his face. 'Shall we go straight to the hotel?' he asked hopefully.

'No, drive on, I want to see the whole town before I go to the hotel. But drive very slowly, and switch off the AC,' I told him.

'The AC was switched off long ago, madam,' he reminded me, puzzled by my forgetfulness. I dislike car air conditioners, and after the inside has cooled a bit, invariably have it switched off. This one had been switched off half an hour earlier.

Still, I felt cold in the car. I had a terrible premonition. Something bad was going to happen. I felt it in my bones. From the safety of the moving car, I peered out, absorbing the tropical beauty of the landscape. Huge trees, lush foliage, red hibiscus, old-fashioned tiled houses. But something was terribly wrong. Everything seemed strangely frozen in the midsummer heat. There was not a soul on the streets. No people, no cars, not even bicycles. The shops were shuttered and the streets deserted, though it was midday.

The row of shops ended and the compound walls of houses began. Still no sign of human beings. There was an eerie stillness—even the leaves did not stir. We reached a junction, and the driver wondered which way to go.

I told him to go straight, and as my eyes swivelled in all directions to scan the countryside, I got my first shock.

Near the crossroads, aloft on one of the compound walls, was an amputated leg. It was placed upside down so the foot pointed up and the amputated thigh faced downwards. Dark, dried blood caked the thigh, which must have belonged to a muscular man. Below the amputated leg was a placard in Sinhalese that my driver translated: 'This is what happens to police informers.'

Sri Lanka's two worst years were 1988 and 1989. War raged in the north between Tamil rebels and Indian soldiers and in the south, the Sinhalese Marxist Janatha Vimukthi Peramuna (JVP) rose in violent revolt against the presence of Indian troops on their soil, saying it undermined Sri Lanka's sovereignty. The JVP represented the ultra-nationalist sentiments of the majority Sinhalese community. In 1971, the JVP had led an insurrection that the authorities snuffed out ruthlessly. After lying dormant for a decade and a half, it was now waging a brutal campaign to overthrow the Sri Lankan government, which had implemented an even more brutal campaign to crush the new insurrection. Sri Lanka was tottering perilously on the brink of anarchy.

In Kandy it was full-scale war between the JVP and the government's death squads. Authorities countered terror with terror. I saw some of the worst scenes of violence in my life during those two catastrophic years.

Shaken, but determined to go on, I told my frightened

taxi driver to keep driving.

'It's very dangerous, madam. We should go to hotel,' he pleaded.

'I am here as a journalist, not as a tourist. My job is to go to the dangerous spots. Don't worry, nothing will happen to us,' I reassured him. He looked miserable, and would probably have stopped the car and walked away, except that the need to keep his job outweighed his fear.

Nodding helplessly, he drove on. But we had progressed barely 300 metres when he slammed on the brakes. Now what?

'They are telling us not to go further,' he said, his voice rising in fright.

He stuck his head out of the car window and hollered in Sinhalese.

It was only then I noticed that the collapsible wooden door of a shop to our right was slightly ajar. From inside, the head of an elderly man peered out. He had one hand stuck outside, which was waving us against going further. All the while, he spoke furiously and fast in Sinhalese.

I didn't understand a word and waited impatiently for the driver to translate. The man continued to jabber and then suddenly, his door snapped shut.

'What did he say? What was he so excited about?' I asked urgently. Before my terrified driver could reply, I heard the sound of a vehicle speeding towards us. It drew up alongside. It was a police vehicle.

I hissed to the driver, 'Don't tell them I am a journalist. Just say we are searching for our hotel.'

My poor trembling driver said so, and the policemen, who looked tough and sinister, ordered him to turn back and leave the place immediately. They sounded irritated and threatening. Just to make sure, they barked at me as

well. I didn't have to be proficient in Sinhalese to figure
out they were telling me to get out. After the men snarled
their orders, the police driver turned the vehicle around
and roared away on full throttle. They were obviously in a
hurry.

My driver began to turn the car around, but I told him
to stop. I wanted to know what the man in the shop had
said.

'He said not to go an inch further. There is terrible
trouble in this area. He said police are in bad mood, and we
will be in big trouble if they catch us. We must go to hotel,
madam. This is very, very dangerous,' he stuttered.

'The police have caught us already, but they have gone
back. We have come so far, we can't turn back now and
abandon our mission. Drive on,' I told him.

'No, no, no madam, I can't drive any more. This is not
like any other country. Terrible things are happening in Sri
Lanka nowadays. We are in bad shape. If we disobey the
police, we will be in big, big trouble. Madam, we must go
back now.'

'Don't worry, I am with you. Nothing will happen.
Nobody will do anything to journalists.'

'These people don't care about journalists. They don't
care about their own mothers and sisters. What they will
care about journalists? No, no, madam, we have to turn
back. This is too dangerous.'

'I have to go further. If you are scared, then I will drive.
You can sit in the front seat,' I said in a voice that brooked
no argument.

'No, no, it's too dangerous. Okay, I will drive, but this
is not wise, madam. You don't know how dangerous the
situation is,' he said, and then with utmost fear and
reluctance, turned the car around once more and slowly

accelerated. He was hunched forward in his seat, clutching the steering wheel tightly—out of fear or to stop his trembling, I couldn't tell. I felt sorry for him, I felt bad about bullying him, but I had a job to do.

Two hundred metres ahead, we stumbled upon a gruesome sight. My driver stopped the car and began weeping with his head on the steering wheel. I got out of the car to take a closer look. There were seven young men lying in the middle of the road, tied together. They were anywhere between eighteen and twenty-five years old. They had been 'necklaced.' Around each man's neck was a burning car tyre. Their bodies bore signs of torture. Knives had gashed their skin, blunt instruments had bruised their joints, and cigarette stubs had burnt holes all over their bodies. Their throats had been slit. Blood had trickled down to stain the road. They were all dead. Their eyes were closed, their bodies still. But I thought I heard one young man gasp. I could have sworn I saw his toe twitch. I saw a gush of blood spurt from his slit throat. And then, nothing.

Such deathly stillness. Such empty silence.

No sounds except for the faint crackle of smouldering tyres that made the silence even louder. No sound of birds, no crickets, no cicadas—no warm buzz of the tropical paradise that Sri Lanka is. The air was filled with the acrid smell of burning tyre and human flesh. Covering my nose with my hands, I tried to shut out the smell. But it had already curled into my mind to lie in wait, like a tapeworm marking its time to strike unexpectedly, sometime in the future.

The air was cold. Eerily cold. I shivered, and felt beads of sweat form on my cold brow. I felt saliva prickling inside my mouth. I felt faint. I wanted to throw up. I wanted to run away. I did.

The young men were JVP members and supporters. The villagers knew that. The message had struck home. For every police informer killed, there would be seven JVP men killed—take your pick. And the villagers had picked. It had suddenly become more dangerous to cross the police than the JVP.

The man widely held responsible for this counter-terror campaign was a policeman named Premadasa Udagampola. He was a big, tough, ruthless man. He hated the JVP—they had slaughtered his entire family, including his small children. He was now a burly, brutal engine of revenge, taking pleasure in exterminating his enemies. His campaign of terror was even more ruthless and effective than the JVP's.

The following day, I met him in his office in Kandy. I was ushered in, and as I sat down to face him, he opened a drawer to his right. Without taking his eyes off my face for a moment, he took out a gun and placed it on the table. 'Yes, what do you want to know?' he asked in an even tone, and the interview began.

This has happened to me twice. The other time was when I met K. P. S. Gill, the Indian supercop who is credited with crushing terrorism in Punjab. As with Udagampola, it was my first meeting with the so-called killer cop. But there was one crucial difference, a difference that allowed me to eventually become a friend of Gill's, while I have never met Udagampola again and can remember him only with a shudder. As he took out the gun from the drawer, Udagampola's face and eyes were expressionless. As he took out his revolver, also from the top drawer to his right, Gill's face was expressionless, but there was an unmistakable twinkle in his eye. I knew he was testing me, taking lazy pleasure in my flustered reaction. But the twinkle emboldened me, and I quipped with a smile, 'That gun is not going to stop me from asking tough questions.' A faint quiver of a smile flickered on Gill's stern face, and he answered my questions, staring at me intently while his fingers caressed the revolver.

But there was something heavy and menacing about Udagampola. It was hard to tell whether it was sorrow, anger or vendetta that oppressed him. Maybe it was a combination of all these and more. He sat like a big, dark, motionless spider in his dark office—dark despite the morning sun shining brightly outside. The dim, unnatural lighting in the room added to the gloom.

The interview was conducted in a strange, deadpan manner. I asked my questions straight; he denied everything straight. He had nothing to do with these hit squads, of course. They were vigilantes who opposed the JVP, ordinary citizens who had got sick of JVP's violence and so had formed squads to rid society of the JVP menace, and so on. What about the fact that these vigilantes rode around in police vehicles? Oh, they were fake vehicles, with fake signs and number plates. All this was said in a calm, reasonable, deliberate tone. He could have been talking about the price of eggs for all the emotion he displayed. But every now and then, despite or perhaps because of the dim glow in the room, I caught a gleam in his eye. An indescribable gleam. Years later, when somebody asked me to picture evil, what came to my mind was that gleam.

Like the gleam in Udagampola's eyes, I can never forget Tillekeratne's smile. For entirely different reasons, though.

It was February 1989. The JVP had ordered people to boycott the parliamentary elections. Ranasinghe Premadasa had already become president after a bloody election, and now the parliamentary poll was turning out to be equally vicious. The JVP had announced that whoever cast their vote first would be killed. Covering this election with me was Dominic Sansoni, a talented and charmingly laid-back photographer who has the ability to become part of the local scenery and people—sometimes even wearing a sarong and smoking a bidi when we reported from Tamil villages. The local people loved him, especially because he looked Caucasian. Dominic is a Sri Lankan, but his ancestors were Dutch.

When voting began as scheduled, fear was as pervasive and oppressive as the tropical humidity. People did not dare to venture out. One's life was too high a price to pay for a vote. Election officials huddled in their little rooms, waiting in vain for voters. At a polling station south of Colombo, two hours went by and not a soul turned up to vote.

Then an elderly man riding a bicycle came along. His dark skin contrasted with his stunning white shirt and sarong. His name was H. Tillekeratne, and he was a retired government official. He was afraid of the JVP, but he was also loyal to his country and conscious of his rights and duties as a citizen. He believed he had a right to vote, and he did not think it was fair of the JVP to stop him and others from exercising their democratic right. He decided to take the risk. After all, he reasoned, he was sixty-one years old. He had had a modest but good life. Most of his earthly responsibilities were over. If people like him did not take the initiative, who would lead the country out of this endless cycle of fear and violence?

A true hero. Unknown and unsung in life as in death.

Societies have survived only through the heroism of such ordinary men and women who live and die, faithfully living out their principles, undiscovered by the media. In many ways their actions, their beliefs, their very existence remains, like them, simple, ordinary, innocent, without being exaggerated and distorted, lionized or demonized, as inevitably happens when presented through the prism of the media. Newspapers, magazines and television networks make such people seem larger than life, and in the process the person loses his essence, his truth, his natural ordinariness. He becomes a media bubble, as unrecognizable to those who know him well, as to himself.

A god-fearing Buddhist, Tillekeratne did not see his decision to vote as heroic. To him, it wasn't an act of courage or defiance. It was simply a matter of duty. There was no fuss, no grandiose explanations, no chest-thumping jingoism. He walked into the election booth, cast his vote and walked out. He leaned against his bicycle for a while, hoping that some more people in the village would take a cue from him.

Nobody did.

He shrugged and decided to go home. He mounted his gleaming black bicycle and pedalled slowly out onto the tarred road. We decided to leave too. As our car overtook Tillekaratne, Dominic waved goodbye. Tillekaratne waved back, smiling in recognition and in farewell.

Then the most bizarre thing happened. His smile moved forward.

At the exact moment that Tillekaratne smiled, a JVP sniper shot him from behind. The bullet pierced the back of his neck, dislocating his lower jaw. The lower half of his face moved forward with the impact. His bicycle wobbled as he lost his balance, and then he and his cycle crashed to the roadside.

Since that day, when someone says 'his smile reached out to the people', or something along those lines, I see Tillekaratne's smile leaving his face and coming towards me.

Tillekaratne was one of the fifty-seven Sri Lankans killed that day for daring to defy the balloting boycott. Elections are bloody in Sri Lanka, but the provincial and parliamentary polls of 1988-89 were the most violent in the nation's blood-spattered history. It was a no-holds-barred period for the Tigers, the JVP and the government hit squads who went about shooting and stabbing, bayoneting and beheading their opponents. In the south, the JVP wreaked mayhem. In the north it was the LTTE.

Sri Lanka, this enchanting tear-drop shaped island in the Indian Ocean, began to resemble a drop of blood. Murder became the great leveller, sparing neither guerrilla nor parliamentarian, rich nor poor, soldier nor farmer, priest nor president. It became an island where the blood of its ordinary and extraordinary inhabitants continuously spilled and seeped into its red earth. An island of blood, swirling with broken dreams and broken hearts.

As part of the India-Sri Lanka Peace Accord, provincial councils were to be created in all the counties to devolve power to the people. Ironically, the provincial councils were opposed both by the LTTE and the JVP for diametrically opposite reasons: the LTTE claimed the councils did not devolve sufficient power and autonomy to the minority Tamils, and the JVP claimed they gave away so much it was tantamount to a partition of the country! Both declared that those who voted in the provincial council elections would be deemed traitors 'who will not be forgiven'.

Most ordinary people were sick of the violence and just wanted peace. Some of them voted, hoping it would bring some peace and stability to their lives. Chandralatha was among those who voted, and her family was not forgiven by the LTTE.

Chandralatha was a twenty-eight-year-old Sinhalese

woman who lived with her husband and three children in a remote jungle hamlet called Mahakongaskanda, which bordered the Tamil areas. The peace of that fateful October night was suddenly broken by alien Tamil voices and the crunch of boots on the gravelled path outside. A group of strange men had invaded their sleeping village. The unfamiliar sounds filled her with dread. Sensing danger, she urged her husband to hide under the bed. But his protective instincts got the better of him. He pressed his body against the door and tried to keep it closed against the marauders. Another ordinary, unsung hero.

The invaders shot through the door, pushed their way in, and sprayed bullets into the humble hut of the family. Chandralatha's husband and one-year-old baby were killed on the spot. She and two older children were wounded severely, but survived because the gunmen left, presuming them to be dead. Altogether, forty-four residents of this hamlet, including eighteen children were shot dead, in cold blood.

The JVP was even more brutal. Striking terror was its main goal, and in achieving that aim, nothing was sacred, nothing taboo. Even the dead were not spared. The more violent and inhuman the act, the more terror it would strike in the hearts of the ordinary people. And terrified people could be reduced to soft pulp, made even more malleable to their bidding.

When mourners gathered for the funeral of a slain JVP victim, little did they realize they would have to pay with their lives. A gang of killers burst in and opened fire. Eight of the mourners were killed, and the corpse beheaded. In the southern town of Hambantota, explosives were set off at a graveyard, blowing up a freshly buried body. In Kamburupitiya, the decapitated body of a Reserve Police constable was placed on his doorstep.

The government responded with tough measures—the death penalty for those who attended demonstrations, instigated protests or published threatening posters. The National Security Minister, Lalith Athulathmudali, who would one day be slain by a bullet, did not exaggerate when he told me, 'We have to act. If we don't do anything, the JVP will capture power.'

Despite the tough measures, the government was steadily losing control. Through posters and their underground radio station, the JVP issued diktats to a quaking public. People were ordered to stay away from work. Defiance was punished with death. Five bus workers who reported for work were shot dead. Government and private employees stayed indoors, and in one instance, five hundred inmates escaped from the Angoda mental hospital. The government retaliated with a new rule that absentee employees would be dismissed. People found it safer to disobey the government. The choice was easy. If they defied the government, they would lose their jobs; if they defied the JVP, they would lose their lives.

Shops, banks, schools, universities, ports and post offices closed down. Authorities ordered tourists to leave the country, and fully booked chartered tours that were a major source of revenue for Sri Lanka were all cancelled. There were no trains or buses, no electricity, water or telephone services. The tropical paradise had become a country paralysed by a siege within. People were either dying or fleeing. More than two-thirds of advertising revenue in Tamil newspapers came from death notices or from travel agencies arranging emigration.

The siege ended only when the government adopted a scorched earth policy against the JVP. President Premadasa

inducted a tough-talking, no-nonsense planter, Ranjan
Wijeratne, to head this new campaign. Wijeratne cracked
the whip on the nation the way he did in his estates. He
was clear and his mind was made up—the JVP's terror could
be neutralized only through counter-terror. He had to create
a situation where it became more dangerous for people to
defy the government than the JVP. So, when the JVP ordered
people to close shops, soldiers went around town shooting
locks open and forcing terrified shopkeepers to return to
the store at gunpoint. Close to hysteria, one trembling
shopkeeper said, 'The army says open, the other side says
close. I am in the middle. I can't think, I can't even speak, I
am so afraid. Please don't mention my name or this shop.
I will be a dead man if you do.' Another terrified citizen
said, 'We don't dare open our mouths except to eat.'

Wijeratne also embarked on a campaign to demonstrate
that the JVP was not a shadowy, elusive group; its members
could be caught and executed publicly. Such public displays
of savagery would deter youths from joining the JVP. For
this campaign, he enrolled policemen like Premadasa
Udagampola. Police and army-backed vigilante squads,
whose sole mission was to hunt down and kill JVP members
and sympathizers, mushroomed. Different death squads
operated in different areas under deadly names,
transforming Sri Lanka into a lethally colourful tropical
jungle of terror: Black Cats, Yellow Leopards, Southern
Black Shadows, Green Tigers, Black Butterflies.

The scorched earth policy culminated in November 1989
with the capture and death of Rohana Wijeweera, the
founder and leader of the JVP. According to the official
version, a Sri Lankan army unit captured Wijeweera in a
well-furnished house in Ulapane, a village in Kandy district,
where he was living with his wife and five children.

Apparently, the dreaded leader capitulated quickly and, under pressure, agreed to tell and show all, including guiding the soldiers to the operational headquarters of the JVP. Incensed by his betrayal, another politburo member of the JVP tried to shoot him, but the troops opened fire and killed both.

It was difficult to believe this story. Wijeweera had so much blood on his hands, especially the blood of policemen, it was inconceivable that raiding troops would have exchanged pleasantries over cups of tea as he trilled information about his organization. There was so much anger and hatred among Sri Lankan policemen for what he had done to their tribe that nothing could have restrained them when they finally set eyes on him.

Suspicions that Wijeweera and two of his associates were tortured and killed strengthened when the government hastily cremated the bodies of the three rebel leaders. Nevertheless, the nation heaved a collective but clandestine sigh of relief. Elated policemen pranced like delirious schoolboys and stopped traffic by lighting firecrackers on the road. But most people sat at home and thanked their stars. Wijeweera was feared more than loved, and he was often compared to Khmer Rouge's Pol Pot, who killed a million Cambodians between 1975 and 1979.

Minister Wijeratne was a happy man. He had accomplished one of his two missions. He had smashed the JVP; now the LTTE remained. One down, one to go. He loved cricket and saw himself as a fast-paced bowler who got his wickets, one by one.

I had come to like Wijeratne. He was fearless, honest and utterly ruthless. What I liked about him was his straightforwardness. There was no hypocrisy in the man.

I remember my first meeting with him. It was when

the government's counter-terror campaign was at its peak, much before Wijeweera was killed.

I was ushered into his office, and the interview meandered along for about half an hour along predictable lines. Wijeratne's language was colourful, uninhibited by the whirring tape recorder. He made no bones about his determination to pursue his tough campaign to its logical conclusion. In his characteristic style, he said the campaign would only get tougher. He warned, 'What you people (the press) have been describing as a crackdown is nothing. It is only a holding operation. If the JVP refuses our peace offers, then we will really apply military pressure.'

That was when I asked the fatal question: 'But what about human rights? Doesn't the government have any respect for human rights? Young boys are being killed by death squads that everybody says has the backing of the police and the army. This is against all norms of civilized behaviour.'

Ranjan Wijeratne exploded. 'How dare you talk about human rights? Who are *you* to talk about human rights? You people write grandly about human rights, and then you all disappear. You write without responsibility. Governments around the world will be able to do their job of governing much better if the press is crushed out of existence. You people are nothing but interfering troublemakers. Don't victims of the JVP and LTTE have human rights? How come you don't dare to write about that? You are all cowards! You don't dare to criticize terrorists because they will slit your throats. Because of your cowardice, you legitimize terrorism. For you people, terrorist actions are okay because it's part of their freedom struggle. But when governments try to stop terrorism, you talk about human rights. You are not just cowards, you are all accomplices to terrorism. But if your milk supply is interrupted for just one day, you will jump up and down shouting the government is useless. You press people are the worst hypocrites in society.'

His voice had risen, and as he shouted, he got angrier. There was no trace of the distinguished silver-haired, fair-skinned man who had greeted me half an hour earlier. He was apoplectic, snorting and ranting without pause. His face had turned red with rage, his bushy eyebrows seemed to have become bushier. He flailed his arms. His nostrils flared and words foamed at his mouth. He looked and sounded like a charging albino bull. As his voice rose, so did he, and I found myself looking up at a towering embodiment of fury. I was still seated in a chair in front of his desk. I couldn't get up as he literally had me pinioned to the chair with his angry eyes.

Hearing his raised voice, his attendants rushed in. But they stood transfixed by his wrath. I sensed rather than saw them because I too was mesmerized by Wijeratne's rage. They did not dare interrupt him or throw me out because he was haranguing me in a torrential sweep of uncontrollable fury.

'It's easy for you people to talk about human rights,' he snarled. 'You talk and leave. Who is left picking up the pieces? Us. The government. We have to keep things going. If the JVP uses terror to paralyse the nation, we will use counter-terror to get the nation going again. We will use more than that too, if necessary. The trouble is, we are soft with you people. That is why you dare to ask such stupid questions about human rights. Would you dare put such questions to Idi Amin? No, you wouldn't! We should treat journalists the way Idi Amin treated his people. I should just chop off your head and put it in my refrigerator. That's what should be done to interfering journalists. Then you wouldn't dare to ask such idiotic questions!'

Something snapped in me. The vision of my decapitated head in his freezer did not frighten me. I found it funny. Given how easily I feel cold, I would like to have my head wrapped up in a nice warm shawl, I thought. Preferably red, because that's my favourite colour. I didn't mean to, but quite without realizing, I started laughing.

The sound of my laughter stopped Wijeratne in mid-sentence. He stared at me open-mouthed. Several seconds ticked by as he remained frozen in pure shock. Then his face slowly relaxed. He started smiling. He sat down and said in unconcealed admiration, 'You are exactly what people say you are. You are one brave, tough woman.' Then he stood up and leaned across to shake my hand. The hugely relieved attendants, who had not dared to breathe until then, quietly left the room.

Wijeratne and I became good friends after that day. He expeditiously cleared all permissions for my travel up north to cover his war with the Tigers. Every time I met him in Colombo before leaving for Jaffna, he would tell me, wagging his finger, 'When you meet Pirabhakaran, tell him it's the last time he will be seeing you. Before you get there next time, I will make sure he is a dead man.'

But the Tigers got him first. One day as he was being driven to work, an LTTE car bomb exploded en route, killing him on the spot. A tragic, but perhaps inevitable end to a colourful man, who talked as dangerously as he lived. That's the critical difference between Pirabhakaran and most politicians. Several Indian and Sri Lankan leaders who have dealt with the LTTE boasted it was only a matter of time before they killed Pirabhakaran. And they would ask me to convey this message to him. Of course, I never did. I am a reporter, not a messenger. Pirabhakaran knew that after I met him in the jungles, I would return to the world inhabited by politicians and would meet them as part of my job. But not once did he convey a desire to have them killed. He never boasted or threatened. He just did it—Ranjan Wijeratne, A. Amirthalingam, Rajiv Gandhi, Ranasinghe Premadasa, Gamini Dissanayake.

Gamini was a prominent Sri Lankan politician, a fifty-two-year-old man who would one day have been Sri Lanka's president had he been allowed to live.

Educated in England, Gamini was a suave lawyer and a shrewd politician. He spoke and wrote with an easy flair. His hooded eyes were always careful and observing, even though he often seemed to be distant or casual. He loved India, but best of all, he loved gossip. So we got along famously. He would fill me in on what was happening on the political scene in Colombo, complete with all the juicy details that could never be printed, and I in turn gave him the gossip from India, which he devoured while I devoured the delicious food cooked by his charming wife, Srima.

Gamini was a one-man broadcasting station. His reach was infinitely superior to that of BBC and CNN combined. Once I told Gamini that every time I interviewed Pirabhakaran, he served me Chinese food, which he loves. Using me as the excuse, it seemed to me, Pirabhakaran treated himself.

About five days after I mentioned this to Gamini, I happened to be back in Colombo. Whoever I met—Indians and Sri Lankans—bombarded me with questions: 'Hmm, so Pirabhakaran loves Chinese food, does he? Where does he get the ingredients from? Is it Chinese Chinese food, or is it Sri Lankan Chinese food? He is fighting a guerrilla war, but look at him, eating exotic Chinese food in the bushes!'

My answers would have triggered several more rounds of debate. Yes, Pirabhakaran loves Chinese food. If he can get hold of SAM 7 missiles, why should he have a problem getting ajinomoto? Yes, it's very Sri Lankan Chinese food with red chillies and coconut, and so what if he is fighting a bush war, the man doesn't drink, smoke or womanize. Surely he is entitled to some good food. And by the way, there is no electricity in Jaffna or in the jungles, but Pirabhakaran always rounds off our Chinese meal with ice cream.

But I never answered the questions, I felt it would reveal more about the reclusive guerrilla leader than was necessary. I would quickly change the topic, vowing never to volunteer any information about living persons to Gamini unless I wanted it unofficially gazetted in Sri Lanka.

In October 1994, while campaigning for elections, Gamini was blown up by an LTTE suicide bomber. It was past midnight, and he was winding up an election rally in a slum district in Colombo. He waved to the crowd and quipped, 'I should say goodnight, but it's morning now, so good morning to you all.'

It was, in fact, goodbye.

Seconds later, the stage was lit by a bright flash, followed by a thunderous roar. When the smoke and confusion cleared, Gamini was dead, and fifty of his supporters were strewn about, dead or dying.

Gamini's handsome face was untouched. But the light had gone out of his mischievous eyes for ever. He looked as if he was sleeping, but his chest had been pierced by countless pellets that had detonated from the suicide bomber's jacket.

The assassin had no chest left. She had worn a jacket filled with explosives densely packed with iron pellets. So powerful was the impact of the bomb she had strapped around her chest that her head had been blown fifty metres away, and dangled from the overhanging electric wires, hair still braided neatly.

Haunting images that burn into your mind forever, images that flash from within when you least expect it, hitting you like a sledgehammer. You can feel the blow, but you never know where it comes from, or what triggers it off.

Haunting images like former prime minister Rajiv Gandhi's mangled body, when another LTTE suicide bomber blew up herself and him. Rajiv lay face down, even his clothes blown off by the impact of the explosion. The keen journalistic eye sees the horror of the scene, even as it takes in the bit of white underwear peeping through, the white walking shoes with the brand name lotto.

There is no dignity in such death. One of India's most powerful men lay sprawled dead, and the voyeurs of the world saw and shuddered. I shuddered for Rajiv, and even more for his widow, Sonia, and their two children. To see one's beloved in such a condition must be one of the most painful experiences in life. And what makes it even worse is to have your loved one dead and paraded around the world. But the media is driven by its own pitiless logic. It's a good picture. That's all that matters. No time to waste on sensitivities here.

Those pictures of Rajiv Gandhi were flashed around the world. It turned my stomach. Rajiv was not exactly the smartest politician around—he was often naïve, and his inexperience showed. But he was a warm, decent, charming human being. You couldn't help liking him. And he was clearly a ladies' man. His eye would notice the prettiest woman in a room and return to her every once in a while, and then he would smile that smile which made the woman feel he smiled only at her.

Ten days before he was killed, I had met Rajiv while he was campaigning at Hardwar in northern India. That was my last encounter with him. The streets were crowded with people. I pushed my way closer to him and yelled, 'Hey, I need a quote from you. Can we talk for just a few minutes?'

'Okay. After this meeting, hop into my car,' he said. So after his speech—a plebian speech, but what applause!—he got into the back seat, and I sat by his side while his school buddy and media advisor, Suman Dubey, sat in front, and we sped off.

I got my quotes and Rajiv, who knew I had the best access to Pirabhakaran, asked me, 'How long will these Tigers keep fighting?'

'As long as Pirabhakaran is alive,' I replied.

Rajiv turned and looked at me as if I had reaffirmed his personal belief.

'Keep this to yourself, the Tigers are sending feelers to me for reconciliation,' he said.

'Are you responding to them?' I asked.

'You know, the bottom line is, the Tigers are intransigent. I don't trust them,' said Rajiv.

His instincts were right. Ten days later, he was dead. Assassinated by the Tigers. They feared he would win the election and, if returned to power, would crack down on them. What they didn't realize then was that a slain Rajiv would prove far more disastrous to the LTTE. For several years, the Tigers had used Tamil Nadu, which was barely twenty-two kilometres across the Palk Straits from their homeland, as their sanctuary. They recouped there after battles, sent their injured cadres for medical treatment, and procured all their supplies from there. But after Rajiv's death, the state administration cracked down hard and smashed much of the carefully built LTTE empire in Tamil Nadu. Worse, Rajiv's assassination turned Indians hostile to the Tigers. They were seen as dangerous and untrustworthy. A decade later, sitting in his London suburban house, A.S. Balasingham, chief idealogue of the Tamil Tigers, admitted to me that in assassinating Rajiv Gandhi, the LTTE had committed 'a historical blunder'.

A few years later, the Tigers exploded yet another powerful bomb in Colombo. I was at the CNN office that evening, though I was to join CNN officially only the next day. It was 6 p.m., and everyone else had left. So when the phone rang, I picked it up. The call was from Atlanta, CNN's headquarters. The caller asked for me.

'You know a bomb has just exploded in Colombo.'

I didn't know, I had just come to the office to put my files on the desk.

'Well, the bomb went off in downtown Colombo, and at least fifty people have been killed. Can we just ask you a few questions?'

'Sure,' I said.

'Stand by,' the voice said and I heard CNN's breaking news announcement. I realized to my horror that I was live on air. I felt tricked. I had never done something like this before. I was a print journalist who revelled in anonymity, in writing my stories in the peace and solitude of my room. I never had to speak.

My voice froze, my blood ran cold.

The smooth, rich voice of the anchor cut through my agitation. 'So Anita, what can you tell us?'

'Damn it, I don't want to tell you anything,' I felt like saying. 'I am not prepared. I was just driving by and stopped to drop off some files. I join CNN officially only tomorrow. That's what I want to tell you.'

But crisis always transforms me into Ms Professional. So of course I started 'telling' him things. I think it was my desperate desire to get off the phone quickly that made me give brief, to-the-point replies. But it didn't quite work that way. The show producer had assigned two minutes for the Sri Lanka blast, so the anchor had to fill the air time by shooting off more questions. Fortunately, I know my stories like the back of my hand, having reported from the trenches for two decades. So the back and forth sally with the anchor lasted two whole minutes—on air it seemed like a lifetime. Each time I finished answering, I thought surely that must be the last question, but oh no, my heart sank as he rapid-fired yet another one. He must have been exasperated, wondering why like so many other correspondents I didn't just keep talking—most love to hear the sound of their own voice, and those two minutes are the moments that reaffirm their existence, their importance, their utility to mankind. It would have saved him the trouble of thinking up new questions to ask. But this was before I had officially joined, before I knew what the system was, let alone how it worked!

At last, after what seemed an eternity, the anchor said, 'That was Anita Pratap from New Delhi, and she will keep us informed as the events unfold.'

I put the phone down, but before I could experience any relief, it rang again. I looked at it in horror as if it was a coiled snake. I was afraid to pick it up. What if it was Atlanta asking for another live broadcast? I could easily slip away. No one would know.

But of course I picked up the phone. It wasn't Atlanta, it wasn't someone asking for another live broadcast. It was

Ed Turner, vice-president of CNN, the man who had hired me.

'Anita, you were great. I really liked the way you kept your answers brief. That way we get more out of a question-and-answer session, and that's much more interesting for viewers. But slow down, don't speak so fast. Remember, people don't know the story, and they are not familiar with your Indian accent. That apart, you were terrific. You kept your cool, and you spoke really knowledgeably and confidently without any ums and ers. Good job, girl.'

The nerve of the man! He had been testing me. I guess he must have nerves of steel himself. I could have made a complete ass of myself, my voice could have frozen in fright so that not even ums and ers emerged. A month later, when I met him in Atlanta I told him as much—I could have made a fool of myself and by extension, he could have made a fool of himself for hiring me.

'Oh, but you are a tough girl,' he said.

FIGHTING TO WALK AWAY

I guess I am tough. My encounter with Ranjan Wijeratne may give the impression that I tend to laugh my way out of fights—which is not true. I am not incapable of fighting. But I pick my battles carefully and fight only when it's a matter of survival, justice or dignity. (I can almost hear Zubin wisecrack, no wonder she is fighting all the time!).

In 1988, I was touring Jaffna in a car I had hired from Colombo. Jaffna was bursting with Indian soldiers; the LTTE was on the run and had mostly retreated into the jungles. The Indian troops were using a quisling Tamil group called the EPRLF (Eelam People's Revolutionary Liberation Front) to flush out Tiger guerrillas and sympathizers. The EPRLF was swaggering around in Jaffna, armed with guns, secure under the protection of the Indian army.

We were driving along one of the narrow, potholed roads when suddenly a group of young men ran out of a house and waylaid the car. Driver Hari screeched to a halt. With their AK 47s aimed at Hari's head, they ordered him out of the car. I remained in the back seat and asked them what they wanted. Rudely, they ordered me out of the car as well. Making no effort to step out, I asked them coolly why they had stopped us.

'Get out,' said one of the boys, pointing his machine gun at my head. Hari was already out. He was trembling.

'I will, if you tell me why you are stopping my car.'

'Don't argue, you stupid woman. Get out of the car,' he snarled, his rifle butt pressed to my temple.

I got out of the car and drew myself to my full height. I was taller than him. I then snarled back at him, 'I am a journalist and an Indian. How dare you treat me like this? I demand an explanation.' It wasn't what I said, but the manner in which I said it, that suddenly made him lose his composure. I spoke with anger and authority. The message was clear: don't mess with me.

One of the other boys pulled his companion to the rear and tried to pacify me, 'My comrade is hurt. He is bleeding. We have to take him to the hospital. We need your car.'

'You don't have to steal my car for that,' I said, knowing that if I gave the car to them, I would never see it again. There had been several reports about the way the EPRLF was harassing the Tamils, looting and plundering and ordering people about.

'I will take him myself to the hospital. One or two of you can accompany him in the car. Bring him quickly,' I ordered, assuming control and pretending to be calmer and more authoritative than I felt.

They brought their moaning, bleeding comrade. His rifle had accidentally gone off while he was cleaning it, injuring him in the leg. Three of his colleagues got into the rear seat, and they placed the wounded young man across their laps. I got into the front seat. We drove to an Indian army medical outpost and dropped the militants there. They even thanked me!

But it was in the summer of 1990 that I found my negotiating skills severely tested. I was on my way to Batticaloa, an eastern coastal town which was still under the control of the Tigers, to report on the resumption of war for *Time*. The Indians had left, but the truce between the Tigers and the Sri Lankan government had ended violently after three months. The LTTE and the Sri Lankan forces were both back to fighting. Once again, war, this island's constant companion, was stalking the land. As Shantha Ruban, a shopkeeper who was seeking refuge in a church near Batticaloa said: 'We Tamils seem to be under some curse; we seem destined never to enjoy peace.'

Photographer Doug Curran and I had set off from Colombo to Batticaloa in a red sedan with 'Hotel Hilton' painted on the sides. I felt it was safer to be in something striking and obviously neutral, especially during the aerial strikes. When the helicopter gunships clattered above us, I would jump out of the car, let my hair down so that it was obvious I was a woman, and wave a white flag.

As it turned out, the skies were not as deadly as the earth. We reached the last Sri Lankan barricade. With great difficulty we were allowed through into the LTTE-controlled territory. From past experience I knew that a buffer zone separated the government-controlled area from the rebel-held territory. This no man's land was treacherous.

The Sri Lankan army lifted the barricade, and we moved forward slowly. From then on, we were on our own. Ours was the first civilian vehicle to cross into the no man's land after the outbreak of hostilities. That would make our passage even more lethal. I ordered the driver to drive slowly—not more than five kilometres per hour. The narrow potholed road rolled out in front of us like a long, motionless snake, stealthily lying in wait to spring an unpleasant surprise. The green landscape had the usual growth of bushes and trees. The whole area was eerily deserted and silent.

I kept my eyes glued to the road. We must have travelled

barely a quarter of a kilometre when I spotted a thin wire stretched across the road and ordered the driver to halt immediately. He slammed the brakes. We waited for about fifteen minutes in the car, bristling with tension.

Then from about fifty metres in front, I heard a shout. A camouflage-uniformed rebel emerged. An AK 47 was slung on his shoulder. He said in Tamil, 'Who are you? Why are you here?'

I jumped out of the car. 'Stay there. Don't move,' he shouted.

I shouted back, 'My name is Anita Pratap. I am a journalist. My photographer is with me. We want to go to Batticaloa and report from there.'

'What did you say your name was again?' he shouted.

'Anita Pratap. I have reported on Sri Lanka's Tamil problem for a long time,' I volunteered.

'Were you the one who interviewed our leader Pirabhakaran?'

'Yes, yes, that was me. I have interviewed Pirabhakaran many times.' I was thrilled, and confident they would now let me in.

'Don't move,' he ordered and shouted something else, apparently to his comrades, not that we could see anybody nearby.

Suddenly the bushes and the trees stirred and within a few minutes, the place was crawling with about fifty camouflaged LTTE guerrillas. They rose from the ground, wriggled out from behind bushes and loped down the trees. It was stunning. Their camouflage was so brilliant it would have fooled even a trained eye on the lookout for them.

The leader who had shouted at me walked up slowly. He avoided the road, walking instead along the grassy edge. He stopped about ten feet away from me. He looked at me closely, then bent down and picked up one end of the string that lay stretched across the road. He walked across the road, lifting the string alongside. He stopped on the other side and grinned at me, pointing to the string. 'This road is mined. If you hadn't stopped, your car would have blown up,' he said. 'But we were expecting Sri Lankan army jeeps, not civilian vehicles on this road. Wait for some more time. We will clear the road up ahead too.'

Yet another narrow shave in Sri Lanka.

Without any further problems, we reached Batticaloa town, where everybody was blaming the Tigers for resuming the war. They had used a petty quarrel between a Tamil tailor and a Sinhalese woman to engineer a confrontation with the state. People were heartbroken because peace had once again eluded them.

I was staying in a lodge owned by a Tamil businessman named Joseph Pararajasingham. Years later, he would go on to become a prominent member of Parliament. After a few days of reporting, Doug and I were ready to return to Colombo. The night before our return, Pararajasingham asked me for a favour. He wondered if we could give his son, Subajeet, a lift to Colombo. His twenty-year-old son was studying in the US and had come to Sri Lanka for a holiday, taking advantage of the ceasefire. Unfortunately, while he was vacationing with his parents, war resumed. Now he was stuck in Batticaloa, as all civilian transport to Colombo had been suspended. If he didn't get back, he would not be able to take his flight back to America—and his whole career, even life, would be ruined. He would forfeit his college seat, he would have to forsake a safe and comfortable life in the US. He would remain in Batticaloa, condemned to a life without a future, living with tension and war.

With tears in her eyes, Pararajasingham's wife pleaded with me: 'My son is unsafe here. He is very young. We will lose him either to the LTTE or to the STF, who will suspect him of being a militant, even if he isn't. To them all young Tamil boys are Tigers.'

She was not exaggerating. The STF (Sri Lankan Special Task Force), a paramilitary unit, was notorious for its cruelty and arbitrary arrests of Tamil youths, who were then tortured and killed. The 'disappearance' of Tamil boys had become a shadowy reality that kept human-rights activists busy. Subajeet stood precariously between two futures—a life of prosperity and peace in the US, and a life of unemployment, possibly torture and even death, in Batticaloa. I agreed to take him with me. But it turned out to be a terrible responsibility.

We started back without any problems. The Tigers once again cleared the no man's land, and we reached the Sri Lankan barricade. The sentry recognized us and waved us through, then suddenly stopped us. He had spotted the boy.

'Who is that?' he demanded to know.

'A friend,' I said sweetly, trying to hurry on. But he detained me, and scrutinizing the boy asked, 'He is Tamil, isn't he?'

I knew what was going through his mind, so I reassured him. 'Yes, he is, but I've known him and his family for a long time. His father is a very respectable man. He owns a lodge. Listen, I must rush back. I have to reach Colombo and take a plane back to India tonight.'

I didn't have a plane to catch, though I did have a deadline to keep. If I didn't file by evening, I would miss the week's edition. But there was no point in telling him about deadlines. He wouldn't understand. Missing planes was more comprehensible. Besides, it sounded more urgent.

I smiled pleasantly and chatted about Batticaloa, how conditions were terrible there. Pleased to hear that and softened by my pleasant chatter and urgent appeals, he waved us through.

Five kilometres down, we were stopped again, by troops manning another Sri Lankan barricade. This was much bigger, and the security personnel were occupying a house by the side of the road. Once again, the guards had no problem with me or Doug, but the presence of the Tamil boy agitated them. He was asked to get out of the car and go in for questioning. I went in with him and answered all the officer's questions.

Subajeet was so nervous that he fumbled his replies. The officer wasn't convinced. His logic was simple. The boy was too well built to be an ordinary Tamil youth. He was muscle-bound, and that made him a Tiger. QED. He said he would have to hand him over to the STF. If the STF was satisfied with his bona fides, they would let him go.

I pleaded with the man, told him about the desperate rush to catch the plane back to Delhi. The man looked at me coolly and said, 'I am not detaining you. You can carry on.'

But how could I abandon Subajeet to the STF? He would be dead within twenty-four hours. The STF was not interested in arguments and reasoning. They tortured first and talked later, and most of the time they hit so hard there was no need to talk later. The person would be dead.

But the officer was adamant. He escorted us to another checkpost, from where we were escorted to the STF camp about three kilometres away. During the ride, I asked Subajeet the reason for his being so well-built. He said he was a sportsman, and he was in fact carrying certificates that proved his accomplishments.

The STF officer who took charge of us was small, wiry and nasty. There was something sinister about him.

'So when did you join the LTTE?' he barked.

The boy stuttered in fear. I intervened.

'Listen, he is not a Tiger. He is a friend's son. His father is a well-to-do businessman. This boy is studying in the US,' I said, explaining that he had come for a vacation before war broke out.

Meanface heard me out and then hissed, 'I asked him the question. Why are you answering?'

'Because you are scaring him.'

'He is afraid because he is a Tiger,' he snapped. Then turning to the boy, he repeated, 'So when did you join the LTTE?'

'He is not with the LTTE. If he was, why would I defend him?' I asked reasonably.

Meanface directed his venom at me. 'You had no business bringing him with you. You are smuggling a Tiger. That's an offence.'

'First of all, he is not a Tiger. He is a student in the United States. I know his parents well. Secondly, I am not smuggling him. I didn't hide him in the boot of the car or the floor of the backseat. I was giving him a lift into Colombo because there is no civilian transport available.'

Meanface was the embodiment of antagonism. He seemed to carry in his head a great deal of accumulated resentment against Tamils and Indians.

'You Indians think you can come here and do what you want and get away with it. A crime is a crime no matter who commits it, Indian or American, we don't care,' he said.

'Something doesn't become a crime just because you

say so,' I argued. 'I am surprised that you as an officer are jumping to conclusions. His certificates show he is a student in the US. What more proof do you want?'

'Certificates can be forged. These Tamils can do anything. Have you seen how well they forge passports? These certificates are not worth the paper they are forged on.'

'How can you say they are forged without even checking?' I asked.

'The same way I can tell he is a Tiger without giving him a second look,' he said.

'It's because you don't give a second look that you assume he is a Tiger. If he were a Tiger, why would he take a lift with me? Tigers don't go around taking lifts from journalists and other civilians. They have other ways of reaching Colombo, and you know that.'

But my logic failed to dent his determination to take Subajeet to the detention centre—read, torture chamber. Once this man took him away, I knew there was no hope. The boy would be tortured and killed. Eventually, he would be just a name in the list of 'disappearances'.

'This is one Tiger I am going to make sure will not reach Colombo, one way or the other. The very fact that you are arguing his case makes you an accessory. We can arrest you for smuggling a Tiger.' The menace in his voice was unmistakable.

We were back to square one. And I was getting hot under the collar.

'I am telling you again, I wasn't smuggling him. I was giving him a lift because there is no civilian transport,' I said, clenching my teeth to prevent myself from losing my temper.

'And why is there no civilian transport? Because

Pirabhakaran started the war again,' he said, and then glaring angrily at the boy he thundered, 'Why don't you blame that leader of yours for your situation now? No, you people won't dare blame him. You all are slaves, a bunch of cowards. We trust you Tamils, and you hit back. Poisonous snakes, that's what you all are. You should be crushed underfoot. Shown no mercy. Treacherous bastards. Our president trusted Pirabhakaran, and look what happened. He was slapped in the face. The whole world is laughing at us. Okay, so Pirabhakaran wants a fight, we will give it to him.'

My blood froze. I realized the man was seething with hate and anger. Logic or reason would not be able to penetrate this blind wall of prejudice. And the victim would be this young boy, whose whole future lay in the hands of this STF officer who now turned to me.

'I don't understand why you are so concerned about him. You say you have a plane to catch. Why don't you go? We are not stopping you. Why are you so interested in this boy?' he said with a sneer.

'Because his parents pleaded with me to take him. If he had remained in Batticaloa, either you guys or the Tigers would have got him. Whereas if he manages to reach Colombo, he will be able to go back to America and resume his studies and lead a normal life.'

'And why can't he have a normal life here? All because of that bloodthirsty dog, Pirabhakaran. He won't allow them. He wants to suck their blood, but these idiots don't realize that. They still support him. This should teach him and his family a lesson not to support Pirabhakaran.'

'You are not teaching him a lesson. You are punishing him for no fault of his. You have battles to fight with Pirabhakaran, fight them with him. Why are you taking it out on this innocent boy?'

'Innocent? You call him innocent? No Tamil is innocent,' he shouted.

I was tired. I seemed to have run out of options. And then I tried the last resort—appealing to his good instincts. I was sure that whatever good instincts he might have had as a child would have been smothered long ago. But I couldn't give up. I had to do something, so I pleaded.

'Listen, you are a young man. I don't know whether you are married, whether you have children. I am a mother, I have a son who is nine years old. I am doing what I am doing now—appealing to you to let this boy go—not as an Indian, not as a journalist, but as a mother. I cannot forget the tears in his mother's eyes as she handed him to my care. She is very worried. For a mother, there is no greater calamity than danger to her son. I am defending this boy because I can so easily imagine that this could be happening to my son. I beg of you, don't behave like an STF officer, please behave like a human being, like a father. Some day, God forbid, it could be your son facing an ordeal like this boy. Please let him go.'

I was getting worked up. There were tears in my eyes.

'You are either a good woman or a good actress,' he said with a thin smile.

'After I go back to my country, I am going to give up journalism and take up acting. It's so much easier. I don't have to go through all this. It's too much,' I said.

'You don't look old enough to have a nine-year-old son,' he said, eyeing me sceptically.

'I promise you I have a son. I wouldn't lie about a thing like that,' I said, fishing in my wallet for Zubin's picture. 'And the picture is not forged,' I added with a smile.

My emotional speech seemed to have changed the atmosphere. The tension eased. Meanface became almost

affable. 'Your son is very cute. Doesn't look a bit like you.'
I let that sneaky dig pass.

Then, in a very businesslike fashion, he said he was
letting the boy go, but took down his contact address and
telephone number in Colombo, ordered him to report to
the neighbourhood police station immediately on reaching,
and to be in daily contact with the station till he took the
plane out of Colombo.

When he finally said we could leave, we were deeply
relieved. Maybe it was the Stockholm syndrome, but I felt
immense gratitude towards him.

'Thank you, sir. We really appreciate this. You will never
regret this,' I said.

He half raised his hand in farewell. His parting shot
was, 'By the way, I am not married.'

I smiled, waved, wished him all the best and scrambled
back into the car. As the car started, I looked at Subajeet
sitting in the front seat. He was quiet and still, visibly shaken
by the whole experience. Thank God things had worked
out well. His fate had hung in the balance, but now he had
crossed over to the safe side. He would go back to the
United States, lead a normal life, get married and one day
have children of his own. And life would go on, in the
simple, ordinary way it should—but very nearly didn't.

In the past decade, so many nations, institutions and
people have tried to bring peace to Sri Lanka so that boys
like Subajeet can live, work, marry and have children in
their own homeland. But so far, all efforts have failed.

Recently, prospects for peace brightened for a while
when the Norwegians intervened as facilitators. This was
around the time when I married Arne Walther, who was
Norway's ambassador to India. We got married three
times—the first time was in Spain, in a romantic ceremony

at the cypress-lined hacienda of the Norwegian ambassador who conducted the wedding. A Norwegian parliamentarian named Erik Solheim and oil executive Nils Gulnes were the best men, and the chief witness was my soul sister, Nina Pillai. Then we got married in India, a civil ceremony held in the sprawling gardens of my friend Ram Jethmalani's bungalow in New Delhi. Ram was then the union law minister. The third was a moonlit gypsy wedding at the exotic New Delhi home of my friends Sonny and Livleen Sharma, amid 400 guests, two elephants and 128 dancing gypsies.

When I got married, I had no clue that the Norwegians were facilitating a peace process in Sri Lanka. Nor did the world. The Norwegians wanted to keep it secret, exactly the way they had kept their peace talks in West Asia under wraps. But a month after our wedding in Spain, President Chandrika Kumaratunga blurted out the truth during an interview with BBC in London. A few months later, when the government changed in Norway, it was our best man Erik Solheim who was made the key Norwegian facilitator.

In the West, this would be called coincidence. In India, we call it destiny.

One way or the other, Sri Lanka will always be part of my destiny.

Afghanistan

THE DOOMED LAND

A NATION OF REBELS

It's a brilliant day in June. The blue sky is dotted with little white tufts of cotton-wool clouds. The surrounding mountains are lush green, carpeted with white and yellow spring flowers. The trees stand tall, swaying gently in the cool breeze. The air is crisp, pure and invigorating, the kind of air you can only find in the outer regions of the First World, the kind of air you can truly appreciate only if you come from the smog-filled Third World.

We are holidaying in Flåm. Norwegians may call it a town, but to us, who come from cities with populations of more than ten million (two and a half times the population of the whole of Norway), Flåm is tinier than our tiniest hamlet. Ringed by majestic mountains, this charming cluster nestles on the bank of a deep blue fjord. Flåm is picture-postcard Norwegian beauty at its pristine best. Cruise ships end a voyage of rainbows and waterfalls, cliffs and glaciers along the world-famous Sognefjord that meanders its way through the snow-capped mountains, by berthing at Flåm's little pier. Across the pier and down the main street, past a souvenir shop and a café, begins the Flåm railway line, one of the most picturesque train routes in the world.

Having arrived in a cruise ship, we are spending the day in Flåm before taking the quaint little train ride to

Myrdal and then back to Oslo. My friend Ram Jethmalani was spending five days with us in Oslo, and we had decided to see the best of Norway's sights with him.

It's midday, the sun is shining, fat seagulls strut on the pier, and the air is as softly caressing as angels' wings. We settle down on one of the rugged wooden tables with attached benches on the pier and take the goodies out of our picnic hamper. Wine, varieties of cheese, fruit, tortilla chips. We lay it all out neatly, with glasses, plates, paper napkins, forks and knives. We pour out the wine and take deep, appreciative sips. The world looks better. We sit there, sipping red wine, munching yellow chips, swirling blue cheese and talking, not purple prose, but multishaded philosophy. It's a marvellous technicolour world. We open the second bottle of wine. The world looks even better.

Suddenly our world goes topsy-turvy. No, we are nowhere near that level of drunkenness. A gust of wind has blown in and swept everything from our table. The wine bottle topples over, tortilla chips fly across the pier, paper plates race like Frisbees into the fjord. Glasses tumble, cutlery drops, and morsels of food swirl in the air like tasty flying saucers.

We are dumbstruck. One minute we are sitting around philosophizing about life, munching our simple but delicious meal and drinking good wine. The next minute our cosy meal disintegrates right before our eyes, flying off in different directions. Looking at each other's dismayed expressions, we burst out laughing. Still helpless with laughter, we scatter to retrieve our vanishing meal. Each one has his or her priority.

I want to save the wine. I hold the glass to the edge of the table to catch the falling drops. Ram is struggling to save the cheese, and Arne leaps to his feet, flying after the tortilla chips. Arne's eighteen-year-old son, Markus, sits hunched on the bench, watching us disapprovingly from the corner of his downcast eyes. As we scurry to save our meal, Markus slinks away to save his reputation.

Arne strides back looking pleased, like a satisfied predator of yore returning after a hard day of hunting in the woods, laden with food for the family. His trophy? Three tortilla chips that he brandishes triumphantly. Seeing his catch of the day, Ram and I laugh heartily, unmindful of the size of our own catch—in my case, about ten drops of wine and in Ram's, a carton of cheese without any cheese in it.

Arne suggests we get down to cleaning the pier. This is Norway, you don't leave your trash around. So we set about, doubled up with laughter as we stagger around picking up leftovers, napkins, glasses and plates. We look like three well-fed, middle-aged ragpickers. I am the clumsiest, dropping more than I pick up.

But Ram is truly impressive. He has collected a large pile and precariously perched though it is in the crook of his arm, he manages to tread carefully to the trash can and empty everything out.

'What an efficient garbage collector you are. A real pro. Looking at you pick garbage, who would ever think you are the honourable law minister of India,' I say between giggles.

'And I thought I was here on vacation,' he says, laughing.

'Well, look at it this way. You are carrying your heritage with you. You are being a worthy descendant of Mahatma Gandhi. He cleaned toilets, you clean the pier.'

'As long as I wind up with cheese and not bullets in my stomach, I am happy to be the Mahatma's descendant,' says Ram.

'Your stomach is so full of cheese there would be no

space for bullets. But Ram, seriously, see how well you have cleaned up. It comes naturally to you,' I remark.

'Remember, I was the urban development minister before I became the law minister,' jokes Ram. 'So I have a natural aptitude.'

We clean up the mess as best as we can and troop along to the café for a hot cup of coffee. Markus materializes to give his Dad hell. He hisses in Norwegian: 'You don't know how to behave.'

Arne musters his dignity and gets philosophical. Patiently, he explains to Markus, whose fury is rising to new levels as he listens, 'It's all about retaining your innocence. We are competent, responsible adults—Anita is a well-known journalist, Ram is a very distinguished minister and a brilliant lawyer, and I am an experienced ambassador. But we are not prisoners of our persona. You see, more than anything else, we are ordinary, simple people who enjoy the simple pleasures of life. Despite our age, we are still innocent enough to enjoy these simple things. The child in us is alive and kicking.'

If he could, his child would be kicking him now. Markus darts him a poisonous glare, rapid-fires some more in Norwegian, opens his laptop and departs from our world. Ram wants to give his aching legs a rest and read for a while. After our cuppa, Arne and I are full of beans and want to explore Flåm, so we go for a walk up the mountain.

The scenery is spectacular. We are encircled by mountains of varying shades—the one we are climbing is apple green, the ones just beyond are a darker shade of green, the ring of mountains behind that is a bottle green, and the ones in the far distance, a purplish blue.

We walk up a narrow, winding mountain path. On either side are meadows of tall grass, swaying and rippling in the breeze. In the distance, there is a cluster of red and white doll-like wooden houses, a meandering brook and a foamy waterfall. The sounds of nature are exquisite—the hum of the bees, the swish of the grass, the gush of the waterfall, the gurgle of the brook.

I can't help adding my own voice. Like Julie Andrews in *The Sound of Music*, I sing with my arms outstretched: 'The hills are alive with the sound of music.' Arne joins in with his baritone. We traipse along the mountain path, holding hands and singing—the tune is all wrong, the words are missing, but who cares. We are happy and we express it the only way we don't know how to—by singing.

We almost bang into a young boy on a bicycle. He is not more than seventeen, so healthy and rosy-cheeked you feel like biting him. His face reminds you of fresh red apples and creamy peaches. It's flushed red from cycling uphill.

I am overwhelmed by the benign beauty of the landscape and its well-cared-for people.

So different from Afghanistan.

Afghanistan too has mountains, but they are dangerous, mysterious and wild. There is a stark roughness in the mountainscape that is reflected in the weather-beaten faces of the people. Afghans, like their land, are rugged, rebellious, brooding.

Both mountains and faces are etched with suffering.

Like young Abdul Mateen's—caught in an explosion, face charred, burnt skin peeled off, exposing flesh.

It happened on 26 September 1996, the evening the Taliban invaded and captured Kabul. Taliban tanks rolled into the city, filling the ominous vacuum left by the evacuating troops of the government of Burhanuddin Rabbani. Abdul Mateen, who sold vegetables for a living, was having a bad day, he had hardly sold any. The vegetables were drying up, some were even blackening. It was getting late, but Mateen felt he couldn't give up. Maybe, just maybe, someone would come along and buy something from him. He decided to stay on.

It was his first bad decision of the day. What did come along were not customers but rumbling tanks. The few people and vendors nearby ran in panic. Mateen knew he was in peril. Remembering that fearful evening, he said later from his hospital bed, 'I was terrified because I saw government troops running away. There were sounds of shelling. I was desperate to get home.'

There was no such thing as city transport. Mateen had to walk home. It was a long walk, he was used to that, but he was frightened because there were hardly any people around and the few still left on the streets were running for cover. The sound of shelling was getting closer.

People in war zones help each other in ways people in normal areas don't. Even though slowing down and waiting for a few seconds to give a lift to a stranded civilian can sometimes bring danger, even death upon oneself, people do it—I have seen them do it in Kashmir, Sri Lanka and Afghanistan.

Mateen succeeded in getting a ride on a gasoline truck. That was his second bad decision. But do poor and desperate people have choices?

Sometimes I wonder about God, this Being who manipulates our fates. Innocent people find themselves in a crisis. They are afraid and desperate to escape, to survive. Then God throws them a rope—almost like a rope to safety. For a brief, shining moment, the rope seems like a ray of light that promises to lift them out of the crisis into safety. And then the rope curls into a noose.

Take for instance the tragedy that happened in Indonesia.

More than ninety per cent of Indonesia's 210 million people are Muslims, but in the Moluccan Islands, Muslims and Christians are evenly divided. Violence erupted between the two communities in 1999, and in the following year and a half it took the lives of more than 2500 people. The massacre of Christians in May 2000 in the village of Duma on Halmahera Island was one of the worst incidents recorded.

About 500 Christian inhabitants were fleeing Duma where Muslim attackers had just massacred 200 of their fellow villagers. The fleeing group comprised mostly women and children. There were also about thirty wounded survivors of the massacre. They feared another attack, so they decided to abandon their village and flee to the safe haven of Sulawesi, about 200 kilometres to the west, across the Molucca Sea. The only thing that could save them from certain death was a battered old ferry that could take them to their refuge. So the desperate group pushed and jostled frantically to board the ferry. It was a biblical scene of panic and anguish. Crowds fought their way up narrow gangplanks, passing their belongings and their children up above their heads. Some even shimmied up the ropes that moored the vessel. Eventually they all managed to scramble into the boat.

As the ferry left the shores of the killer island, they must have felt incredibly lucky. What thrill it was, what heady relief to escape from the jaws of death. They thanked God, their stars, their ancestors watching over them.

But a few hours into the journey, they ran full tilt into a raging storm. The creaking wood-hulled boat was tossed and buffeted like a useless toy. The ferry engine went dead. They were stranded on the high seas with nine-foot waves leaping like tongues of death around them. The ferry sent out distress signals, but no rescue boats responded. Then the panic-stricken passengers saw water seeping into the aged ferry. This time, there was no place to run to.

The boat, with its load of frightened passengers, sank into shark-infested waters. There were no survivors.

When Abdul Mateen got a ride on the gasoline truck, he was thrilled and relieved. Now he could get away to safety. Or so he thought.

Hit by gunfire, the gasoline truck exploded. Mateen was the only survivor. But he had no skin left. It was charred completely in the explosion. He suffered ninety-eight per cent burns.

When we first saw him, Mateen was swathed in bandages. He was moaning in pain, and asking for his mother. He began to murmur what had happened to him. No story is that important, and I tried to hush him. But he wanted to talk. Maybe it took his mind off the excruciating pain. He told me about that night of the Taliban invasion. He didn't know how he had wound up in the Kabul hospital. And then he said: 'I hope for peace, stability and freedom so that we can repair our destroyed lives.'

While we were with Mateen, the doctor began to remove the bandages. Mateen's face unfolded before our horrified eyes. It was raw and red. As the bandages pulled the skinless flesh, I looked away, unable to bear the sight. Anybody else would have shrieked in agony, but Mateen was brave. He only winced. I looked back at him. Even his eyelashes had been roasted off his face.

But at least his head was intact...unlike Zubaida's husband's. Four years earlier, in the factional fighting that raged in Kabul between the mujahedin forces, Zubaida's husband happened to be in the wrong place at the wrong time. He was at home.

The family heard the sounds of gunfighting, but there were no bunkers to run into, so they just sat tight in their mud hut and prayed to Allah. It was a rocket attack and the sounds of war whizzed around and over them.

In that rocket attack, Zubaida's husband's head was blown off. Zubaida became a destitute widow. She had five children to look after, but she had no qualifications to get a job, no family to run to for support. She started begging on the streets. For three years the family subsisted on her begging. There were days when they went hungry, fell ill with hunger and cold.

Then in early 1996, she got a job in the Kabul orphanage. She had to sweep the floors, tidy the rooms and wash the orphans. She was good at that because she had enough experience with her own children. She was overjoyed. The family was guaranteed at least one meal a day. Allah had answered her prayers.

But the soldiers of Allah, as the Taliban like to call themselves, had other plans. They banned women from working and ordered them to stay indoors. If they did venture out, they had to wear the all-concealing chador or burqa.

What could a poor woman like Zubaida do? What could 50,000 other poor widows, who were the sole breadwinners of their families, do?

Like Zubaida, most of them worked clandestinely. For these women, earning a livelihood had become a crime. If caught working, they would be stoned publicly. But the Taliban offered no alternatives, no security net, not even a poorhouse meal for these destitute women. So they had no choice but to run the risk of incurring the Taliban's wrath.

Zubaida was too scared to walk back home every day after work, so she spent the night in the orphanage, leaving

her fifteen-year-old daughter to look after her younger
brother and sisters. Thinking of the danger her small
children faced, their vulnerability and their helplessness,
Zubaida's face crumbled in grief. 'I can't sleep at night,
worrying about my children,' she said.

Once a week, she wore her black chador, hid a few
potatoes stolen from the orphanage kitchen in its folds,
and walked home. With the few coins she had, she bought
some bread on the way. Her children greeted her with
elation—the joy of seeing a loving mother and the joy of
seeing food. She handed over some money to her daughter,
to tide them over until she could venture out again.

These days, said Zubaida, she had only one prayer: 'I
pray to God, please help me give bread to my children. If
that is not possible, then please let me die so that I can be
released from this terrible situation.'

Dilfor's situation was even worse. She was old, tired
and hungry. Her sallow, deeply lined face was gaunt with
despair. She was destitute: her husband had abandoned her,
and she had no children to take care of her. She was forced
to work secretly because she needed money to feed herself.
But the Taliban didn't understand that. Her plight was worse
than Zubaida's because poverty forced her to defy the
Taliban on two counts: she worked, and she walked about
without a burqa. She did not own one, and she was too
poor to buy one.

So she fearfully sneaked in and out of her house, always
on the lookout for Allah's soldiers. She hid in alleyways,
watching for the young turbaned men up ahead, looked
furtively behind, and when the coast was clear ran a short
distance to hide behind the next pillar or post—and then
repeated the procedure until she reached the orphanage
where she worked. She stayed over late because it was easier

to get back home safely in the cover of darkness.

She lived with the terror of working. She lived with the terror of having to walk the streets without a burqa. She knew she was tempting fate. One day her luck—what little she had of it—would run out. In the meantime, she died a thousand deaths a day. She was startled by anything and everything. Living constantly on the edge had made her a taut live tension wire that jerked with every stimulus. Every time she heard the sound of a man, she feared it was the Taliban and shrank into the darkness.

The plight of the 850 orphans she and Zubaida were looking after was as unhappy. They cowered in the shadows of the large, dirt-stained orphanage. They were young, but they didn't seem to have a future either. Collective suffering hung in the air, heavy and oppressive like rain clouds. The rough stone floors were cracked and dirty, the walls unpainted and gouged with bullet holes.

The orphanage was run by the government, and when the government changed, the orphanage had to run. Over the past four years, it had changed locations twice because it found itself on the shifting frontlines of Kabul's civil war. Twice gunmen had looted this hapless orphanage with its band of hapless orphans and stolen beds, tables, chairs, blankets and food stocks.

Now three children shared a bed and a blanket. The fight was over who would sleep in the middle—the only way to keep warm. It was October, and the winter frost had already set in. But the windows had no glass panes to keep the chill out. They had been shattered in the recent round of rocketing. The children didn't have warm clothes. Most didn't even have shoes.

Soon it would be snowing.

For these children, the Taliban takeover had made life

very difficult. Food stocks were running low. Normally, the administration supplied them with food, but now the government had more important things to do—like consolidating territories and capturing new ones. Within two weeks of the Taliban's takeover, stocks plummeted to an all-time low. The children had no meat and no vegetables, and instead of the two helpings of lentils they got every day, they were now down to one.

Most of the 330 employees in the orphanage had been women. Now only four desperate women turned up for work. It was virtually impossible for them to do all the chores. Keeping the children clean and laundering their clothes was difficult. The children now bathed only once a week, and their clothes were laundered every two weeks.

Education had come to a standstill. The Taliban had decreed that girls should not go to school. Boys could, but they actually didn't because most schools didn't function— eighty-five per cent of the teachers were women, and women were not allowed to work.

Maleeha was a beautiful young teenager. One of the oldest in the orphanage, she was an eighth-grade student who had wanted to become a doctor. Now she would remain semi-literate. 'My future is dark, but what can I do?' she asked.

Thousands of middle-class families had fled Kabul, but Maleeha was too poor to leave. She had no place to go. She had no relatives who could support her. She had no knowledge of the world outside the orphanage, and now she seemed doomed to remain in its dark, cavernous rooms, sentenced to a kind of life imprisonment.

For the citizens of Kabul, the Taliban invasion had brought peace—but at the cost of freedom.

*

Perhaps no other region has been invaded so many times and so fiercely as Afghanistan. Its unique geographical location made it the route of the invaders. The area was a hub on the ancient silk route, carrying exotic silk, spices and other luxury goods to the West and Buddhism to the East. Through history, armies marched over Afghanistan—Tammerlain, Genghis Khan, Alexander, British and Russian soldiers.

Afghanistan is the confluence of four geographical and cultural areas—the Middle East, China, Central Asia and the Indian subcontinent. Much more than America and for a much longer period, Afghanistan has been a melting pot of Persian, Central Asian, Mongol, Arab, Indian, Turkish and European influences. In the nineteenth century, Afghanistan was the battleground of what came to be known as the Great Game, played by imperial Russia and Britain. Both tried to extend their control over Afghan territory— a land route that had tremendous strategic value, especially because of its proximity to areas of huge gas and oil reserves. It became a theatre of intrigue and treachery as adventurers and ambassadors, soldiers and mystics, explorers and spies indulged in devious covert operations. But it was a Great Game that neither won. Later, the game was played by the Russians and the Americans, and the Americans won.

But all along, Afghanistan kept losing—its people suffered, were robbed, maimed and killed. Nobody has kept a record of all the fighting over the centuries, but the casualties were high enough in the decade-long war in the 1980s between the Russian occupiers and the mujahedin— the anti-communist Afghan 'holy' warriors: One and a half million dead, six million refugees, a nation flooded with weapons, opium, widows and orphans. The landscape turned lethal. No less than ten million landmines lie about, silent and treacherous, waiting to claim unsuspecting men, women and children—which it does at the rate of twenty a day.

Rahima Zikriya was a poor woman with four children. Her husband went into the fields one day and never returned. Next day they found bits and pieces of him strewn about in the fields, some four kilometres from their home. That was the day Rahima decided she could not live in her country any more. She packed her bags and her children and took a ride into Pakistan one summer's day in 1992. For four years they lived as refugees in Peshawar in Pakistan, close to the Afghanistan border. It was safe, there were no lurking landmines. But it was a terrible life, cramped and dirty in their slum in the Afghan refugee camp.

After four years, they couldn't take it any more. Besides, her three daughters had grown up and would soon be needing jobs and husbands. She didn't see how they could get either as refugees in Pakistan. So they bundled up their shabby belongings and returned to Kabul. She was thrilled when she managed to get a job as a government clerk within a few days. Her children enrolled in a school nearby and Rahima felt settled after a long, long time. God knows she deserved it after all the trauma and suffering she had endured ever since her husband's brutal death.

But tragedy lay waiting just round the corner. She could not have returned to Kabul at a worse time. Within two weeks of her arrival, the Taliban invaded the city. Rahima was a poor widow who needed a job to feed her four children, but she was not allowed to work. Her three daughters were banned from attending school. Her youngest son could not go to school because the teachers were women and could not work.

Like her husband's corpse, bits and pieces of Rahima's hopes lay strewn all around her. She was trapped. There was no future for her, no future for her children, and no money at all. How was her family going to survive? She wept, but tears couldn't solve problems. She sobbed and moaned against the world, her fate, her country, the Taliban, but what was the use? Tears and complaints couldn't feed her hungry children who were crying quietly in a corner.

When her tears were spent, she began to think. What could she do? Her sole thought was how to feed her children. There was only one solution. She would go and live with her brother. He was not rich, but being a god-fearing Muslim, he would not turn her away. So once again, she bundled up her shabby belongings and set off, this time for Dahdodi village in Mazar-i-Sharif, some 300 kilometres north of Kabul, where her brother lived. The area was peaceful because it was then ruled by the wily Uzbek warlord Abdul Rashid Dostum, a man who played a key role in the treacherous, shifting alliances of modern Afghan politics.

In 1979, the Russians had invaded Afghanistan and installed their puppet regime headed by Najibullah, an Afghan of tremendous cunning. The mujahedin, armed and bankrolled by the CIA via Pakistan, fought the Russians, forcing them to leave. But when the Russians eventually evacuated in February 1989, Najibullah managed to remain in power, propped up by his network of ruthless secret police and a few tribal chiefs, including Dostum.

But the mujahedin stepped up pressure and when Dostum, a big, shrewd man, switched loyalties, Najibullah collapsed and the mujahedin rode into Kabul accompanied by the roar of tanks and the fireworks of automatic weapons in 1992. Najibullah and his brother moved to the safety of the UN house in Kabul. But in the absence of a common enemy, the mujahedin soon began to turn on each other. Factional feuds destroyed Kabul. The Afghan capital had been spared fighting throughout the communist and Najibullah regimes, but now it was bombarded constantly by the so-called saviours. Age-old tribal, ethnic and religious rivalries erupted and Kabul became the theatre of a vicious new cycle of internecine war. The mujahedin commanders turned into power-hungry leaders, each one wanting to emerge as the undisputed king of Afghanistan by capturing Kabul. The fighting was so intense and so prolonged that large parts of this beautiful, graceful and historic city were reduced to rubble. Women were widowed, children orphaned. But the fighting raged on.

The mujahedin also began running out of money. With the Russians gone and the Cold War ended, the CIA had no further interest in the region. The world didn't care any more. It became the Forgotten War. Uncle Sam's funds dried up and the average mujahedin's monthly salary dwindled to the local equivalent of four dollars. They were left to their own devices to earn money. The easiest thing to do was to turn their guns on the helpless villagers and snatch money from them.

So when the Taliban came in and disarmed the mujahedin, the local people were relieved. The Taliban were fierce and Islamic, but they were disciplined. At least in the beginning. 'Taliban' means religious students, and that's what the young men were—but with guns in their hands. Most of them were peasant boys educated in madrasas, Islamic religious schools, in Pakistan. They emerged as a reformist group, honest and devoutly Islamic. For them, gaining control of Kabul was not merely a question of flexing political muscles and making territorial gains—it was a puritanical quest to unify the Afghan nation, cleanse it of its ills and vices, and create a cradle of Islam. They wanted to rule the people; they also wanted to instruct their souls. As one gun-toting Taliban explained, 'We must follow the shariat, Islamic rule. Only then can we go to heaven.'

But many Kabulis feel the Taliban's path to heaven is routed through hell. The night they conquered Kabul, the UN refuge where Najibullah and his brother were staying degenerated into a torture chamber. A large contingent of Taliban soldiers raided the UN premises and tortured the two men—kicking, punching, slapping and stabbing. They shot and killed them like dogs.

Next morning, shocked residents of Kabul saw the bruised corpses of their former president and his brother swinging from a concrete pole outside the presidential palace. Their faces were swollen, their clothes torn and bloodstained, their nostrils stuffed with cigarettes. It was a bloody and humiliating end to Najibullah, once the most powerful and feared leader in Afghanistan.

Unlike the rural areas of Afghanistan, Kabul had been modern, liberal and cosmopolitan. The decade-long communist rule had driven Islamic fundamentalism from the cities to the hinterland. As Muslims they were devout, but Kabulis did not feel the need to express their religiosity through beards and veils. Women were outgoing, they were educated and worked side by side with men in professions such as medicine and teaching...until the Taliban came along.

The Taliban saw all this as debauched modernity. They were strict about imposing their new edicts. Not just on women, but on men too: they had to grow beards and wear skull caps; prayers had to be said five times a day; smoking was prohibited in offices, and alcohol was strictly forbidden;

music, televison and video were banned. To show they meant business, the Taliban strung up television sets on trees. There were curbs even on leisure activities—playing cards and chess were banned. As one Taliban reasoned, 'Islamic laws are eternal, from Prophet Mohammad's time until doomsday. They do not change.'

Punishments for violating their laws were extreme—public execution for murder and other serious offences, amputation for theft, and public flogging for drinking or having illicit sexual relations. Women guilty of adultery were stoned to death.

In just a few years, the Taliban captured more than two-thirds of Afghanistan. Wherever they went, they imposed their shariat, and it found favour with the villagers—at least with the men. Women in any case didn't have much of a choice in this fiercely patriarchal society. The Taliban imposed peace, and initially the people welcomed them because they managed to rid the towns and villages of crime.

But five years later, the Taliban were indulging in all the crimes the mujahedin had been guilty of. They looted, blackmailed and extorted money from people, especially the traders and businessmen. No cargo could be sent unless the local Taliban commanders had been bribed, in addition to payment of taxes and other levies. No business transaction could take place unless the local Taliban officials had been given their percentage. There were reports that the Taliban looted homes during night curfew. Even criminals didn't dare venture out then, and yet, the houses of many wealthy Kabulis were burgled. The religious fervour of the initial days degenerated to a great extent, and the trappings of power are today more evident. Taliban ministers live in fancy houses, drive luxury vehicles with posses of gun-toting bodyguards. Taliban members dine out in restaurants, unmindful of children scavenging in garbage dumps and widows begging for food outside. Religion is enforced, however, on the people. Armed with leather whips, officials of the Vice and Virtue squad cruise the streets in their tinted four-wheel drive vehicles, on the lookout for women without burqas and men with trimmed beards.

The Taliban's invasion of Kabul dramatically altered the lives of the Afghans. It also revived international interest in the region. Suddenly the media and the world remembered this benighted land and its forgotten war. Journalists descended on Kabul, not because the war had entered a crucial phase, or a decisive victory was at hand, but because they were suddenly curious about this new face of Islam. They wanted to know what the Taliban was all about, how dangerous they were, and to what extent they could threaten peace in their own country.

It was possibly one of the worst times to be in Kabul. Never in all my life had I faced such a challenging reporting assignment.

All the odds were stacked against me. Indians were hated because the Taliban were assisted by Pakistan. I was a television reporter, and television and video were banned. I worked for an American television channel, and the Taliban saw the Americans as the worst example of Western decadence and imperialism. The ground situation was really dangerous—we were covering a live, hot war with two enemies, heavily armed and brutal with each other. Above all, I was a woman reporter working outdoors—and that was forbidden.

I mitigated my plight by wearing a black burqa and a black scarf around my head. It was best not to attract attention. But the ploy was not always successful. Once, as we waited inside a van for our guide to return with directions, a Taliban soldier stared at me. I looked away as demurely as I could. He walked around to our driver and snapped something at him. Our driver looked and sounded apologetic, and then turned around to me and explained I had offended the Taliban because my head scarf had slipped down to reveal my hair. The soldier had apparently threatened our driver: 'Tell her if she does not want her face smashed in with the butt of my gun, she should make sure she obeys our laws and keeps her head covered at all times.' Okay, boss. I didn't mean to disobey the laws of your land, the damn scarf slipped down, and I wasn't aware of it simply because I am not used to having a scarf around my head. No arguments, of course. The man with the gun rules. I quickly raised my scarf and tied it tightly around my head.

The trouble is, you really can't be incognito as a television reporter, the way you can as a print journalist, when you can observe the situation and talk to people surreptitiously. You can thus avoid the attention of the authorities. But television reporters can't because they travel with a crew and have to cart so much equipment around—camera, tripod, sound equipment. You stick out for miles.

So there we were in Kabul, filming marketplaces, hospitals, street scenes, people at work, destroyed neighbourhoods. We would get out of our van, and I would lurk around in my burqa, my eyes constantly swivelling at 360 degrees to make sure there was no Taliban in sight. Then my crew would quickly take out the equipment and start rolling the camera. All the time, our eyes oscillated to spot Taliban movement, and if they did, we hurriedly packed up and left. It was tense and scary. We couldn't be at a spot for more than a few minutes. I wanted to interview the local people, which was dangerous because you could never tell who the informers were. But it was a risk we had to take.

So we sneaked into the alleys, keeping our driver on vigil so that he could inform us if he saw any Taliban patrolling. If they happened to come by, we packed up and hid, or at least hid the equipment and pretended we were casually chatting with each other. Still, there were times when we got caught. We were shooting in a marketplace, taking some nice shots of a man baking fresh bread, when the Taliban soldiers pounced on us. They were so infuriated they attacked my crew with rifles, hitting them on their arms and legs. I was spared, probably because I was a woman. We quickly apologized and escaped in our van.

The most difficult part of our work was shooting my standups, the few lines in the script that the reporter says looking into the camera. The standup is like a stamp of authority—it is the reporter's signature on the script, proof that she is actually reporting from the conflict zone. But in Kabul it was even more dangerous because it was visible proof that I was flouting the Taliban ban on women working. Not only was I working, but I was doing it openly, and that too on television.

For the first and only time in my life, I did my standups in a burqa and a black scarf around my head. I had to. As I said my lines, I was not concentrating because my eyes were secretly scanning to check if any Taliban soldiers were in the vicinity. As usual, retakes were inevitable. Either I stumbled on my lines, or a cloud passed that changed the light exposure, or a passing vehicle drowned my lines. What I wanted to say for the standup in my very first report from Kabul was 'Kabul is a historic city because of its strategic location. It is the gateway to the Indian subcontinent to the south, and to the Central Asian republics to the north. Through history many conquerors have invaded Kabul and now the latest conqueror, the Taliban, is all set to leave its stamp on the city—by imposing a fundamentalist regime guided by its own interpretation of the Islamic law.'

We had two takes in the can. We were attempting our third. Just as I started saying my lines, we saw three Taliban soldiers approaching. We quickly packed up and left, and looked for another spot. But just as we were ready for the take, two others turned a corner, so we had to pack up again. Now we were really running out of time. We went quickly into another street. This had to be our last shot. We had all of ten minutes, and then we had to rush back to edit and transmit. The crew was ready in a few minutes, and I said my lines. All was well, except towards the end, a vehicle without a silencer passed by. The sound was distracting. Ever the perfectionist, and used to being on the brink all the time, I insisted on one last take. I was halfway through my lines when I saw a group of soldiers approaching from behind my crew. This was the last chance and I didn't want to abort my standup midway, so I pressed on. But I might as well have given up. Because what I said was: 'manyconquerorshaveinvadedKabulandnowthelatest conqueror—theTaliban—isallsettoleavetheirstampon thecity.'

The tumble of words made the standup unusable. We had no choice but to pack up and run for our lives. We threw ourselves into the van and made a quick getaway.

The most remarkable aspect of television reporting is that if the reporter and crew are ethical, it is the best example of honest journalism. Sitting in a bar or a press club, a print journalist can get quotes and descriptions from soldiers or aid workers who have been to the battlefront, and write as though from the war zone. But a television crew cannot get war footage unless they are actually in the thick of the action.

As we drove to the shifting frontlines, we could hear and see artillery shells exploding all around us. Sometimes they fell so close that the van shuddered with the impact. Sometimes they were so far away that all one could see was a brown cloud of dust rising from the ground, followed by the sound of an explosion a few seconds later. We were moving against traffic, heading to the warfront while villagers fled towards Kabul. There were people on foot, in ancient taxis and on donkeys, all of them clutching bundles, the women and children wide-eyed with fear, the men silent and grim.

Every few kilometres, we ran into a group of Taliban soldiers. Winter was setting in, and there was a slight chill in the air. The Taliban were well-armed, but none of them wore warm clothes. Some were even barefoot. When I asked one of them how he could fight a war without basic things like footwear and sweaters, he replied, 'We are fighting for Allah. We don't care for things like shoes. We don't care for our lives.' I wondered whether such motivation stemmed from ignorance or conviction or religious indoctrination.

Eventually, we reached the last Taliban fighting position, about fifty kilometres north of Kabul, a little short of the Bagram air base. From two tanks on either side of the road, the Taliban were firing at the fortifications of their enemy, Ahmed Shah Masood, like there was no tomorrow. Masood, the military commander of the ousted Rabbani regime, had positioned his forces a few kilometres ahead.

We were really excited, because this was the real stuff.

You couldn't get closer to war than this, you couldn't get better pictures than these. As the tanks fired, the Taliban soldiers who had clambered onto them, and those who were swarming around them, were shouting 'Allah o Akbar' and other religious slogans. Great pictures. You had war and religion, and what better way to depict the Taliban, who in my head I had already titled as 'The New Sword of Islam'.

For once, the Taliban were supportive. They did not stop us from filming. They were on some kind of a high, and actually encouraged us to film them. Perhaps the troops were so helpful because they were young, and so was their commanding officer. Their immaturity perhaps enhanced their sense of importance, their holy mission. We made the most of it, and Sanjiv Talreja, CNN's gifted and dedicated cameraman, was shooting away furiously. But ten minutes later I decided it was time to leave. Sanjiv, who had climbed up on the tank, was reluctant because it was so rare to be able to walk right into the battlefront when a battle is raging.

But years of experience as a war correspondent warned me it was time to leave the scene. It required only common sense to know that you should not keep firing from stationary tanks, especially when the enemy is only a short distance away. They can very easily and quickly identify the source and return fire, often with heavier weaponry—like artillery shells. If they'd had any sense, the Taliban would have fired some shots and then moved away to a different location before firing any more. Continuous fire from stationary tanks made them sitting ducks, and I didn't want to be near them for too long. So I hurried my crew away.

As we walked to the van parked about hundred metres away, the return fire began. We ran for our lives. But it trailed us, coming as close as six metres behind us, kicking up dust. As we ran to our parked van, a new threat loomed.

A senior Taliban commander had arrived on the scene. He was older, more experienced, and carried an air of stern authority. He could not believe what he was seeing—a fleeing camera team! He started shouting and waving his rifle angrily. When he saw a woman in the team, his fury made him momentarily lose his balance. He could have shot us down, and he probably would have, except the sight of a strange woman lifting her black burqa to reveal blue jeans below and running for her life, made him splutter with so much rage that he did the most extraordinary thing. He bent down, picked up a few stones and threw them at us. Instead of bullets, we found stones pelting past us.

Now I was furious. I stopped running and turned to face him. He was a little distance away, but I could see he was red with rage. I was purple with rage myself. What did the man think of himself? Just because I was a woman, he thought he could treat me like a dog, chasing me away with stones from his backyard? Bullets had some dignity, but stones? I was furious, and all set to give him a piece of my mind. Then a little voice of reason rang warning bells in my steaming head, a little voice that asked, 'Would you really prefer that he chased you with bullets? Get the hell out of here.'

When the Taliban commander saw that I had stopped running and had turned to face him, his rage leaped to new heights. He was literally dancing on his feet, like a large grotesque Rumpelstiltskin, flailing his rifle menacingly and shouting what were clearly expletives. I didn't have to understand his language, I knew what he was saying—'If you don't get out of my sight this very minute, I will shoot you.' I ran to the van where my crew had already loaded the equipment and the driver was running the engine. We raced back to Kabul as fast as we could.

We learnt later from aid workers that both tanks were blown up less than thirty minutes after we had scrambled away. I guess for those Taliban boys there *was* no tomorrow. Commander Masood's troops had ensured that.

Shah Rasool was one of Masood's men. Until September 1996, he was on the right side of the law: a government soldier loyal to Commander Masood. Then the Taliban invaded Kabul and he had to flee. The invading Taliban militia chased and pumped bullets into him. Some pierced his arm, some his legs. The urge for survival blinded him to pain. Rasool ran in spite of his wounded legs.

We met him in the hospital. He was recovering, but one leg had been amputated. Rasool was a sad and perplexed man. He said, 'I don't know who is right or who is wrong. But everybody is fighting.'

They still are.

Rasool was lucky to be alive. Unlike another of Masood's men who lay dead and unclaimed on the battlefront, in what was really a no man's land. There was nothing there, no people, no huts, no animals, no trees. Just a narrow road snaking into the horizon, a few scattered shrubs, and one dead man in combat fatigues. During the week when we reported from the battlefront, the frontline shifted—sometimes in the hands of Masood, sometimes reclaimed by the Taliban. As the frontline shifted, so did the status of this unknown dead soldier. When the uninhabited piece of land fell to Masood, he became a martyr. When the Taliban recaptured the land, he became a traitor.

Through history, Afghanistan has been a land of shifting fortunes and frontlines, a land where yesterday's rulers are today's rebels. Not that any of this mattered to the dead soldier. He just lay there face down, unidentified and unclaimed. In the distance, the rolling mountains brooded—as they had for centuries. Nearby, the sands shifted in the howling wind—as they had for centuries.

Gradually, the dead soldier crumbled into the dust of his doomed land.

ON ANOTHER PLANET

Headquartered in the ancient city of Mazar-i-Sharif, Abdul Rashid Dostum, the powerful leader of the Uzbek tribe, ruled northern Afghanistan in 1996. He drew his strength from his large, well-armed and well-trained militia. Through the turbulent recent past of Afghanistan, he had always succeeded in emerging on the winning side. So at one time he remained in power because he backed Najibullah, and when he realized the tide was turning against him he hastened his collapse by switching over to the mujahedin. It is a tribute to his cunning that he maintained excellent relations with the pro-CIA mujahedin even though he, a former communist, still had strong Russian connections. Perhaps due to Russian influences, Dostum was not a religious fanatic the way the Taliban are. He was more tolerant, and certainly women were better off in his reign, being encouraged to educate themselves and get jobs. But he ruled like a tribal despot.

While reporting the Taliban invasion from Kabul, I realized it was important to go across and meet Dostum because it wasn't yet clear whose side he was on—the Taliban's, or the ousted regime of Burhanuddin Rabbani. But Ariana, the national airline of Afghanistan, did not operate between Kabul and Mazar-i-Sharif. The safest and quickest way to get to Mazar was to go to Peshawar in

Pakistan and take a plane from there. The alternative was driving for two, maybe three days, on a bumpy, landmine-ridden road in a battered taxi, all the way from Kabul to Mazar. There was heavy fighting along certain sections of the road, so chances were we would be turned back.

In Peshawar, we realized there was an airline called Balkh Air that could take us to Mazar. We boarded the small Balkh plane, along with a few smelly, rugged tradesmen, and landed on a desert surface that looked like something from another planet. The airport comprised one runway and two small, squat, single-storeyed buildings. On arrival, everybody went through a narrow doorway into a small room. Two mustachioed men waved the other passengers in but detained us and demanded to see our passports, which we handed over. They looked at them up and down and sideways and every which way, muttering constantly to each other in a language we couldn't understand.

Then one of them asked us to show our visas, which we did. The decibel level of his muttering rose. He was angry now. In broken English, he protested: 'This Afghan visa!'

I was right, we had landed on another planet. There is no point getting angry with officials; it only worsens your case. So very politely and patiently, I said, yes, but aren't we in Afghanistan?

'No,' he retorted. 'You in Balkhsthan. This visa no good here. You need Balkh visa.'

I had never heard of a land called Balkhsthan, but over the next few days we discovered there really was a separate country within Afghanistan called Balkhsthan, which was ruled by strongman Dostum. He had his own nation, with its own flag, army, bureaucracy, airline, laws and currency. The world did not know of this separate nation, it was certainly not recognized by the United Nations, it couldn't be seen on any world map, but it existed in flesh and blood and spirit. And there we were, facing these two ugly Balkh despots without valid travel documents.

I wanted to say I had never seen an embassy of Balkhsthan anywhere in the region, so where were we supposed to have got the visas from? But tart remarks would only have angered him more.

'Can we get visa on arrival?' I asked sweetly.

'Where you from?' he asked gruffly.

Was he illiterate? Couldn't he read that from our passports?

But I demurely replied, 'India.' I was still being nice and patient.

'You really from India? Not Pakistan?' he asked suspiciously.

Why on earth would visitors claim they were from India if they were really from Pakistan? And if we wanted to fake our identities, wouldn't we have said something distant and neutral, like Mauritius?

My patience was wearing thin, but I knew that if I lost my temper, we would lose access to this wretched place. It was hot and dusty, and there was nothing to be seen through the small window but a dreary expanse of sand. The room itself was small and stuffy, furnished only with two scarred and battered desks.

'No. No, we are really Indians,' I said.

'You speak Hindi?' he asked.

'Mera joota hai japani, mera pataloon hai angrezi, phir bhi dil hai hindustani,' I sang.

To our amazement, the gruff tyrant's face wreathed into a smile and he guffawed. Then he sang the same song. And he knew the words better than I did.

'We love Raj Kapoor. We love India. But we hate
Pakistan. Bad country. No trust Pakistani,' he said. It was
only later I figured out that the people of Balkhsthan were
pro-Russia, which in Cold War politics made them well-
disposed to India and ill-disposed to Pakistan, which had
allied itself to the US.

I knew that Raj Kapoor was popular in Russia, but I had
no idea that the people of Balkhsthan loved him too.

And then we were treated like stars. They gave us tea
and biscuits and, most crucially, a vehicle to get into the
city.

As he waved us off, the official said, 'Next time don't
forget Balkh visa.'

But next time there was no Balkhsthan.

Months later it disintegrated, and Dostum himself fled
to Turkey. A vicious bloodbath erupted in the region,
between Uzbek and Taliban soldiers. The fighting left
thousands dead in the most brutal way—with entrails
hanging out, eyes gouged out and heads cut off.

But that was later. As we rode into town, everything
was peaceful, perhaps because there was nothing—no
people, no camels, no trees. Just a lot of sand shimmering
in the heat.

The town itself was so faded and medieval that it looked
straight out of a film set. Mazar-i-Sharif must have been a
grand old city once, but the relentless sun had bleached the
buildings and baked the people. Their faces were walnut-
brown and deeply lined. They clearly liked their leader,
Dostum. People praised him for building roads and bridges
and improving women's education. People here were not
fundamentalist, but certainly they were devout. Even
soldiers had a gun in one hand and prayer beads in the other.
What gave colour to the once grand but now jaded town

were the beautiful red rugs on display in shops and on sidewalks, and the juicy yellow watermelons, the sweetest I've ever tasted.

All over the town, gigantic posters of Dostum stared down at us. The man was obviously a megalomaniac. Apparently he saw himself as the new Tammerlain, the fierce Uzbek horseman who conquered Afghanistan in the fourteenth century and founded an empire that lasted 150 years and stretched from Baghdad to Sinkiang in China. Dostum reminded me of Pirabhakaran. It wasn't just the muscle, moustache and macho military uniform; it was the megalomania. Pirabhakaran projected himself as a descendant of the great Chola kings. When he controlled Jaffna in the early 1990s, large portraits of Pirabhakaran had mushroomed all over the peninsula. He ruled like an unseen but omniscient king...till he was overthrown by the army of Chandrika Kumaratunga in December 1995. Virtually overnight, the portraits disappeared without a trace. The same fate would befall Dostum.

Shortly after checking into the city's main hotel, a stately old building, we got to Dostum's fortress called Qila-i-Jangi, or Fortress of War. I managed to talk our way in at the main gateway, but we were stopped at the entrance to the palace. Dostum was too busy, his aides told us curtly. He couldn't meet journalists.

I had come all this way to meet him, and I wasn't leaving until I had interviewed him. I presumed an American delegation had come to meet him because I could see a gleaming black bulletproof Cadillac in the driveway. It looked like a mafia car and seemed incongruous in the driveway of a 150-year-old mud fortress in the middle of a desert.

'Is he busy with the Americans?' I asked the man

guarding the entrance to the palace.

'No, he is having a cabinet meeting.'

Even tribal warlords have cabinet meetings. And Dostum, after all, was the president of Balkhsthan.

'Whose car is that?' I asked, trying to strike up a conversation.

'It is our president's,' the guard answered proudly.

No wonder Dostum had switched sides from the Russians to the CIA-backed mujahedin.

'Why is it bulletproof?' I asked innocently.

'Too many people try to kill him,' he said. 'Our president loves cars.'

'What else does he love?' I asked even more innocently.

'His new wife. She is very beautiful. And very young,' he said, almost enviously.

Our conversation was getting gossipy and interesting, but at this point a senior aide arrived and told me rudely that there was no point waiting because Dostum had not met a single journalist since the Taliban invaded Kabul, and he would not be meeting anyone until things settled down.

Meaning, until he decided which side to switch to.

I pretended not to hear him and started talking about the Cadillac, slowly inveigling him into conversation. Before long, we were talking about India. He even spoke some broken Hindi, and told me about the cockroaches he had tried to crush under his shoes at the Ashoka Hotel in New Delhi. And then I told him, 'Listen, I have come such a long way only to meet Dostum. I don't need a long interview. I just need a few comments. It won't take more than a few minutes.' Saying he would give it a try, the aide disappeared into the interiors of the building. He came back within minutes and informed me, 'Our president has agreed to meet you for a few minutes on his way out. I told him you are Indian, and he is happy to meet you.'

About half an hour later, Dostum strode in with a posse of heavily armed bodyguards. He was a big man, but much younger in real life than in the posters. He was buoyant.

'You are a very determined person, eh? You Indians are like that. But I like it, I like it,' he said.

I beamed, but before I could reply, he boomed: 'You say you are from CNN, but I don't watch CNN. It's too repetitive, and those women speak through their noses with American accents that I can't understand. You know what I really like watching? Zee TV!' He guffawed.

India's cultural imperialism had shifted from Raj Kapoor to Zee. It was a generational thing.

I asked Dostum my set of questions, and he answered them, brisk and to the point. He declared he would not ally with the Taliban—they were too fanatical for his taste. He did not know then, but that decision would have disastrous consequences for him, his troops and his homeland. I also got him to arrange for us to visit his army camp to take pictures of his soldiers. Then, as if on cue, ·the black Cadillac glided up and the rear door swung open, letting out streams of ice-cold air from the air-conditioned limousine. In a blur of lithe movements, Dostum was whisked into the purring car, and it roared away, taking him possibly into the waiting arms of his beautiful wife.

Ayodhya

CYCLE OF REVENGE

ATTACK! IN THE NAME
OF THE LORD

Arne and I are holidaying in Cordoba, an enchanting olde worlde town with narrow cobbled paths lined with orange trees, ivy-smothered walls, fountains, statues, patios, ancient taverns, and quaint two-storeyed white-washed houses bedecked with geraniums and potted plants glistening in the November sunshine. We are staying in a lovely little inn in the old part of this ancient town in southern Spain. Arne has gone in for his shower. I am still lazing in bed.

'What shall we do today?' Arne asks, coming out of the shower with a fluffy white towel draped around him, like a Roman emperor.

I leaf through the tourist brochures. 'Let's see the mosque-cathedral first,' I suggest.

'Make up your mind, what do you want to see first—the mosque or the cathedral?' responds Arne.

'The mosque-cathedral,' I reply.

'What's that?' Arne asks. He doesn't bother to argue, he knows by now there is a method in my madness.

'It's the Mezquita cathedral, the largest mosque in the Islamic world after Mecca, and it's right here, a street away from us.'

'I don't get it. If it's a mosque, why is it called a

cathedral?' asks the puzzled Norwegian, who in his personal life is accustomed to doing nothing more complicated than getting a train ticket from an automated machine.

'It's a mosque built by the Moors, which the conquering Christians converted into a cathedral,' I reply patiently.

Cordoba's greatest moment came with the invasion of the Moors in 711 AD, when it became the capital of a vast, flourishing emirate. The original mosque was built in 788 AD, but succeeding caliphs kept expanding it over the next hundred years. During the tenth century, while the rest of central and northern Europe lived through the Dark Ages, Cordoba was booming with luxurious palaces, graceful public baths, excellent sewer and street-lighting systems. It was comparable only to the prosperous city of Constantinople, and its mosque became the richest and the most splendid Islamic monument of the time.

But like most empires, it fell into decline because of palace intrigues and murderous rivalries. In the thirteenth century, the Moors were vanquished by the invading Christian armies and over a period of time, Cordoba became part of the empire of the Catholic monarchs. In the sixteenth century, the Catholics built a massive cathedral right amidst the columns of the grand old mosque. It took 250 years to complete. More than 800 columns were erected in addition to the existing ones. Today, the mosque-cathedral is a unique combination of the lavish mihrab—the Mecca-facing sanctum sanctorum—in exquisite Byzantine mosaic, where the Koran is kept, and the main altar in red marble with its dazzling Baroque pulpits.

The mosque-cathedral is spectacular. But it is also a visible assertion of power—the power of the Christian conquerors over the defeated Moors.

Much the same way as the Babri Masjid in India was a

display of power, of the Muslim conquest of a Hindu empire.

The Babri Masjid was built in the sixteenth century by a Muslim nobleman in Ayodhya, allegedly over a Hindu temple that marked the birthplace of Lord Ram. Over the years, the mosque fell into disuse and dispute. But Hindu rituals continued to be performed in the shrine, in a dark passageway beneath the three big Islamic domes. I visited the shrine several times in the late 1980s and noticed the iron pillars with traditional Hindu motifs which held aloft the Islamic domes. Of course, historians say that's no proof that the mosque was indeed built over a temple—it could just be that the Muslim builders acquired temple materials for constructing the mosque. Perhaps that is so, but their intent was clearly not to save money. The new mosque was a symbol of subjugation. Though not a Hindu myself, I experienced that same feeling of dismay I was to experience many years later in Cordoba. Not fair.

But what happened to the Babri Masjid was not fair either. Hindu fanatics decided to right a historical wrong with a contemporary blunder. They tore the mosque down on the afternoon of 6 December 1992, with crowbars, axes, and even their bare hands.

For several years, a section of the Hindu community had been seething at what it perceived to be the ruling Congress party's pandering to Muslims. To these politicians, Muslims were not human beings, they were votebanks. To win their votes, the politicians offered them bribes—symbolic ones like carving out a Muslim district, or making Urdu an official language, or declaring a holiday on Prophet Mohammad's birthday, or banning Salman Rushdie's novel *The Satanic Verses*—issues that did not qualitatively improve the lives of ordinary Muslims, but created an illusion that the ruling politicians were sympathetic to the Muslim cause. But Hindus, who received no political bribes of any sort, real or symbolic, believed that politicians were partial to the Muslims at their cost. Thus began a hate campaign against the Muslims, the bottom line of which was that there would be more fishes and loaves for the Hindus were it not for the Muslims.

The Hindu resentment was engineered and stoked by Hindu right-wing groups. An awesome phenomenon is the ability of these groups to spread rumours—not just around the world, but across the length and breadth of Indian villages that are not connected by road or telephone. In just a few years, even educated Hindus came to believe that these cap-wearing, circumcised Muslims would outnumber them as they did not practise birth control. Indian census reports reveal that the Muslim birth rate is in fact only 0.15 per cent higher than the Hindu rate and is actually declining. The Hindus also came to believe that the breeding capacity of the Muslims is enhanced because all Muslim men have four wives. It is true that their religion permits it, but very few Muslims in fact have more than one wife. As Ahmad Yusuf, a bakery owner in Bombay, told me, 'I can't afford to keep one wife, how can I keep four?' The Indian census report of 1981 shows there are actually more polygamous marriages among Hindus.

Far from being pampered, the truth is that the plight of Muslims in India is worse than that of the Dalits, who are perched on the bottom-most rung of India's social ladder.

The only major government-sponsored study on the socio-economic status of Muslims exposed this truth. Muslims form nearly twelve per cent of India's population, but Muslim children who finished school account for a mere four per cent. In the prestigious Indian Administrative

Service, Muslims number only three per cent; only two per cent Muslims secure industrial licenses; and less than four per cent get bank loans.

The root cause of the Muslim problem is educational backwardness. For that, Muslims have to take much of the blame for sending their children to madrasas, which pay more importance to religious instruction than science or math.

When they got the report, the ruling Congress government did not even try to uplift the Muslims. They just hid the report. The majority Hindu perception of Muslims is therefore not based on facts. But any journalist will be able to tell you that perceptions can seem bigger and more real than the truth. As Edward De Bono says, there is no point in arbitrarily dismissing perceptions just because they are baseless. You have to deal with them. But, as he also points out, it is more difficult to deal with the 'water' logic of perceptions than the 'rock' logic of reality, because 'water' logic is not well-grounded—it is iffy, undefined, changeable.

This widespread Hindu perception snowballed into a national resentment against Muslims. The Hindu right-wing groups coalesced this anger beautifully with their campaign to tear down the Babri Masjid and build a Hindu temple on that very spot. It was their way of asserting Hindu might and avenging the Muslims for all the past slights, real and imagined.

Muslims didn't worship at the Babri Masjid, so most ordinary Muslims didn't really care (though Muslim politicians refuse to admit that). But reactionary Hindus taking the law into their hands was not only objectionable and illegal, but heavy with ominous portents for the future.

Hindu groups had set 6 December as the day they

would tear down the mosque. Nobody believed them. 'Typical rhetoric' was the reaction of the government and the media. But I had an uneasy feeling about the campaign. People say I am lucky I am always present where trouble is. It's not luck, it's hard work, preparation and common sense. I am in constant touch on the phone with people living in areas where trouble is brewing, and when they tell me things are looking bad, I hop into a plane or car or bus and reach the spot, and invariably walk into a riot or uprising. You pick up signals when your antennae are up—and the controversy over the Babri Masjid had my antennae twanging wildly.

For one thing, I had been increasingly perturbed over the Hindu hostility to Muslims—even among some of my friends, who are the most apolitical, tolerant, couldn't-care-less, bourgeois sort of people you could think of. For three years, I had been observing the subterranean anger that was steadily rising to the surface. It had to explode one day.

The government wasn't expecting Hindu fanatics to actually tear down the mosque. And it's when the authorities don't expect trouble, or don't take threats of trouble seriously, or choose to look the other way that trouble erupts. When the authorities anticipate trouble, you can bet your last buck that nothing will happen, because they are geared to put it down. And no mob of troublemakers can thwart the will of the state.

From my conversations with people living in Ayodhya, it seemed that the mood was getting uglier every day. So I decided to see for myself. I reached the city on 3 December. Kar sevaks, mostly members of the RSS, had come from different parts of India. The mood was particularly nasty in the tents housing kar sevaks from the states of Maharashtra, Gujarat and Uttar Pradesh. Their pet slogan was 'Hindu ke liye Hindustan, Musalmaan ko kabristan' ('Hindustan for Hindus, the graveyard for Muslims'). Many of them vengefully quoted an extremist Hindu leader's view—'The only way to get rid of Muslims is to stamp them to death.' What was really shocking was that this was the view of a Hindu sadhvi named Rithambara. The kar sevaks took this to be a vindication of their stand—even the sadhvi had turned.

But they were not angry with the Muslims alone. Their fury was also directed at the government and the media. They were angrier with the English media, accusing them of maligning their 'sacred mission', and angriest with the foreign media, accusing them of being tools of the CIA and hell-bent on breaking up India, propping up the Muslims and driving the Hindus into the ocean. In fact, the kar sevaks in the Maharashtra tent got so worked up, I had to be hastily removed from the scene by two of their seniors. 'There is no point talking to you filthy English-speaking journalists. In any case, you write all kinds of poisonous lies,' the angry kar sevaks yelled after me. 'We will teach you all a lesson.'

They did three days later, on Sunday, 6 December.

Hindu leaders, many of whom were to become Central ministers six years later, were making lofty speeches about the glory of Hindus. I had positioned myself atop a three-storeyed building right opposite the Babri Masjid. An open gravelled ground of about forty metres separated the building from the shrine. The view was terrific. The kar sevaks were below, the Babri Masjid up ahead, and on a podium to the left you could see the leaders thundering, wagging their fingers and shaking their fists. A large number of kar sevaks were milling about on the rooftop, and I recognized a few whom I had interviewed over the past few days—not the ones from the Maharashtra tent. I chatted with them. Several other journalists discovered the vantage point and came up. The tempo of the speeches was picking up, and the kar sevaks in the open space below were getting agitated.

'I am going down. I think there is more action down there where those kar sevaks are,' said my buddy Peter Heinlein, the Voice of America correspondent.

'I wouldn't if I were you,' I replied. 'Their mood is ugly, and it will get uglier.'

Peter looked at me, amazed. This was not the Anita he knew, journalism's Joan of Arc or Queen Anita, as he and his friend Ed Gargan of the *New York Times* often addressed me in jest. I couldn't explain, it was just instinct. You don't always have to be 'in' the scene to report. Sometimes it's better when you are 'by' the scene. You get a clear view of what is going on. That's more important. Being 'in' the scene gives you a view—but only for a short while. Years of trench-reporting have taught me that the most important thing about getting such a view is to know when to get out. Otherwise, you can get killed, maimed, injured, arrested, or thrown out. And finally, you end up not getting the whole story. There was no time to explain all this to Peter, who is himself a veteran, so I merely said, 'I think the view is much better from here.'

'But there's more action down there,' he said and set off, clutching his tape recorder and microphone.

Shortly after he left, several baton-wielding cops landed up on the terrace and ordered the journalists to get out.

I turned to the kar sevak by my side and asked if he could lend me the saffron-coloured bandana he had tied around his forehead. The bandana had 'Jai Shri Ram' printed in white in Hindi. That would hoodwink the pestering cops into thinking I was a kar sevak, and they would leave me alone.

Which is exactly what happened. In secret triumph I watched the cops herd all the other journalists away, while I remained on the roof, one of the few to watch the entire tragic episode unfold. The journalists, I was told later, were shepherded into a building nearby, and they heard rather than saw what happened next.

The cops must have had advance information about the kar sevaks' intention—because immediately after they removed the reporters, the kar sevaks in the grounds below went on the rampage. 'Kill the journalists' became the blood-curdling war cry. I ran to the parapet, and leaned over to see all hell breaking loose below. Kar sevaks were beating and hitting journalists with wooden batons and iron staves.

I searched frantically for Peter and found him in the melee. I didn't know whether to laugh at his stupidity, smile in admiration or curse in fury. The intrepid reporter was thrusting his microphone out to get a sound byte from a Rastafarian-looking, gesticulating holy man. But the sage-turned-maniac was in no mood to talk. He hit Peter on the head with a weapon—in my alarm and confusion, I didn't notice whether it was a wooden baton or an iron rod.

Blood started trickling down Peter's forehead.

Wanting to rush to his rescue, I ran towards the stairway, but stopped when I saw him being herded away. I realized then the danger I was in. The only guarantee of safety was the company of the few kar sevaks I had befriended on the rooftop. My notebook and pen—certain indicators of my profession—had disappeared into my bag long before.

After the few journalists in the grounds below had been violently disposed of, the decibel level of the Hindu hysteria increased. Mass appetite for violence had been whetted. I watched in shock as a few kar sevaks broke the police cordon, climbed over the wire fencing and began a frenzied

attack on the shrine. Dozens, then scores, and then
hundreds joined them. It was a spectacle out of a Cecil de
Mille film—medieval, dramatic, frightening. Dust rose in
the air from the sandy plains as a seething mass of kar sevaks
ran and pushed and stamped. Thousands of people lined
the ridges nearby and hung precariously from trees,
rooftops and walls to get a better view. The screams and
shouts of frenzied attackers mingled with a cacophony of
strange and fearful sounds—thundering drums, crashing
cymbals, noisy chants and the mournful wail of conch shells.

Encouraging the crazed youths to attack the mosque
were plump matrons perched on a nearby rooftop, matrons
who would normally have spent the Sunday slicing onions
and helping their children with homework. I wasn't
surprised by the transformation. Just a day earlier, Sunanda
Goswami, a middle-aged housewife from a village in western Maharashtra, had told me, 'For the sake of the temple
we are prepared to die.' The women were egging on the
kar sewaks by shaking their fists and screaming in support.

Against such mass hysteria, the dilapidated shrine did
not stand a chance. With every falling piece of masonry, the
jubilant roars reached a new pitch. Some who were injured
by the falling stones were carried shoulder-high from the
rubble, intensifying the public hysteria. Those who could,
attacked, and those who couldn't, watched enthralled at the
seething spectacle of mass hatred. 'The stigma of Hindu
subjugation has been destroyed for ever,' yelled Kishore
Das, an excited, long-bearded Hindu priest near me. 'Jai
Shri Ram,' roared the onlookers.

When the first wave tired, they returned to base, armed
with war trophies—bricks and pieces of stone from the ill-
fated shrine. Then a new wave surged towards the crumbling
domes. As though in a relay race, Amitabh Upadhyaya, a

twenty-one-year-old, unemployed youth from New Delhi, lurched forward to take his place in the hall of fame. With the air of a brave, patriotic martyr, he pulled open his shirt to display the slogan 'Jai Shri Ram' tattooed on his chest with cigarette burns. 'My corpse will show the world that I died for Ram,' he boasted. Of course he didn't die. He wasn't even injured or arrested. Neither was Satprakash Kasat, one of the first young fanatics to storm the mosque. Haloed by Babri dust, he triumphantly returned to our rooftop. He was given a hero's welcome, his colleagues embracing, kissing and backslapping him in ecstatic admiration. Kasat, looking like some bizarre film negative, said breathlessly, 'I felt proud to smash the mosque. No leader can control our pent-up rage against Muslims.'

He was right. Even as he spoke, spirals of dark smoke began to rise in the distance from torched Muslim homes. To me they seemed like funeral pyres of India's most cherished values of democracy, rule of law and secularism. Across India, Hindu-Muslim rioting broke out. It was a miracle it didn't turn out as disastrous as the Hindu-Muslim riots during Partition.

Within hours of the Babri Masjid's destruction, Hindus and Muslims tore into each other, but nowhere was the violence more brutal and shocking than in Bombay, India's most cosmopolitan city. Muslims reacted to the demolition of the shrine in Ayodhya by stabbing two Hindu workers to death. In another incident, a Hindu family was roasted alive in their hutment. That provoked a volcanic eruption of Hindu hatred—centuries of Hindu resentment that lay coiled deep within boiled to the surface and erupted like molten lava, scalding India's most tolerant city. It's not that the Hindus had suddenly become intolerant. It was largely the handiwork of the Shiv Sena that had a large number of lumpen elements as its storm troopers. They let loose a campaign of fierce vendetta, while the Hindu-dominated police force chose to look on in secret support as the attackers targeted Muslims.

When I reached Bombay, the riots had reached their peak. The city was a gory spectacle of looting, killing and burning. Hindu fanatics were cruising the smouldering streets, shouting, 'Burn them'. Trouble erupted in slums, spread to middle-class areas, and eventually engulfed even the posh neighbourhoods. Thriving Bombay was paralysed to a nervous standstill. Flames licked and curled with evil intent, destroying the lifelong savings of many honest, hardworking middle-class Muslim families who had never hurt a Hindu in their lives. Crazed with rage, people stabbed, slashed and beat one another to death. They hurled petrol and acid bombs. They moved in gangs, forcing men to drop their pants. If the penis was circumcised, a dead giveaway that the person was Muslim, they killed him.

Muslims fled to the safety of their ancestral villages. Airports, train stations and bus terminals were choked with terror-stricken, fleeing families, whose only crime had been to seek a livelihood in India's city of opportunities. Railway platforms were swamped with Muslim refugees, their most precious possessions pushed into cloth bundles and worn-out suitcases, waiting for the next train that could take them away from this nightmare. It was a pathetic scene of confusion and fear—men with worry lines on their brows, women with tear-stained cheeks and children exhausted, hungry, cranky and crying, 'I want to go home'.

But where was home?

To be an orphan in one's own country is a tragic fate for a community. These Muslims were born in India, they lived in India. They chose to remain in India while some of their own relatives went across to Pakistan, and they had assumed they would die in India—not be killed. Their quiet patriotism, their love for their country, was now being rewarded with bombs and knives. A Muslim villager from Kosi in Uttar Pradesh said in anguish when I interviewed him, 'The RSS tells us, go away to Pakistan. What is Pakistan to me? I have never been there, and why should I go there just because there are a whole lot of Muslims there?' Stamping the ground, he cried, 'This is my land, my motherland. This is where I was born and my father and his father before him.'

He bent down, scooped some earth from the ground and let it fall through his fingers, as tears rolled down his face. 'This earth holds the dust of my ancestors. This earth is my home. From this soil I came, and to it I will return. What does the RSS mean, go to Pakistan? I don't care about Pakistan. And I won't move from here. They will have to kill me first.'

For India's Muslims, it was a bitter betrayal to be now seen as Pakistani agents—which is how the fire-breathing Shiv Sena leader Bal Thackeray saw them. He was out to avenge historical wrongs: the plunder of Hindu temples a thousand years ago by invading Muslim Mongols, the construction of the Babri Masjid, the oppression the Hindus endured over centuries in their own homeland at the hands of the Muslim conquerors. He was out to 'teach them a lesson', and his army of Shiv Sainiks was there to do the job.

I first met Thackeray on my thirty-fourth birthday. It was 23 December 1992, a little over two weeks after the Babri Masjid had been destroyed. I had seen for myself the role played by the Shiv Sainiks in the demolition. I knew then that I must meet Thackeray, the leader of this gang of reckless young men, swelling with pride and vendetta and fed on a dangerous diet of hatred. My instincts told me there was a story brewing, and the sooner I got acquainted with him, the better it would be for me.

There was nothing happening vis-à-vis Thackeray to justify a story. Not just yet. There was no way I could get *Time* to pay for my trip to Bombay—after all, I was acting on a mere hunch, keeping tabs on a story that was still only developing. So I would have to pay for the trip out of my own pocket. I decided to kill two birds with one stone. I would stop by in Bombay on my way to Cochin, where I was spending my birthday and Christmas with my parents. Zubin had already flown to Cochin a few days earlier when his school closed.

So, on the morning of 23 December, I flew into Bombay and went straight to a meeting with Thackeray. I was ushered into a tiny room where Bal Thackeray sat, dressed in a maroon dhoti-kurta. My first impression of him was—oh God, what a dandy! It was all that maroon silk, spotless and shiny and so marvellously uncreased. And his hair! He was sixty-five years old, but it was jet black. Clearly dyed. And not only that, I could tell it was blow-dried. He was as old as my father, and no one I knew in my father's generation blow-dried his hair. So here was a man who really cared about his appearance.

And about the appearance of those who met him. I saw his eyes run over me, head to foot. I was modestly dressed in a pink and white salwar kameez with a white, gold-flecked dupatta draped over my shoulders. Thackeray looked at my business card, read aloud my name, and asked, 'Your name sounds Hindu, but are you Muslim?'

Why on earth would he think that? I am much more dark-skinned than an average Muslim. I have been mistaken for Spanish, American, Bengali, Sri Lankan, but never Muslim. Then I saw his eyes taking in my dupatta. Ah, the gold flecks. I was about to deny I was a Muslim when it struck me my religion was none of his business anyway.

I said so to him, of course much more tactfully. I smiled politely, opened my notebook and brought up the subject of the Babri Masjid.

But he was relentless. 'What are you, Hindu or Muslim?' he asked curtly.

'How does it matter what I am?' I asked sweetly.

But it was like sprinkling sugar on vinegar.

'What are you, Hindu or Muslim?' he repeated, a sharp edge to his voice.

I bristled and said stiffly: 'Really, Mr Thackeray, I don't understand how it matters whether I am Hindu or Muslim. I am not here to ask for a donation, or permission to start an organization. I am here only to interview you.'

'That's why I want to know. When you are interviewing me, it matters whether you are Hindu or Muslim.'

Now I was really offended. He was insinuating that if I was Hindu I would be favourable to him and if I was Muslim, I would misrepresent him. The objective, independent journalist who never let anyone or anything cloud her opinion or judgment, who held fair and objective reporting to be the bedrock of journalism, was hopping mad.

'Mr Thackeray, let me make one thing clear. What matters is what you say, not my religion. It doesn't matter one bit whether I am Hindu or Muslim. I am meeting you as a reporter for *Time* magazine.'

'Then you can kindly go back to your *Time* magazine. I have no interest in giving an interview to a journalist whose background I don't know.'

'I would be happy to provide you with my background—academic and journalistic. But I think it's unfair and unreasonable to insist on knowing what my religious background is. I promise you, it will not make any difference to the questions I ask or the way I report your answers.'

'So okay, I am unfair and unreasonable. Think what you want. I don't care. You can leave right now.'

I couldn't believe it. The man was throwing me out because I was refusing to disclose my religion!

I was so riled, the emotional part of me told me to leave. My pride was wounded. What the hell, I didn't need to talk to such a man. But the rational part of me said, defuse the situation, tell him and get on with the interview. If I got up and left, I would be the loser. He didn't care, he gave a million interviews, and he thought very poorly of journalists anyway. But I would never get to know the mind of this man. Don't lose sight of the wood for the trees, I warned myself.

So I calmed down and told him, 'Well, I am neither Hindu nor Muslim.' I was giving in, but not in a hurry. I wasn't going to make it easy for him.

'What are you then?' he retorted derisively, as if to say, if you are neither man nor woman, you must be a eunuch.

'I am a Christian,' I answered, as irritated with him as I was with myself.

'Oh, I see,' he said. And that was that. Having won that victory, he was happy to go on with the interview, answering boldly and frankly. It was perhaps the cartoonist in him, but he had nothing but contempt for journalists, politicians, women, Muslims—almost everybody except cricket and movie stars.

Like most people who have strong views, Thackeray is not without contradictions. He talked extensively of how

Muslims should be put in their place. He sounded as if he had an ingrained hostility to Muslims. Suddenly, I went off at a tangent and praised his hairstyle. He relaxed and smiled, almost preening.

'I have stuck to the same barber for years. He is Muslim. He is the best.'

I wondered how he had the courage to say such nasty things about Muslims and then put his head at the mercy of a Muslim. His barber could so easily slit his throat. I told him so, and Thackeray roared with laughter. 'No, no, he would never do that. He is a good man.'

This from a Muslim-basher!

During the first part of the interview, Thackeray constantly said, 'you Muslims and Christians'. But as the interview progressed, he relaxed and concluded I wasn't quite the ogre he had predetermined me to be. Along the way he started saying things like 'and these Muslims' and 'we must not allow them to get away with this'. Gradually, he had co-opted me into his Hindu fold.

I spent an hour interviewing him, and told him this was part of my mission to get acquainted with him as I was absolutely sure he would be playing a very important role politically, not only in Maharashtra but also on the national stage. He loved that. He preened again.

I left, promising to see him soon.

It turned out to be sooner than I had anticipated. Riots broke out barely two weeks later, in January, and Shiv Sena gangs began setting Bombay ablaze.

I was with *Time* photographer Robert Nickelsberg and our Bombay stringer, Amrita Shah, who was accompanying us to the airport. We called on Thackeray en route to the airport. And that's when I got the interview that pitchforked both of us into a maelstrom of controversy.

When we met him, Thackeray was in a state of high
excitement. He and his boys had humbled Bombay,
paralysed the government, horrified Indians across the land,
petrified the Muslims. He was heady with power. His eyes
were gleaming with satisfaction. He was at the centre of it
all, and he alone had the power to rein in his boys and restore
order to a devastated Bombay. He had demonstrated Hindu
power to Muslims. He was aggressive, tough, unapologetic.
He thundered, 'Muslims started the riots, and my boys are
retaliating. Do you expect Hindus to turn the other cheek?'

When I told him that Muslims were beginning to feel
like Jews in Nazi Germany, he retorted, 'Have they behaved
like the Jews in Nazi Germany? If so, there is nothing wrong
if they are treated as Jews were in Germany.'

I was completely flabbergasted by the interview. Amrita
said Thackeray had been saying these things for a long time,
and his newspaper *Saamna* was full of such inflammatory
statements. People either didn't read *Saamna,* or they didn't
take it seriously. In any case, it only preached to the already
converted Hindu chauvinists. But the impact was dramatic
when *Time*, a reputed international magazine, published the
interview with the headline 'Kick Them Out'—calling for
all Indian Muslims to be pushed out from India to Pakistan.
It was serious, threatening, vile, dangerous, stark. In *Saamna*,
perhaps such incendiary threats got lost in a sea of threats.
In *Time*, it seared like a volcanic eruption. Everybody who
read it was aghast.

When the interview was published, there was no reaction
from Thackeray. There was no need for one. He had said
everything that was printed. He knew and I knew there
was no misquoting. In any case, everything was on tape.
The secular Hindus, Muslims and every right-thinking
person reacted sharply to the interview. Pressure mounted

and Union Home Minister S.B. Chavan said Thackeray could be arrested for what he had said in the interview, and his organization banned.

It was only then that Thackeray issued a denial. He denied he had said all Muslims should be kicked out. He had merely said those Muslims who were Pakistani agents should be thrown out.

Nobody needs Thackeray to tell them that Pakistani agents should be kicked out. They routinely are by the police. Not only kicked out but tortured as well. But Thackeray's Pakistani agents obviously included Muslim women and children, and owners of garages, bakeries and eateries who had lived in Bombay all their lives and who were now refugees crowding railway stations, desperately seeking a safe haven from the rampaging Shiv Sainiks.

The media came to me and wanted my reaction. I said the tape was in my possession and if the authorities so desired, they could listen to it and decide for themselves exactly what Mr Thackeray had said.

My statement was reproduced faithfully, and the reaction was swift. I started getting threatening calls from Shiv Sainiks. The Delhi police, without my asking for it, had secured enough information on their own to give me police protection. Chavan, who was having a political slugfest with Thackeray, began pushing his advantage. Okay, so Thackeray was denying one part of the interview, but what about the rest? He had said there was nothing wrong in treating Muslims like Jews in Nazi Germany—that was sufficient to put him in jail.

I understood why Thackeray ignored the existence of the tape, but I couldn't understand why Chavan did not ask for it. A commission of inquiry was appointed and three years later, the commission still hadn't found it necessary to ask me for the tape. It lay locked in my office drawer—powerful, yet mute testimony since nobody wanted it, nobody cared for it, because nobody was really interested in getting at the truth. Then the commission wound up. Life moved on for Bombay, for the victims, the Muslims, the Hindus, and Bal Thackeray.

Life moved on for me, too. I was offered a job by CNN and left *Time*. CNN was in a hurry for me to join them, and I didn't have the time to sort through the stacks of papers, files and tapes that I had accumulated. So I threw away all the tapes, including the one with the Thackeray interview.

I realized later that one should never underestimate the unpredictable twists and turns in Indian politics. Six months later, the commission of inquiry was revived and this time around, Justice Srikrishna, who was heading it, meant business and took the trouble of getting in touch with me. He asked me to depose with the tape. I was livid. Here I had safeguarded the tape for years, and a few months after I had thrown it away, I was being asked for it.

I guess the commission understood my vexation. Justice Srikrishna was very kind and, in fact, I would go so far as to say he protected me when the Shiv Sena lawyers harangued me in his court. Not that I needed any defence. I was used to such fire and brimstone, so it didn't ruffle me. At the end of the deposition, the two top Shiv Sena lawyers came over and had a long chat with me, saying their first impression of me was all wrong and that I was actually a very nice person! Independent, but nice. I don't know whether it was the relief of knowing for sure that the tape was gone that disposed them so kindly towards me.

Still, Justice Srikrishna was taking no chances. I had to spend an extra day in Bombay to continue with the deposition, so he arranged for me to stay at the legislator's home, and insisted that policemen stand guard outside my door through the night. It was ironical, because by this time, the Shiv Sena was ruling Bombay.

During the deposition, Thackray's lawyers tried to establish I had a bias against him, but Justice Srikrishna's verdict was unambiguous. He said: 'Having carefully perused the lengthy cross-examination of the witness, it is not possible to agree with the contention that Ms Pratap was biased or that the interview...attributed to Bal Thackeray did not take place. The assertion of Ms Pratap that there was no denial of the interview to her or to *Time* magazine remains unshaken...In the circumstances, the Commission finds no reason to disbelieve the testimony of Ms Pratap or that the text of Exh.3109-C truly represents the interview during which Bal Thackeray had given his answers to pointed questions posed by the interviewer.'

It was not just Muslims who suffered because of Thackeray's chauvinism. Bombay suffered, the way few cities in the world have. The riots that Thackeray aggravated in January eventually resulted in the deadly serial bombs that exploded at a dozen different locations in downtown Bombay, two months later, on a sultry afternoon on Friday, 12 March 1993. It was the worst act of urban terrorism India had ever seen. It was Beirut, Belfast, Jerusalem and Colombo combined.

Cars and scooters packed with powerful explosives were parked in strategic locations—at the stock exchange, the Air India building, important offices, bustling shopping centres. The first bomb ripped through the busy stock exchange at 1.29 p.m. Eyewitness accounts are horrific. The thunderous sound of the explosion was followed by a bizarre rain as debris fell from the sky—mangled steel, a million shards of glass, flying bricks, window panes, and then an arm, a leg, a torso, a head.

Hospitals were crowded with bodies, some mangled, some charred, some mutilated, some intact...like the little dead schoolgirl who was still clutching her satchel.

It was a rain of death and destruction. Police officials confessed they thought it was an enemy strike. Terror-stricken Hindus involuntarily drew comparisons from the epics to describe the disaster. Stunned onlookers tried describing their amazement as they saw the top level of a double-decker bus flying past them. One of the most bizarre and enduring images of the Bombay serial blasts was the scene inside a city transport bus that had been hit by a bomb. The top half of the bus was blown away...taking with it the head of the driver. But his torso remained intact and as the bus came to a crashing halt, he was still seated, headless, his hands clutching the steering wheel tightly.

Investigations showed that Bombay's Muslim underworld had orchestrated the serial bombs—their revenge against Thackeray and the Shiv Sainiks. The message was clear—you attack Muslims, we attack Hindus. An eye for an eye, and Bombay goes blind. Nobody wanted that, not even Thackeray. The message struck home. There hasn't been any violent Hindu-Muslim rioting here since the bomb blasts.

But why does it take so much death and destruction for simple messages to strike home?

Bombay has learnt its lesson, but not the rest of India. We still suffer political tension and uncertainty, all because of a disused Muslim mosque that doesn't even exist today. We as a nation don't seem to realize we are ruining our present by dragging in the past. If we are to have a future, we must keep the past where it belongs—in the past.

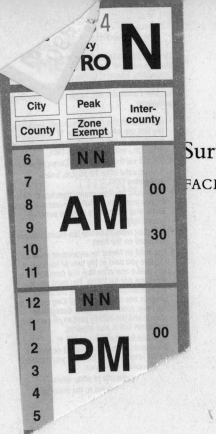

Survivors

FACE OF TRAGEDY

SILENCE OF THE BIRDS

The soft, tinkling sounds enhance the tranquillity of the emerald landscape. We are far away from the noise I have grown up with—the snarl of traffic, the blare of sirens, the whistle of pressure cookers, the piercing scream of gunfire in conflict zones. We are gliding along silently in our wooden rice-boat on the backwater canals of Kerala. Everything is green—apple-green paddy fields, dark-green fronds of coconut trees that line our passage, cloudy-green water of the canal. Occasionally, thatched huts rise like brown mushrooms. The red of the hibiscus flowers contrasts with the shades of green in the scenery. The vibrant colour, the shape and texture of the flowers, imbue not only the hibiscus but the whole landscape with a warm sensuality.

We punt gently in our quaint two-bedroom boat. The canal is narrow—usually thirty feet wide, though sometimes it broadens to about hundred feet. Coconut, mango and cashew-nut trees lean forward into the canal like eager citizens waiting to catch a glimpse of passing royalty. I fantasize I am Cleopatra going down the Nile in her barge and wave majestically at trees, if not people.

The landscape is lush, the sounds of peaceful routine hypnotic—children reading aloud lessons from their school textbooks, mothers blowing into hollow iron pipes to light kitchen fires, women washing vessels on the banks of the canal, men arguing matters of state. Occasionally temple and church bells ring out, mingling with the melody of a film song that floats out of a radio.

We are sitting on the deck of our boat enjoying the morning sunshine. Zubin is strumming his guitar as he lazily watches the countryside slipping by. He does not drink or smoke, but he loves his guitar, rock 'n' roll and girls—in that order, I think. Markus is as usual tinkering with his laptop, I am reading a book, and Arne is stripped to his waist, worshipping the sun with eyes closed. I think this is an involuntary Norwegian reaction—when the sun comes out, Norwegians take off their shirts, turn their faces upwards, close their eyes, sigh deeply and soak in the sun.

'Your husband looks like a retired Tarzan,' says Zubin with his lopsided smile.

I look at Arne anew and burst out laughing. Zubin has a cartoonist's eye, seeing caricatures instead of people. His comparisons are extreme and ludicrous, but there is always an element of truth in them.

Suddenly I hear what sounds like a hundred echoes of my laughter. We turn around and see a bunch of children mimicking me. On seeing our boat, these children, who were playing on the banks, jumped into the river and are now gliding like eels towards us. They swarm around our boat like droning summer flies, begging, giggling and talking rapidly in their high-pitched voices. They shout 'pain pain', but their dark gleeful faces look anything but pained. They keep pointing to our table on which there are some fruits, mineral water and glasses. I ask our boatman what they want, and he says they are asking for 'pens'.

That in many ways beautifully symbolizes a statistic—Kerala is India's most literate state. Poor children here don't beg for money, they beg for pens. All of them go to school because education is free, but they are often too poor to buy basic accessories like books and pens. The other objects of desire are the empty bottles of mineral water. Store-bought water bottles are too expensive to take to school, but these unwanted bottles are very useful. They can take them home and fill them with well water to quench their thirst during the long walk to and from school in the hot, humid months—which is virtually all year.

We don't have pens, but we hand over the empty bottles and move on, occasionally mooring to explore a village. Houses and huts are built on narrow strips of land abutting the canal. Behind the houses stretch waterlogged paddy fields. Virtually every house has a mango, a hibiscus and a few coconut trees. Narrow patches of garden, usually gravelled, bear the criss-cross lines of a sweeping broom. Goats or cows are tethered close to the house. Clucking hens wander about purposefully, constantly pecking for food. Sometimes we peer into the houses—the rooms are tiny and dark, and furnished at best with a chair, a table or a wooden cot. People here still live very rustic lives. We enjoy exploring the villages, but are glad we don't have to live in them.

Arne has gone completely native, with a towel thrown over his left shoulder and eating rice with his hands. He shakes his head as he speaks in that uniquely south Indian way. He even wants to wash his clothes the way the women here do, on the banks. So we moor again and watch as Arne carefully steps ashore and selects a spot to wash his T-shirt. He then begins to imitate the women—first dipping the T-shirt into the water, then placing it on the rough stone, rubbing soap all over and then swinging it around, beating the stone with the T-shirt. This is more fun and action than dropping clothes into a washing machine. Everyone gathers to watch him—the villagers, our boatmen, Zubin, Markus and I. That brings out the ham in Arne. Now he has a captive audience. The Tarzan in him comes out of retirement and he swings the T-shirt so hard, it flies right out of his hands. His audience bursts into laughter. A washerman he never will be.

Arne dives into the water to retrieve his T-shirt. He loves water as much as he loves the sun. A country passenger boat is approaching us. It is full of local people—men in white shirts, women in colourful saris and children in freshly washed clothes. Arne swims towards the boat and when he gets close, lifts his right hand out of the water and begs, 'Pens, pens'. Zubin and I burst out laughing, our merriment enhanced by the look of utter amazement on the passengers' faces. They have never seen a sight like this—a silver-haired foreigner mimicking their children and begging for pens! Markus is red with embarrassment.

'He is just having fun. Let him be,' I tell him.

'It's not funny,' says Markus dourly.

'The important thing is, he is enjoying himself. Why should we care what the world thinks? Remember, when we laugh the world laughs with us, when you sulk, you sulk alone.'

Markus's face brightens—not because he is inspired by my earthy wisdom, but because lunch is being served. Arne abandons his failed pen project—he didn't get even one—and joins us for lunch, which is a delicious spread of freshly caught curried fish; a variety of garden vegetables cooked in coconut, some sautéed, some fried crisp, others curried; several types of pickles, chutneys, pappadams; and plenty of rice—all laid out colourfully on green banana leaves. We eat so much we look like a family of boa constrictors.

After a heavy meal like that, there is only one thing to do. Siesta. So we slither to our bedrooms and curl to sleep. Arne nods off the minute his head touches the pillow. It always takes me a while to sleep, so I usually read a book. But now I prefer to look out of the window of our country boat. The window is so low, it's on the same level as the bed, enabling me to see the soothing scenery drift by. I watch the magic of ordinary life: people walking on the bank, women gossiping under the shade of luxuriant trees, cows grazing, little boats with men and their wares gliding past. All so peaceful, accompanied by the gentle sounds of nature and people in harmony—the lulling chatter of human voices, the drone of dragonflies, the melody of birdsong, the soft rustle of the breeze as it dances on the paddy fields, the whisper of palm fronds, the fragment of somebody's laughter, the gentle lapping of water against the sides of our boat that glides ever so gently over the placid waters.

So different from the boat I once took across a choppy Bay of Bengal, pitching and rocking and heaving like a pregnant woman trying to deliver twins...

It started one morning in May. As my family and friends know, there are two rituals that give me great pleasure. A huge lunch on Sundays, followed by a three-hour siesta, and a shampoo, which I do twice a week. I oil my hair the night before, with a special concoction made from coconut oil, crispy fried curry leaves and hibiscus leaves. It has a peculiar smell, but I love it. I don't know whether it helps to keep the hair black as it's meant to, but it certainly gives me a fantastic, deep sleep. In the morning, I wash it off with shampoo. It's a ritual that lasts twenty minutes and consumes tons of water.

At 8 a.m. I had just started my bathing ritual when I got a call from Deepak Puri, *Time*'s bureau manager. Deepak has the invaluable knack of dredging people out even if they are tucked away in the strangest corners. Never mind how remote the place or how impossible the circumstances, the long arm of Deepak will somehow find you. I was once on vacation and inside an Air France plane that was about to take off from Paris to Rome, when he managed to reach me and get me back on a plane to India instead, to cover a breaking news story in Sri Lanka. This was much before the advent of mobile phones.

Deepak told me on the phone that *Time*'s editorial bosses in New York wanted me to go to Bangladesh immediately. The cyclone was getting real big. It was now going to be the cover story. I had to take the 9.15 flight to Calcutta to catch a connecting one to Dhaka.

I abandoned my shower, threw some clothes into a bag, wrote a note for Zubin who was at school, telephoned our stringer Farid Hossain in Dhaka requesting him to meet me at the airport with a good vehicle and a pillow, took a taxi to the Bangladesh High Commission to get my visa, and drove at breakneck speed to the airport, where Suresh, Deepak's right-hand man, was waiting with my tickets and foreign exchange. I took a deep breath only when I was seated in the plane. But Abdul Rashid, the passenger next to me, must have held his breath throughout the flight. My damp, smelly hair wasn't exactly like the perfumes of Arabia, I guess.

Farid, trustworthy and efficient as always, was waiting at the airport with a van—and a pillow. We would have to drive all night to reach Cox Bazar, which was in the vicinity of the worst-affected area of the cyclone, and I needed to make the journey as comfortable as possible. Once I reached the trouble spot, I knew the work would be gruelling. I might not get to sleep for two or three days.

Steve Coll, the correspondent for the *Washington Post*, was with me on the flight into Dhaka. Steve is a brilliant man and humble, not like the typical all-knowing journalists who always predict things wrong and later claim they had astutely predicted the correct outcome all along, safe in the knowledge that nobody remembered their predictions anyway. Unlike most journalists who love the sound of their own voice, Steve is hard-working and a good listener. And beneath that sweet, polite exterior ticks a sharp mind. Years later, he was to win a Pulitzer Prize.

In rain-swept Dhaka, there was not a single taxi to be hired. Had I seen any other journalist wandering about with growing anxiety in the airport, the way Steve was, I would have chuckled with glee and slunk away happily. But I like Steve, so I offered him a ride to Cox Bazar.

We clambered into the van, and I instructed the driver to drive as fast as he could. I then told Steve he could stretch out on the rear seat while I took the pillow and the middle seat. I told him candidly that I wanted the middle seat because it was longer than the front seat and I could stretch out more comfortably. The rear seat was equally long, but it would shake and bump the most during the rough ride. Steve appreciated my honesty, and I lay down, closed my eyes, and eventually drifted off to sleep.

We reached Cox Bazar before daybreak. The six-foot-tall Steve uncoiled himself from the rear seat and groaned in pain—he was a mass of bruised bones and muscles. 'Thank God I at least had Mariah Carey for company through the night,' he said with a rueful smile, taking the earphones of his Walkman out of his reddened ears.

We learned from the locals that a little island named Ujantia was among the worst hit by the cyclone. So we decided to head there. The village was accessible only by boat, and the sea was still rough. But that didn't deter us. We walked down the flooded street into the pier where a rickety old country boat was moored. It was dangerously dilapidated and should have been broken down to firewood a long time ago. But it was the only one that could take us across the Bay of Bengal to Ujantia. The boatman, however, refused to take his boat out. It was too dangerous, he said, shaking his head vigorously.

I bribed him with a huge amount of money. He refused at first, but his head now shook much less vigorously. I kept coaxing him. Eventually, the sight of all that money made him change his mind.

It's amazing how greedy people are. Here I was, giving him ten times more than what he would earn for a normal ride, but he calculated, why not make some more? There were only three of us, and the boat could easily accommodate twenty passengers more. He told us to wait and disappeared. Within fifteen minutes he was back with a whole bunch of passengers whom he had refused earlier.

The boat had a low horsepower engine, which was pathetically inadequate against the huge waves around us. The angry sea tossed the boat as if it were a worthless plank of wood, which of course it was. We lurched and bumped against one another as we kept losing our balance. The sky was grey, and the winds were howling. Later, in his book on India, Steve wrote about the boat trip, about how we were going on this crazily dangerous ride when he asked me whether I could swim and I said no. And he marvelled that I had the courage to be on a rickety boat in the choppy seas without knowing how to.

Truth is, I can swim—one length in the unruffled calm of a swimming pool. But swimming in the sea even in the tourist resorts of Goa or Sri Lanka is beyond me, let alone in a sea whipped by a cyclone.

Anyway, there we were riding into Ujantia as if on a bucking horse. It was early morning. My eyes took in the horrifying spectacle of devastation. The land was a squelchy marsh of uprooted trees and flattened homes—damp straw, broken timber frames, misshapen lumps of mud that must once have been walls of huts, offering some protection against wind and rain.

As I stepped gingerly onto the slushy bank, the first sound I heard was of high-pitched wailing. Dawn was greeting this devastated island not with the chirping of birds, but with the cries of hungry babies.

The mothers of the children were close to tears themselves. They didn't have anything to satisfy the hunger of their wailing infants. Their dark, taut faces were full of despair and frustration. Their breasts had dried up long ago, and they had been feeding their children cow's milk. But ever since the cyclone struck, there was no milk, there was not even a banana available. The banana trees were a tangled mess on the ground, and the few that stood were stripped of leaves and fruit.

Twenty-year-old Sultana Razia had only water to give her child. The baby was so happy to get liquid, any liquid, she sucked greedily at the feeding bottle. But her hunger couldn't be slaked. Annoyed, she turned her face away from the nipple and started whimpering. Gradually, the decibel level increased. She was angrily demanding food, but her mother had none to give. So once again she thrust the nipple into the infant's mouth, who sucked for a short while before turning away again in irritation, cried some more and then fell silent, not from satiation but from exhaustion.

About 2000 homeless people of Ujantia were huddled in their new home: a rectangular cyclone shelter. It was a depressing building in ugly concrete, with chipped and soot-stained walls. The refugees had cordoned off little spaces for themselves, where they had placed their precious belongings: bundles of clothing, a blackened cooking pot, a tin lamp.

Delwara Begum and her little daughter lived in the shelter now, but they didn't have any possessions other than the dirty, torn clothes they were wearing. Delwara looked so haggard and old, she could have been mistaken for the grandmother of the child. Red veins mingled with yellow streaks in the whites of her eyes, making them look dirty and infected. It was difficult to look her in the eye.

She recalled that horrible night when the cyclone struck. The winds were roaring, but exhaustion was a good antidote to fear. She and her husband had been too tired after the day's toil to be worried about a storm. They were too poor to own a radio, so they did not know that the government had announced a signal 9 storm, the second most severe storm signal.

At night, the six-metre tidal waves struck, destroying their hut. In panic, Delwara reached out and clutched her six-year-old daughter and clung to a bamboo beam. She was washed up, battered and bruised, but alive, no less than eleven kilometres away. She was destined to live, but her husband and five other children drowned. Their bodies were not even washed up ashore. Of Ujantia's 15,000 inhabitants, 3000 died. Some of them still lay dead and bloated on the southern coast: a devastated island fringed by its dead. The shores were strewn with the bodies of men, women and children in bizarre postures—legs wide apart and arms stretched out, fingers clawing the air; eyes wide open, transfixed in terror. Bloated with water, the dead children looked plump and healthy in stark contrast to the emaciated babies in the cyclone shelter.

Perhaps the most difficult thing about covering calamities is coping with the smell of decomposing bodies. It clings to your nostrils long after you've left the scene, long after you are back in the fragrance of your own home, long after you breathe the scent of sweat of your son back from play, long after you smell his freshly shampooed hair when you kiss him goodnight.

The smell of death doesn't go away. It lies curled somewhere in your entrails, rising to the surface to ambush you when you least expect it. People wonder why you wrinkle your nose in disgust when you bend down to smell a gladioli. Only you know that somehow, the white of the fragrant flower reminds you of the white handkerchief you held against your nose to shield yourself from the stench of nature's death row.

I wondered whether Delwara was relieved that her husband and children had perished without a trace. Wasn't it better to live with her memories of them, rather than cope with the final, horrible image of rigor mortis on the shore? She seemed to have read my thoughts. 'I wish I could have seen my husband and children one last time. I have searched all over this island and the next one. I know there is no hope of ever finding them alive, but at least I could have given them a decent burial. Isn't that the least one deserves after living on this earth?' she said sadly.

I thought of my own ambitions and the ambitions of my friends, acquaintances and competitors. How utterly pointless and shallow they seemed, how warped and grandiose compared to this woman's desire.

Illiterate and poor she was, yet Delwara was also a philosopher. 'We are not meant to die alone,' she said in Bengali, a language I learnt in school. 'We are not alone when we come into the world. At least our mothers are with us. So also, we are not meant to die alone. Our children should be with us when we die. This is the chain of human existence that keeps us linked together. I am a cursed mother. No, I am doubly cursed. I am a mother whose children have died before her. And I couldn't be by their side, or my husband's, when they died. My children died, alone and frightened, and I was nowhere near to comfort them.'

Delwara started crying silently, one hand pressed to her bowed head, in the universal posture of grief. I tried to comfort her. At least she was able to save her little daughter. She nodded her head in acknowledgement and looked up, grateful for the few words of comfort from a stranger she would never meet again. As I left her, I sent a silent prayer to God, 'Please God, don't make me suffer like her. Take what you want from me—my money, my job, my social status, my friends, my abilities—but please God, don't let Zubin die on me.'

For Ujantia, the cyclone was the beginning of a long season of travails. At this time of the year, the villagers would normally be cultivating their land. But the fields were now flooded with sea water. The three-metre mud wall that blocked the salt water of the ocean from the low-lying island had been washed away. Until a new dike was built, the tides would bring more salt water to the soil, eventually making it too saline for cultivation. If the surrounding fields became unfit for farming, Ujantia's very existence would be threatened. The villagers would have to uproot themselves from their homes and migrate to urban slums and survive by working on construction sites.

The villagers knew the fate that loomed ahead, but they were waiting for the government to start the food-for-work programme. This was a scheme by which the state rewarded workers with rice for building roads or village embankments. But the government right now was stressed out trying to bury the dead, clear the debris and reach relief to the starving. Official reports claimed as many as 1,25,000 people had died in the cyclone. It would be a long while before the government got down to rebuilding dikes. I was irritated by the public attitude. There was no time to wait for the state to act. The sea water would ruin their land long before the government came to their village with its programme. Why couldn't the men get together and rebuild the dike? A life of handouts would keep them in the perpetual bondage of poverty, I preached.

Shamsuddin, a young farmer, looked at me calmly. There was no insolence or anger in his steady gaze, as there might have been. There was a passivity instead, which I initially mistook for fatalism, an attitude I see so often in the people of the region, an attitude that drives me up the wall. But here it wasn't fatalism, it was helplessness. In the West, helplessness makes most people hit out in anger, but here it encourages stoicism. Anger requires energy. These people were so poor and exhausted, they were even deprived of energy. Shamsuddin told me, 'Right now, it's an effort for me even to talk to you. How can I dig and shovel earth without food in my belly?'

But, as if to endorse the validity of my reasoning, Abdur Rahman, a small landowner and one of Ujantia's elders, spoke up, 'If we don't plant soon, we will have no crop next season. There will be only starvation.'

In that case, Ujantia would awaken for a long time to the cries of hungry infants.

★

In the earthquake-devastated village of Killari in Maharashtra, there were no wailing babies. They were all dead.

As I drove into Killari, I knew where the dead lay. I just had to look up at the sky for the circling birds of prey, to locate the Mound of the Dead. For me, even worse than the distress of hungry infants was the silence of the birds… the lull of vultures as they circled silently above a disaster zone. Invariably, there was an ominous hush beneath.

I had expected to see death, but I was unprepared for the sight of the corpses in the hospital grounds. The dead had kept pouring in until the hospital ran out of space, so the bodies were piled on top of each other. Dead men, women and children were stacked like logs. And then I saw something that was to haunt me for the rest of my life— maggots crawling out of a dead man's eyes.

The eyes were wide open, frozen forever with the terror of sudden, frightening death. The man's body was straight and flat, but his head, instead of facing upwards, was turned sideways, as if watching the visitors walking into the hospital. For a moment, he seemed alive to me. His eyes didn't have the blank stare of death. They were expressive, wide open with a kind of pleading terror. I had heard so many ghastly stories of living people being buried by mistake. So I edged closer to him to check whether he was alive. As I stared intently into his eyes to see if they blinked, I noticed the whites of his eyes were bright yellow, as if afflicted with jaundice. Then I recoiled in horror—they were little wriggling maggots.

At that moment, the stench of death hit me fully, and I was paralysed with shock and revulsion. I shut my eyes tightly, stopped breathing for a few seconds, took a few steps backwards, opened my eyes, and ran out to where my taxi was parked. I felt ill. But I knew that if I started vomiting, I would be too drained to work. It was a Friday, and *Time* had kept the edition open for my file. I had only a few hours to gather the facts, and then I had to send in my report. There was no time to be squeamish. Get on with the work, I told myself.

I reached for the bottle of mineral water in the back seat of the aged taxi. As I opened it, I saw a yellow eye swimming inside, with wriggling maggots. I screamed silently. 'Stop it, control yourself,' I scolded myself. 'You can either stay here and puke your guts out, or you can get on with your job. Grow up for Chrissake.' My self-directed anger jerked me out of my nausea. I washed my face and resolutely walked back into the municipal hospital. But I didn't have the nerve to look at the pile of dead bodies again.

I walked into the dispensary of the hospital that was overflowing with the injured. The building itself was still intact, though the cracks on the wall seemed dangerously wide. The doctors were red-eyed and looked fatigued beyond words, but they were coping admirably with the situation. Their immediate priority was to dispose of the dead; the smell was overpowering.

Babu Singh, a forty-five-year-old tea-stall owner, was helping the authorities to bury the dead. He had already cremated his own.

So often, calamity befalls a family or community after a particularly happy event or phase. The earthquake struck Killari at the happiest time of the year. It was that old perverse fate again. You were taken up higher, just so the fall could be that much harder.

Hours before the earthquake occurred, the villagers of Killari had concluded the ten-day Ganesha festival. The

15,500 inhabitants celebrated late into the night, drinking, dancing and blowing horns. It had been a good year. The monsoon was good, so crops would be aplenty. The people were rejoicing in thanksgiving. The ceremonies culminated with the villagers immersing Ganesha's idol in the small pond nearby. Tired and drunk, the men straggled home a little past midnight.

Babu Singh was tired but happily drunk. His family was asleep inside the house, but as usual he took his cot out and slumped to sleep on his front porch under the asbestos awning. That saved his life. At 3.56, he was woken from his slumber by a deafening roar. He clutched his shaking cot in terror and incomprehension. He could see nothing but a thick curtain of dust where his three-room house had stood just moments before. Recalling his terror, he said, 'I thought the earth was an exploding bomb.'

Singh's entire family lay entombed inside. His mother, wife, two sons, daughters-in-law, grandchildren. A few moments before, he had been the head of a large family. Now he was all alone in the world. With a broken heart, he pulled out, one by one from the debris, the bleeding and dusty corpses of his loved ones. Breaking off the wood from the beams and window sills of his collapsed home, he cremated his entire family. Columns of smoke rose from the burning wood to meet the last of the monsoon clouds.

Babu Singh was perhaps more fortunate than most of his neighbours. At least he had enough wood to give his family a decent cremation. He used torn saris and bed sheets to shroud the corpses. Babies were tenderly wrapped in towels. But now as he helped to cremate his neighbours, such dignities became a luxury. Wood and cloth ran out. There were too many dead. The only thing to do was to dump them in the municipal hospital. There the authorities decided to cremate Hindus in collective pyres and bury Muslims in mass graves.

In Killari, I ran into Lt. Gen. A.S. Kalkat, who was heading the relief operations. The last time our paths crossed was in Sri Lanka. He was then head of the Indian peacekeeping troops. We had developed a rapport that soon blossomed into friendship based on mutual respect.

The adventure in Sri Lanka was over, and he was now the chief of the Indian army's southern command. He was a career soldier who had fought three wars, but on seeing the death and destruction in Killari, his shock was deep, and similar to mine. 'I have seen death. I have seen destruction. But I have never seen anything like this,' he said.

Killari looked as if it had been carpet-bombed. The village had been reduced to rubble. No less than 10,000 people had been killed in a matter of minutes. The poor people in Killari used stones to build their houses, even though the village was located on a seismic zone, because they could not afford safer building materials. When there was an earthquake, the stones came tumbling down with lethal effect. I couldn't help but experience a sense of frustration. The earthquake had registered 6.4 on the Richter scale, but far more powerful ones have struck San Francisco to cause fewer casualties.

In 1988 an earthquake of 6.9 intensity on the Richter scale had hit Armenia and San Francisco. In Armenia, 30,000 people died, mainly because they were entombed in concrete houses. In San Francisco, only sixty-seven people died because they used sophisticated housing materials that collapsed without injuring. In fact, the casualty was so high only because some of them died of heart attacks due to the shock.

Getting the story was difficult enough, but transmitting turned out to be a bigger nightmare. I reached Latur, the nearest town, and discovered that all telephone lines were down. Those were the days of telexes and faxes, much before the era of email, mobile and satellite phones. I had a lot of good stuff to report, but how was I to transmit it? It was Friday night, and our edition would close in a few hours. The news would be too stale for the next edition. Not one to give up easily, I scoured the city and found one open STD booth. That phone turned out to be the only one working in Latur. I got on the phone and dictated the whole story to Meenakshi at our Delhi bureau. She patiently wrote it all down in longhand and typed it out to New York. It was published as the cover story with Babu Singh's quote 'the earth was an exploding bomb' emblazoned in red across the picture of a man holding a dead baby girl with little silver anklets on her tiny, plump feet.

Another powerful picture from the earthquake, a heartbreaking one taken by photographer Dieter Ludwig, was published alongside the article. It was a picture that immortalized a poor family's embrace in death. The husband and wife lay on their sides, facing each other on a single iron cot, with their infant in between. The baby had his face upturned to his father, whose face tilted downwards protectively toward his son. His arm was slung affectionately over his wife's head. A torn bed sheet covered the lower half of their bodies. The cot had collapsed into the pile of debris, and they were covered with the mud, stone and dust of their destroyed home.

The earthquake had struck Latur on Thursday, I had reached the spot on Friday, and on Monday *Time* hit the stands worldwide with the earthquake as the cover story. We beat even the Indian magazines, and satellite news channels had not yet arrived in India. I was thrilled. These are the triumphs of a journalist, triumphs that keep you floating on cloud nine till you land with a sudden, painful thud when you suddenly, for no reason, see yellow eyes squirming with maggots.

I have not revisited Killari, but I have no doubt Babu Singh and the others continue to survive somehow. Most of them would have rebuilt their homes, some may have migrated to cities nearby, but at least they still have a village to go back to.

The villagers of Hazara have no such luck. The river swallowed up their village.

It happened bit by bit, day by day. They watched an angry river devour their homes inch by inch. There was nothing they could do to stop it. Angrier than the river was the local Sikh legislator V.M. Singh. For months he had struggled to stop the juggernaut of the river, but man and nature conspired against him. 'As we are speaking, Hazara is shrinking, and by next week it will cease to exist,' he raged in a friend's home in New Delhi while on a visit. The unusual fate of the village was intriguing, and I had an urge to see it with my own eyes. Singh volunteered to take me to Hazara, which was located in his constituency in Uttar Pradesh.

A few days later, Singh, my friend and photographer Dayanita Singh and I set off for the remote village, close to the India-Nepal border. We travelled by train, then by car, and eventually arrived in Hazara in a four-wheel drive vehicle. It was mid-August, and the sky was grey and heavy with rain clouds. The villagers were as sullen as the sky. More curious visitors to see their misery, they must have thought. But their faces brightened when they saw we were with V.M. Singh. He was their only ray of hope. They loved him, even though they knew he was a ray that could not light up a new dawn for their doomed village.

Hazara's troubles had begun during the previous year's monsoon. The rain-engorged river nearby burst its banks and surged across farmlands to gouge a new course. Tumbling from its headwaters in the Himalayas and sluicing down through the foothills of Nepal, the fast-flowing Sarda now cut through the outskirts of the village, swallowing twenty-eight houses as it trammeled a new course. The villagers were dumbstruck. They were used to floods which, although ruinous, receded in a few weeks. This was different. The half-kilometre wide river had turned deadly, gobbling literally the ground beneath their feet. The hungry river did not stop with twenty-eight houses. It was eroding the receding frontiers of the village, snaking inexorably to its heart.

Frightened by the carnivorous river, the mostly illiterate villagers did the only thing they could think of. They petitioned the local authorities to protect the village. The solution was clear—new dikes would have to be built quickly, and the old silted river bed would have to be dredged to seduce the Sarda back to its original and less lethal course. The authorities did the only thing they knew: they formed committees. The pleas of the villagers and of V.M. Singh that there was no time to waste, fell on deaf ears.

In June, Singh petitioned the local court to force the bureaucracy into action. But he didn't succeed. Rains were expected in less than four weeks. Time had run out. In desperation, Singh organized the villagers to dredge the channel themselves. But it was too late. Heavy rains began lashing the region in late June, churning the river bed into a gooey mess that immobilized the villagers and the bulldozers. They had to give up their work. The time had come to resign themselves to their fate. In a matter of weeks, the village would cease to exist.

Poor and desolate, there was little the villagers could do. Still, they made feeble attempts to delay the advance of the snarling river. They put up a few barriers. Officials now started trickling in to make a show of helping the villagers. They erected a single dike consisting of flimsy bamboo poles and sacks of mud. Mukhtiar Singh, a farmer, said sarcastically, 'Forget stopping the river, this will collapse in the next rain.'

It did. The monsoon clouds burst, the river swelled. By mid-July half the village had been washed away. There was nothing the villagers could do but watch the river and feast their eyes on their beloved land to imprint it in their minds—the only place where it could now survive. Daily, women would engage in a helpless ritual: gather at the retreating rim of the village and watch it crumble into the Sarda. They stared with brooding fascination as the tops of once luxuriant mango trees poked through the swirling waters, branches waving helplessly like the arms of drowning swimmers. Bits and pieces of the village slipped into the river in a silent procession—animal carcasses; planks of wood that had once kept a hut aloft; thatches of huts that looked like straw hats of drowned men, all floated away from them into oblivion.

In early August, when it was clear that nothing could save the village from the advancing river, the 600 villagers abandoned Hazara. They went to makeshift shelters in nearby hamlets, surviving on the charity of relatives, neighbours and gurudwaras. The government promised them new homes, but the people were angry and bitter. They knew these would be empty promises. Narrowing his eyes, farmer Ranvir Singh said, 'Even God will not forgive this government for its negligence.'

Until the last day, Ranvir Singh and the other men and women of the village clung to their daily ritual. With lumps in their throats, they stood and watched until one bleak day in August 1995, the river washed Hazara off the map.

*

If water sealed Hazara's fate, then drought ruined Mudalapalli in Karnataka. Again, it was a story of how the state never comes to your aid, but is always there to add to your miseries.

Droughts continue to ravage many states in India, as they did five, ten, fifteen years ago. Why does a country like India, which is renowned for its architectural, engineering and personnel skills have to suffer crippling droughts even in the twenty-first century? India can send satellites into space and explode nuclear bombs, but its farmers are still dependent on rainfall. There are no proper aqueducts, no sensible management or preservation of ground water, no afforestation programmes that could prevent the recurrence of this man-made catastrophe. I burned with anger when I saw the remarkable Roman aqueduct in Pont du Gard in southern France. The aqueduct had been built more than 2000 years ago to transport twenty million litres of drinking water daily for the needs of the population of Nîmes. If the Romans could do this in 19 BC, why is it not possible for Indians today?

The trouble is, the state does not care. Nor does the intelligentsia or the middle class. Those who matter don't care any more, driven as they are by their ambition for upward mobility. Their eyes are so focused upwards, they cannot, will not, see what is happening below. Those who make policy and those who read about it are not really affected by drought. And those who are affected are too poor and powerless to protest. Like Narasimhappa.

Normally by August, the fields in Mudalapalli are green, and the sheaves of maize so tall they hide the toiling farmers. But due to the long drought in 1987, the land was flat and barren, and the bodies of worried farmers could be seen silhouetted against the horizon. Many farmers lay hopelessly on their string cots, gazing at their empty, parched fields. The drought had turned the earth leprous. It was dry and cracked, and the surface was a mottled brown and flaky white. Skeletons of cattle lay in the arid fields like relics of dead hopes. Every now and then, farmers glanced futilely at the relentless brown sky. Earth and sky—it was all one dusty brown expanse.

Villagers survived on the few leftover grains from the previous year. There was no fodder for the cattle in the village commons. So they had to take loans from moneylenders to buy some. That sent them sliding deeper into debt. Most of them had already mortgaged their winter crop even before it was sown, even before they knew whether there would be any rains to allow sowing the following season.

The normally thriving grain markets had become ghost towns. Usually, there was a queue two kilometres long as trucks and tractors lined up on the road to empty their produce. Now there were no vehicles to be seen. The dusty road was empty save for a few push carts. A few farm workers and traders gossiped idly, some played cards, others dozed in the shade.

Life was more cruel to the farm workers. As they were landless, they subsisted by toiling on the lands of the better-off farmers. For their labour, they earned a few rupees and a small portion of the crop—sufficient for immediate survival, but insufficient for storage. Unlike the land-owning farmers, who could survive a year of drought because they could dip into the previous year's stocks of food grain, these landless workers were hit hard by drought. There was no work to be had on the bone-dry fields, which meant no wages and no food. For these marginal men and women of India, drought meant displacement.

Narasimhappa was one such marginal man. I spent some time with him and his family in 1987. A landless farm worker, he was a thirty-three-year-old Dalit with a wife and two small children. He had been working on the land in his village since childhood. He was thin, dark and wiry, but strong.

After cultivating onions and peanuts for land-owning farmers for years, Narasimhappa gradually and surreptitiously encroached on a hilly patch of land, three miles away from his village, and began to illegally cultivate maize. The land belonged to no one and was lying unused. He was not hurting anyone; he was only helping himself. Though maize did not bring good returns, at least it filled the belly, and there was a little left over for sale. It would have been more lucrative to plant peanuts, but he could not afford the expensive seedlings. His annual income from the crop was a thousand rupees. It was a pittance, but it protected his family from abject poverty.

Over the years, the rainfall decreased. The yield from his patch of land fell. So he encroached some more and worked harder to harvest the same amount. By the end of three years, he was cultivating an acre of land. He had built up his farm slowly and steadily. But one day, forest officials swooped down on the spot, evicted him, uprooted his maize and planted eucalyptus saplings instead.

Now there was no choice but to depend entirely on his old job—working on the farms. But work was neither easy nor regular. If he found work, he earned five rupees a day, and his wife Chinnagangamma earned four. As the monsoon became weaker in the subsequent years, his earnings dwindled. There were prolonged periods of unemployment. So once again he was left to his own devices to survive. He began chopping trees in the outlying areas of the village to smuggle firewood.

Every evening Narasimhappa set out, trudging eight kilometres to the nearby hills to chop wood. He needed the cover of darkness to smuggle his bundle back to the village. Early next morning he set off for Bagepalli, a town ten kilometres away, to sell the firewood. He returned by afternoon, ate and rested, and then set off for the hills again. He trudged thirty-six kilometres every day to earn eight rupees.

But the law stood in his way once again. Authorities noticed the denudation of the hills and set up squads. Narasimhappa got caught, and his bundle was confiscated. He was let off with a warning. But the warning was drowned by the growling bellies of his two hungry children. Two days later, food ran out in his hut, and he went to the hills again to smuggle firewood. He got caught again. The warning was more stern this time. For good measure, the official boxed his ears as well. He nodded his head shamefacedly, promised never to commit the crime again and walked back home in despair.

That night Narasimhappa and his wife came to the conclusion that they would have to migrate to Tirupati, the nearest big temple town. He was bound to find work there, as a road or construction worker. There would be plenty of jobs in a big town. In any case, it was rumoured that meals were virtually guaranteed because the Balaji temple fed poor people. Even if they didn't find work immediately, they wouldn't starve to death. Already they had stopped having dinner. Said Narasimhappa, 'At night my two children would start whimpering in hunger. I could only watch helplessly as my wife tried to cool the fires of hunger burning in their stomach with a glass of water.'

Now even the morning meal was in jeopardy.

He had no choice but to migrate from the fringes of the village to the fringes of a city slum to lead a borderline existence.

Narasimhappa carefully worked out a plan. After breakfast, he and his family would walk to Chelur, twelve kilometres away. The pace would have to be slow to enable the children to keep up. After a night's rest, they would set off early for the Mulakalacheruvu railway station, ten kilometres away. From there, he and his family would travel ticketless to Tirupati by the afternoon passenger train that left the station at 3 p.m.

The planning was easy, the execution much tougher.

Narasimhappa was penniless. Even though he planned to travel ticketless, he still needed a few rupees. He had to buy enough food to last the three-day journey to Tirupati. He approached a few villagers for a loan, but they all refused. His debts already totalled two hundred and fifty rupees, and nobody was willing to lend money to a departing man. There was no choice, he had to head for the hills again. He went later than usual, well after sunset. He was lucky. He was able to smuggle uninterrupted for a few days. That was all he had prayed for. When he had saved ten rupees, he decided they could embark on their journey.

Narasimhappa was sad at the thought of leaving his

village, but there was simply no choice. But he promised himself and his family that they would come back to their village next spring to attend the Ugadi harvest festival. His land may have spurned him, his crops may have failed, but Narasimhappa like millions of other destitute Indian villagers would continue to cling to the rituals.

The day of departure was 19 August. The Narasimhappa family rose as usual. At about ten o'clock they squatted on the floor of their thatched hut to eat their last meal there—a dark brown ball of ragi, with a chutney made of green chillies and tamarind. The meal over, they trooped outside to wash their hands. Chinnagangamma carefully packed the remaining ball of ragi in a sheet of yellowed newspaper to take along on the journey. She then heaved the earthen pot from the fireplace and put out the fire. For one long moment, she gazed into the dying embers. Fading firelight flickered on her small pinched face and died, leaving it in darkness. 'I wonder where and when I will cook my next meal,' she whispered. Her eyes glistened with unshed tears in the gloomy darkness of the hut.

Husband and wife looked around their hut one last time, glanced at each other and stepped out. They didn't bother to lock the door. There wasn't a bolt in any case, and besides, there was nothing valuable in the hut—only a blackened pot, a few worn aluminium vessels and some torn and shabby clothes.

Walking along a narrow, dung-stained cobbled path, the family trooped towards the village temple—a small, squat, stone structure painted in white with little statuettes of local Hindu gods. The deities were placed alongside some sacred swords and heirlooms of the village. With his hands folded high, Narasimhappa prayed long and hard. Asked what he had prayed for, Narasimhappa said: 'I prayed to

God to save us from all troubles. I prayed that my hands be put to good use.'

And then, without turning back even once, Narasimhappa and his family walked on steadily into an uncertain future that they hoped would be a little better than the difficult past they were leaving behind.

IN THE VEILS OF SORROW

It is such a delicious pleasure to struggle for a decision—when all you have to decide is something as simple as where to have your next meal. More so, when the places you have to choose from are exotic destinations. I take delight in this trivial struggle precisely because I know how cruel life can be, that other people at this very moment could be grappling with difficult, life-and-death decisions relating to marriage, children, health, career, property. While I struggle to decide where to eat, I am only too aware that millions in my country are deciding whether they should skip today's meal to keep it for the next day when they will be hungrier. I thank God silently for my good fortune and return to the topic of discussion.

'So what should we do? Stay on here and have dinner at Roussillon, or should we drive back to Gordes and find a restaurant there?' asks Arne.

We are touring France in a rented car. The 200-year-old chateau where we are staying is about two hours away. We have just driven down from Gordes, a charming medieval hilltop village facing a huge valley, to Roussillon, the scarlet village. This is a hilltop village too, but it is in shades of red because of the rich ochre deposits in the area. People here use ochre to paint their houses, shops and restaurants. The result is stunning. Roussillon looks as if it is basking in the permanent glow of a setting, blood-red sun. Perched on a cliff, the village looks warm and rich and inviting.

'But I'd like to see Roussillon properly. We've just arrived,' I point out.

'If you want to explore Roussillon, then we must have dinner here. If we go back to Gordes and have dinner there, it will take us too long to drive back to the chateau,' Arne reasons.

Before we arrived in Roussillon, we had decided to go back to Gordes because we hadn't had enough of that enchanting village with its quaint cobblestone alleys and majestic views. But the shades of red in Roussillon are bewitching. To go or to stay? What a tough decision!

'I really wanted to go back to Gordes, but at least we have an idea what it's like. Besides, there seems to be something very special about Roussillon. So why don't we explore a bit here and find a restaurant up in the village for dinner?' I suggest.

Arne is happy to go either way. He is glad we have finally arrived at a decision.

So we park the car and walk up the steep, winding road to Roussillon. The red walls of the houses are dramatically patterned with dark green ivy and vines heavy with green grapes. Narrow cobblestone paths twist and turn through rows of little houses, from the windows of which hang boxes and pots dripping a profusion of flowers. As with all French villages, there is a church that occupies pride of place in the swelling heart of Roussillon. You can see why the playwright Samuel Beckett chose to live here during World War II.

It is a lovely summer evening, and the tables are out in the main square and along a few of the wider cobblestoned paths. We walk around, absorbing this uniquely charming village and eventually find a quaint little restaurant with a fantastic view of the valley below. What makes the restaurant so breathtakingly beautiful is its roof of flowers. It is actually an open-air restaurant with a wooden trellis for a canopy, from which dangle baskets overflowing with bright little blossoms. They are explosions of colour—red, orange, yellow, purple, pink, white. Vines snake their way through the lattice painted in white and bunches of tender green grapes hang tantalizingly just above our heads.

We have a delicious Provençal meal that we wash down with some terrific Côte d' Rhône red wine. With half-closed eyes I gaze contentedly at Arne. 'This is life,' I murmur.

'Did you enjoy the meal?' the voice of the Frenchwoman who owns the restaurant floats like birdsong among the flowers. She and her husband also cook most of the dishes. The husband is a taciturn, grumpy-looking man, but the wife is a cheerful, chirpy woman with frizzy hair and accented English.

'It was marvellous,' I say, while Arne nods enthusiastically as he swallows yet another mouthful of wine. 'The herbs you used are simply divine.'

'You must take back some Provençal herbs with you. They are special. Have you visited the ochre quarries?' she asks.

'No, we haven't done that, but we have walked through the village. It is very charming,' says Arne.

Pointing to the valley and hills beyond, she says, 'You must walk along the val des Fées. It means the valley of the fairies. It is very beautiful.'

And then, pointing to a hill with a massive gash of red ochre deposit on its façade, she asks, 'Do you know what that is? The falaises de Sang. In English it means "cliffs of blood".'

'They have been named appropriately,' I remark.

'There is a story why we have these cliffs of blood,' says the woman and then goes on to tell us the Legend of Roussillon.

Way back in the twelfth century, the lord of Roussillon, Raymond d'Avignone, had a very beautiful wife named Sermonde. But she was as unfaithful as she was gorgeous. She loved not her husband, but a humble page and troubadour named Guillaume de Cabestang. Their illicit love blossomed, especially when the lord was away on his frequent hunting expeditions. With rising passion, the lovers became reckless. Tongues started wagging, and the lord soon got wind of the affair.

The lord was as ruthless as he was cunning. He invited the page to go out hunting with him, killed him, cut off his head and tore out his heart. But he did not stop there; he had a far more diabolical plan in mind. Back at the castle, he had the heart cooked and served to his unsuspecting wife. After she had finished eating, Raymond d'Avignone told her what she had just had. Crazed with horror, Sermonde ran out of the room, out of the castle, on to the highest part of the hill and threw herself over the cliff.

It is believed the ill-starred lovers were buried together, but not before their blood tinged the surrounding land red.

Nine hundred years have gone by since the birth of that legend, but women continue to suffer in relationships that have turned bitter. My first brush with a marriage that turned fatally bad was almost two decades ago.

In 1980, Shobha, a prominent upcoming actress, committed suicide by hanging from the ceiling fan in her bedroom. Her suicide created a national furore—she was only eighteen years old and had won the prestigious Urvashi award for best actress only a week earlier. She was the most promising star on the south Indian film firmament. But while she was soaring in her career, she was riding the rough seas in her personal life. Her marriage to the already married cameraman Balu Mahendra had fuelled a scandal. Then, just when her career was taking off, she hanged herself from a ceiling fan in her room.

To me her death seemed typically filmi. If she wanted to commit suicide, she could just as easily have swallowed sleeping pills. But these ghastly hanging scenes are enacted so often in movies, actresses probably start believing this is how they must seek death in real life.

I learned from some friends that Shobha's heartbroken parents pretended she was still alive. It had the makings of a good story, so in 1982, two years after Shobha's death, I met her parents, and ended up spending seven and a half hours with them. I was shaken by the encounter. It reinforced my belief that many film people live bizarre, melodramatic lives. They can't seem to distinguish between real and reel life, and they do peculiar things—things which we think happen only in the movies.

Shobha's parents lived in a neat little bungalow in a middle-class neighbourhood in Madras. The front door was open, and as I stood wondering whether to go in, an elderly woman appeared and beckoned me to sit down while she went in to fetch Prema, Shobha's mother. I sat down on the sofa and looked around the typical upper-middle-class drawing-cum-dining room. One half of it was occupied by sofas upholstered in brown, and the other half by a dining table with six chairs. Some six feet separated the dining table from the sofas. I looked around the walls curiously, and counted twenty-nine photographs of Shobha in different poses—laughing, dreamy, coquettish, pensive, sultry, happy, sullen, intense. She really had a charming, mobile face.

Jasmine and crossandru flowers were neatly arranged around each of the mounted photographs. On every photograph, a bindi of red kumkum and a dash of sandalwood paste were smeared on Shobha's forehead. There were a few photographs of Shobha with her parents. I peered at them closely—Prema seemed a typical Malayali mother, plump and pleasant with nice, regular features and her father, a typical Malayali father, slim, with spectacles and a customary moustache. They looked about forty.

Suddenly, I heard a murmuring sound. I looked around but couldn't see anyone. I strained my ears and then felt a chill in my bones. The sound was human. There was somebody else in the room. I scanned it frantically, even looked behind the curtains, but couldn't see anybody. It was spooky. I almost expected the front door to slam shut, trapping me inside this strange house with its stranger sounds. But it didn't. It was eleven in the morning and the sun was shining brightly outside. Everything seemed normal.

The murmuring stopped. I relaxed, feeling utterly foolish. It must have been the palm fronds swaying in the breeze. Except, there was no breeze. It was a still, humid day. I must have imagined it. I delved into my bag for a book to read and froze. There was that murmuring sound again. I pricked up my ears. It was coming from inside the room, very close, from the middle of the room—yes, the sound was coming from the space between the sofa and the dining table. Cautiously, I got up and tiptoed to the large sofa and leaned over to look behind. I gasped in shock.

An old man, bare-chested with a white mundu, sat cross-legged on the floor. White-haired and emaciated, he looked like a sanyasi. He was sitting in front of a red Samsonite suitcase and going through photographs, clothes, and some accessories. All the while he was mumbling under his breath. Sometimes his voice rose, maintained a steady monotone for a few minutes, then it subsided. I had been sitting in the room for fifteen minutes, and I hadn't sensed his presence. I had no idea who he was, and I didn't dare disturb him. I tiptoed back and sat down on a single-seater sofa.

I wished Prema would hurry. The house was giving me the creeps, with its oppressive air of death, neglect and disuse. There was a film of dust on the music system, clocks and other gadgets, indicating they had not been used for a long time.

I fished out my book and began reading. I must have been reading for perhaps ten minutes when I had the sensation of being watched. I looked up and nearly screamed. I thought I was seeing a ghost. At the doorway that connected the dining room to a bedroom stood a skeletal woman in white. She was staring at me, unblinking but in a peculiarly sightless way. She stood erect and motionless, clutching her white sari tightly around herself as if it were a shroud. She looked about sixty years old.

Without moving and without shifting her gaze, she said tonelessly, 'You have come to see Shobha. Please come with me.'

Saying this she turned and disappeared into a side room. I didn't know what else to do but follow her.

I entered a small, unlit, windowless room. I couldn't make out anything in the dark except the silhouette of this wraith-like figure in white. I had no idea who she was. Then she switched on the light.

It was like floodlights coming on in a stadium. The light was so bright, the transition from darkness to light so sudden and blinding, that I instinctively closed my eyes.

And squinted them open to see a life-size cardboard cut-out of Shobha.

'Sho mol, see, a journalist has come to see you,' said the old woman to the cut-out and then turning to me she said: 'Meet my daughter Shobha.'

I didn't know where to look—at the life-size cut-out of the dead daughter or the corpse-like mother. I couldn't believe my eyes. This woman couldn't possibly be Prema. In two years, how could a person have changed so much? She had lost twenty kilos and gained twenty years.

The tiny room where Shobha 'lived' resembled a garish film set. Shobha was clad in a gaudy green sari with heavy zari. Fresh jasmine flowers adorned her black cardboard hair. There was a kumkum bindi on her forehead. In the bright light, her necklace, bangles and zari glinted wickedly. The cardboard cut-out was placed in a corner and positioned in such a way that for a moment you felt a real person was greeting you with a namaste and a big smile: parted, painted red lips framing even white teeth.

Shobha's room was actually the puja room. It was crammed with flowers, garlands, lamps, photographs and pictures of Hindu gods. It was hot and airless in the over-bright room, and I felt sweat break out on my brow. Prema was oblivious to the heat, but I couldn't take it any more. I quietly left and stepped back into the living room, which in comparison seemed cool and refreshing. I took a deep breath. I hadn't realized I had been holding it for a long time.

Prema switched off the light and followed me into the living room, where I was able to see her better. I could see traces of the plump, pleasant woman in the photographs. She looked very old, but in a tragic way, more beautiful. Her features had become bleak, but they were chiselled and sharp. Her brooding lips, shaped like a cupid's bow, were dark and drooping. Her sunken eyes were huge and lost. Dark circles around her vacant eyes gave her a hunted, haunted look.

'Why are there kumkum bindis on all these photographs?' I asked to get a conversation going.

'You see, Sho mol loved kumkum bindis. You could never see her without it,' replied Prema. 'Mol' is a Malayalam endearment used for daughters.

The decibel level of the mumbling rose, and I looked questioningly at Prema.

'That's Sho mol's father. He lives there. He keeps all his worldly possessions in that suitcase. He sleeps on the floor there, and I sleep on the sofa here. You see, after Sho mol went, we took a vow never to sleep in the bedroom,' said Prema.

Suddenly her voice faltered. Tears welled up in her eyes, making them seem larger and more lost than ever. She looked like a koala bear, except she was so thin and un-cuddly.

I couldn't believe the old man was Shobha's father. He too had aged at least twenty years in the last two years. In the photographs he appeared dark-haired, but now he was white with a thick white beard that made him look like a renunciate. What apparently gave meaning to his life was his conviction that Shobha did not commit suicide. She was murdered. He was constantly plotting and planning how to avenge his daughter's death, how to find evidence to prove his suspicions. He hated Shobha's husband Balu. That hate was eating into his vitals, but paradoxically, it kept him alive. He could not forgive his son-in-law for the pain and misery he insisted Balu had caused his darling daughter.

When her Sho mol was alive, Prema had lovingly

attended to her tiniest needs. She continued to do so even after she died, filling her days with little rituals that brought meaning to her wasted life. It also helped her pass the time. Every day she glided about, cleaning the photographs and putting fresh bindis and flowers. In the puja room, she conducted an elaborate ritual of 'dressing up Sho mol'. She rearranged the cut-out's sari, smoothing out all the wrinkles, real and imaginary. She adjusted the flowing pallu, applied fresh kumkum on the forehead and flowers on the hair. It was difficult to change the sari every day, so she did it every fortnight. 'Sho mol must always look neat and beautiful. Isn't she a blossoming actress with the Urvashi in her hand?' Prema said to me.

'So how did Shobha get into acting?' I asked, hoping to begin the interview.

I realized I was addressing a non-person. Prema was not with me. She was sitting there ghost-like, but her vacant eyes saw right through me.

'It's time for Sho mol's lunch. I'll just be back,' she said and disappeared only to reappear moments later with a green banana leaf on which water had just been sprinkled. She put spoonfuls of rice and curry on the leaf and took it to the puja room so that 'Sho mol can eat in peace and privacy'.

Either Prema was stark raving mad, or she was a terrific actress. There were times when I got the feeling she was putting on a melodramatic act for me. This business of dressing up and feeding Sho mol seemed one big fake scene, inspired by the movies and designed to shock me. For that reason alone I spent over seven hours there, just to figure out whether her sorrow was genuine, whether the make-believe world she had spun was a real make-believe world or a carefully orchestrated show to fuel my sympathy.

Shobha's father K.P.P. Menon did not arouse my suspicion or any ambivalent feelings. He really had gone nuts. But Prema had been an actress before her marriage, and it could be that she was play-acting the greatest tragic role of her life for my benefit.

After seven hours, I was reasonably sure that Prema had created this artificial world as a crutch—false it was, but it forced the heavy hours to tick by. For, after her only child's death, the world stood still for her. There was no meaning, no movement in it. To keep herself going, she had constructed this elaborate world where Sho mol still existed, still needed her. What moored this fragile make-believe world to reality was the set of elaborate daily rituals. It was not that her melodrama was fake; it was just that it was inspired by the movies. She borrowed images, dialogue and situations from films because those were her reference points. She believed that cinema imitates life, so when faced with a crisis she, like her daughter Shobha, imitated cinema in real life.

Shobha made her debut in films when she was three years old. Roles came easily because Prema was a reasonably well-known actress. Prema maintained that Shobha turned out to be a very good actress because she was basically an excellent mimic. She would have everyone in splits imitating the much older Balu Mahendra—his peculiar walk with shoulders slouched to one side and light metre in one hand.

Balu Mahendra's relationship with Shobha was strange to say the least. At first he referred to her as his friend's daughter, then he called her his 'niece', and then she became his 'daughter'. Shobha was only a few years older than his son, Gowrishankar. Balu's wife Ahileshwari wanted a daughter, but he would not hear of it saying, 'When we have Sho, why do we need another?' He gifted Shobha a beautiful illustrated edition of *My Favourite Fairy Tales,* with the inscription 'To my darling daughter from Papa, B.M.'

In fact, till a few months before their marriage, Balu wrote letters to Shobha addressing her as 'My darling daughter' and signed 'Papa'. She always called him Balu 'uncle'.

It was after Shobha's eighteenth birthday that Prema saw a distinct change in her daughter's behaviour. 'Sho started becoming distant, particularly from me. She was innocent and gullible,' Prema reminisced during the interview. 'All kinds of lies were fed to her—that I was repressive and wanted to grab all her money. Because I was quite strict with her, she believed a lot of things. Sho mol and I were so close, we did everything together. Suddenly she became aloof and irritable. This was around her eighteenth birthday. It was drilled into her head that she would soon be a major and could do things on her own, without seeking our permission. Whenever she set off for shooting, she'd always kiss me first. All these little gestures of affection, of our love for each other, stopped. It was Shobha's body, but Balu's mind. She was very imitative—she began imitating Balu, his actions and his mannerisms. A girl who had read only fairy tales and comics started talking about all kinds of intellectual things. When she spoke, it was as if Balu was speaking.'

In a sudden decision, Shobha got married to Balu in January 1980. There was a press conference followed by a garlanding ceremony in a hotel. The marriage ruptured relations between parents and daughter. Prema could not forgive Balu and was violent in her reaction to him. This pushed Shobha further away, though she continued to live with her parents even after the marriage. Shobha became sullen and bitter. It was around this time that Prema began to suspect her daughter was under the influence of drugs. 'There were nights when she used to thrash about on the bed. Her appetite was ruined, and she lost weight rapidly,' said Prema.

Then one day, six weeks after her marriage, Shobha told her mother to return all the money she had earned during the past two years because 'Balu says now that we are husband and wife, we must file our income tax together.' Prema lashed out: 'He is not your husband. He is Ahila's. You are just his keep.' When Shobha showed her 'tali' (mangalsutra), Prema shouted hysterically: 'Your tali is meaningless. Even prostitutes wear talis in hotels to avoid suspicion. Yours has as much sanctity as that.' Shobha burst into tears and hearing her sobs, Balu who was in the living room, came rushing in and dragged her away. That was the last time Prema saw her daughter alive.

According to Prema, Balu extracted considerable leverage out of this episode, claiming that it proved what he had always suspected—that she was after Shobha's money. Prema erupted: 'For God's sake, what would I do with Shobha's money? She was our only wealth. Do you believe we were after our own daughter's money? How could he even think like that? I lost my temper because I felt so bad that my daughter had been duped into believing she was legitimately married.'

Was the lady protesting too much, or was I witnessing the anguish of a wronged, heartbroken mother? I was inclined to believe the latter.

After they walked out of her parents' home, Balu and Shobha initially stayed at the Atlantic Hotel. Later they took a house in the middle-class neighbourhood of K.K. Nagar. Prema refused to step into her daughter's house. But Menon visited her several times. 'I used to hang around like a beggar outside her house, waiting to see her come and go. Sometimes I went in and talked to her. In fact, the Friday that she died, I was supposed to have lunch with her,' he said.

Neither Shobha nor Balu informed her parents when she won the Urvashi award. They heard about it from a friend. When a thrilled Menon rushed to Shobha's house, he was told she had already flown to Delhi to receive the award and would be back on 27 April. Said Menon angrily, 'That was a deliberate lie. She came back on 26 April. I wanted to go to the airport and see her coming back with the Urvashi. I knew I would not be able to go near her, but at least from a distance, hidden in the crowd, I could have proudly watched her arriving with the prestigious prize. I was deprived even of that. As nobody gave me a copy of the photograph of Shobha receiving the award from the president, I wrote to (Minister) Vasant Sathe. He was kind enough to send me one.'

By the time the photograph reached Menon, his daughter was dead. The precise circumstances that impelled Shobha to kill herself are not known, but her life must have swung wildly from the heights of public acclaim to the depths of personal anguish. Four days after she returned to Madras with the Urvashi award, Shobha committed suicide.

Prema recalled an incident from Shobha's childhood, when she was only five years old. She had to die in the arms of Malayalam films' evergreen hero Prem Nazir. She portrayed the death scene so well that everybody on the sets was teary eyed. An overwhelmed Nazir picked up little Shobha and hugged her tightly, saying: 'You will definitely win the Urvashi award one day.' She did, and within a week was enacting her own death scene, alone and unseen.

Shortly after Shobha's death, Balu sent a note to Menon saying, 'Out of human consideration, sympathy and goodwill, I am returning Shobha's things.' He'd made out a list of belongings, which included five bras and seven panties!

The issue of *Sunday* magazine in which this article on Shobha's parents was published was a sell-out. For the first time in the history of *Sunday* in Tamil Nadu, the magazine was sold in black at ten times its normal price. (That sounds more grand than saying it was sold for ten rupees—those were the days when the cover price was only one rupee. Even the most expensive magazine then did not cost more than three rupees). Balu Mahendra was untouched by the scandal. He went on to become even more famous as a cinematographer.

A few years after the story was published, Prema committed suicide. I was not surprised. She must have found it impossible to sustain her make-believe world.

Rewards are big in the Indian film industry, but sometimes there is a very high price to pay as well. Two decades have flown by and several more actresses have opted to kill themselves rather than live on in their world.

Silk Smitha, the voluptuous vamp of south Indian films cast a spell, especially on men, with her sultry, bedroom eyes; her inviting, luscious lips; pointed, thrusting breasts; and heavy, quivering thighs. During her sexy song-and-dance scenes, collective lust rose like steam in south Indian cinema halls. Sexually frustrated men ventilated through salacious catcalls, sighs, yells and even urgent masturbation. Her popularity was so high at one point that no distributor was willing to show a film unless it had a 'Silk Smitha scene' in it.

My friend and film journalist Vyas Chand arranged a

meeting for me with Silk Smitha at her home. I was thoroughly shocked to discover a thin, drab woman who I first mistook for a maid-servant. She wore a dirty salwar kameez and looked wan, wasted and unwashed. Her hair was brown and scraggly. She was indistinguishable from millions of lower-class women. Even after summoning all my powers of imagination I could not relate this pathetic woman to the screen sex goddess. She told me her story, and it was a sad one, of financial, physical and sexual exploitation. Everyone in the film industry, every man she met, from producer to light-boy, constantly harassed her with innuendos and propositions. When I met her she was broke, sick and lonely. You had to dig to find her self-esteem.

That was the first time I personally witnessed the chasm between fame and reality, between artificial public persona and real private individual, between adulation and loneliness, between public acclaim and private grief. In public, she had the world curled around her sexy little finger; in reality she was curled and trapped around the greasy little fingers of the film industry's sleazeballs. Some time after I met her, she committed suicide. So did another sexy actress called Patapat Jayalakshmi. The most recent case of suicide was in November 2000 when actress Viji ended her life because her lover, a film director, 'betrayed her love'. The already married man had refused to marry her. She too hanged herself from a ceiling fan.

One way or another, Shobha and these other well-known actresses were driven to suicide by their families or their ill-starred relationships. If this is the reality for these so-called famous, successful women, how much worse must it be for unknown Indian women? Surveys have in fact shown that home is the most dangerous place for her to be—starting with the womb. Female embryos are aborted;

newborn girls are smothered or their heads smashed; during childhood, girls are given less to eat than their brothers; during adolescence, they often become victims of incest—usually at the hands of uncles, brothers, cousins or even fathers—and after marriage, husbands and in-laws murder them for money. Women are battered and broken, sometimes even burnt to death.

Two years after marriage, twenty-year-old Sunita Vir was battling for life in a hospital bed with ninety-six per cent burns. She was beyond medical help. Her dying declaration read like a horror story. Her father-in-law Subh Ram and brother-in-law Dalbir had held her down on a cot while Chand Vir, her husband, doused her with kerosene. One can imagine Sunita's terror explode into excruciating pain as mother-in-law Savitri lit the match.

Sunita was being punished for her father's failure to deliver an additional dowry of new appliances. Two years later, a district court for the village of Lowarkhurd in Haryana sentenced Sunita's husband and in-laws to life imprisonment. Sunita's case is unusual, not because she was murdered by her own family, but because the guilty were punished. On an average, only one per cent of dowry death cases result in conviction.

In modern times, dowry offers a short cut to acquiring material wealth. It is considered disgraceful to have an unwed daughter in the house, so parents scrounge and incur huge debts to buy all the appliances needed to get their daughter married. If they have a son, they make it back, but doomed is a family that has only daughters. It's a sure-fire guarantee for a life of debt and misery.

Dowry deaths have increased nearly fifteen-fold, from 400 a year in the mid-1980s to nearly 6000 in the 1990s. Studies indicate that dowry deaths usually occur within the first three years of marriage, predominantly in lower-class, mother-dominated families. In each and every case, the mother-in-law is an accused. A survivor of oppression in the early days of her own marriage, the matriarch inflicts the same mental, emotional and physical abuse on her daughter-in-law. Semi-educated, if not illiterate, and absolutely dependent on her husband's family, the bride has no option but to endure the humiliation and torture, even when she fears it will culminate in her own murder. Her parents are usually unwilling to take her back because an abandoned daughter is as much a social stigma and an economic burden as an unmarried one.

Often, the in-laws continue to extort more goods after the wedding. When their demands can no longer be met, they dispose of the bride by poisoning, strangling or burning her to pass it off as a kitchen accident. Then the son can remarry and make fresh demands on the new bride's parents. Sundari Nanda, a policewoman who has handled many dowry death cases says, 'Consumerism has become a national virus. Today many families use dowry as a tool to fulfil their material expectations.' Many middle and lower middle-class families have no legitimate means of acquiring the new range of consumer goods flooding the market. Traditional cultural mores then provide the means—parents of bridegrooms virtually sell their sons for a list of household appliances—refrigerators, washing machines, music systems, scooters or cars.

Sunita's in-laws were possessed by unquenchable greed. At the time of her marriage, her father Kalam Singh, a farmer whose annual income was Rs 30,000, had incurred a massive debt to put together a dowry worth Rs 1.5 lakh, which included cash, steel trunks, cupboards, a sewing machine, kitchen utensils and—the crowning glory—a black-and-white television set. Yet, ten days after the wedding, Sunita's in-laws, who lived a spartan peasant life, began badgering and eventually beating her up for more dowry. They wanted an air cooler and a refrigerator. 'How could I pay more for one daughter when I have two more unmarried daughters?' asked Kalam Singh in despair when I met him a short while after Sunita's death. In jail, Sunita's murderous mother-in-law was unrepentant, wracked not by guilt but by one single worry—her locked-up house. 'I hope all my possessions will be safe,' she fretted.

Dowry harassment—which does not always result in death—is part of a nationwide pattern of domestic violence. But domestic violence is not confined to Hindu India. It is prevalent in Muslim Pakistan as well. It seems to be part of a feudal, patriarchal South Asian culture and continues to prevail in areas characterized by feudalism, poor education and low status of women.

In a hospital in Pakistan, eighteen-year-old Noreen lay badly burnt and dying.

She was seven months pregnant. Her heart was more broken than her skin. 'It is my fate,' she said. 'From childhood I have seen nothing but suffering.'

Noreen claimed she was burnt when her kitchen stove caught fire, but activist Shahnaz Bhukari did not believe her. She asked, 'The whole body is totally burnt and the husband, lying in the next room, could not hear her shrieks of pain. Is that possible?'

The victims dare not blame their families. If they recover, they will have to go back to the same house.

Zuleika Bibi's face was almost lost in the veils of her sorrow. Weeks had passed, but time had in no way diminished her grief. Her daughter Shamshad had been burnt to death, allegedly by her in-laws. Zuleika was reconciled to her daughter's death. But what continued to torment her was the thought of the pain her daughter had suffered. Breaking into sobs, the anguished mother said, 'What causes me so much agony is that they burnt my daughter. If they had poisoned her or shot her, I wouldn't have been so distressed.'

In Pakistan, this ghastly phenomenon of burning women is an intrinsic aspect of domestic violence, not related to dowry and not confined to any religious community. Victims include Christians. Irene, a young Pakistani Christian woman, was burnt by her in-laws. They claimed the stove burst when she was warming milk for her baby. The infant was eighteen days old and was being breastfed!

Burning is also an instrument of punishment. Fathers burn their daughters or brothers burn sisters for daring to fall in love, husbands burn their wives because they want a new wife. Domestic quarrels are the main reason for this shocking abuse. And the quarrels can be unbelievably petty, on account of something as trivial as a man getting infuriated because his wife overcooked the food, put too much salt or used his soap!

It's not just marriage, even love can turn fatally bad. Very often, a woman gets entangled in a relationship that, instead of being a garland of love, curls into a noose.

One of the most gruesome punishments meted out was to two young lovers in the village of Mehrana in Uttar Pradesh. Roshni was a fifteen-year-old upper-caste girl, bright and light-skinned. She was a typical village girl in many ways. But she fell in love with a young man named Brijendra, who was five years older than her, and a Dalit. It was impossible for them to meet secretly—everybody knew everybody else in the village and news of such illicit trysts fly faster than pollen. So Roshni and Brijendra eloped.

Tradition made their crime unpardonable and punishable with death—or so decreed the village council comprising upper-caste men. Retribution struck as soon as the young couple returned. Brijendra and his friend Ram Kishen, another Dalit who had helped the couple in their getaway, as well as their fathers and brothers, were all beaten up with sticks. Then the two young men were hung upside down, and their lips and genitals scorched with burning cloth.

At dawn, a terrified Roshni was dragged out of her house and along with the two young men, taken to the village banyan tree that spread over a temple to Lord Shiva. Ropes were thrown around their necks and then the fathers, including Roshni's, were forced to hoist their children up. The parents could not summon the strength to strangle their children, so bystanders completed the task. When the youngsters were taken down, Ram Kishen was dead. But eyewitnesses told me that Roshni and Brijendra may still have been alive. All three were then placed on a pyre and cremated.

When the police arrived to investigate, Mangtu Ram, the most powerful upper-caste man in Mehrana, proudly admitted to the executions. He and twenty others were immediately arrested, but they insisted they had acted correctly. The community's reputation was paramount. 'If we had not taken severe action against them, our entire community would have been disgraced,' said Thakur Lal, a relative of Mangtu Ram. 'Nobody would have married Jat girls from this village.'

Bishan Devi, Roshni's mother, was furious with her daughter but obviously distraught at her grisly death. She said, 'I pleaded for her life with the elders. Drive us away from the village or burn our house down, but spare my daughter, I said. But they told me, "She is not your daughter, she is ours."'

Yet, this same community has no compunction about throwing their women out on the streets when they become widows. What happens to the community's honour and pride then, one wonders. In spite of social reforms, poor widows especially in the backward areas suffer a decline in social status when their husbands die. It is common in this strata of society to treat widows as outcastes, more so if they are childless. It is as if they have outlived their utility on earth. Custom demands they dress only in white, eat frugally and shun cosmetics and jewellery. They must not be attractive to men hereafter. They must avoid garlic and other spices lest they arouse lust in them. Sometimes, poor families already short of food force widows to leave. Remarriage of widows is taboo, so the hapless women are encouraged to renounce the world and their families and head for a pilgrim town, so that they can dedicate their remaining years to prayer. And if they die in a holy city, they will not be reborn.

A large number of destitute north Indian widows flock to the sacred city of Vrindavan, the legendary birthplace of Lord Krishna. It is a beautiful place in mythology, with charming meadows, gurgling brooks and sweeping orchards, where beautiful, lissome maidens frolic. In reality, it is an ugly, chaotic urban sprawl, noisy, polluted and congested with its teeming people and diesel vehicles, special only because of the large number of temples.

I visited Vrindavan ten years ago to do a story on the plight of these widows. At that time there were about 2,000 of them in the town. In 1910, a philanthropist businessman had set up an ashram for widows. Here they were assured of at least one frugal meal a day. They were given six white saris and a blanket every year. They also got one rupee a day for chanting, meditating and reading the Vedas for eight hours.

It was a chore, but most of them had no other way to kill time. Besides, they were so desperately poor they needed every penny they could lay their hands on. Every morning these desolate women huddled together to pray in the ashram's grimy hall. Bored and melancholic and dressed in cheap white cotton saris, they looked like lost souls from a bygone era. On one side of the hall was a tiny, makeshift temple. At its centre were idols of Lord Krishna and his consort Radha. Sunlight hardly penetrated the dark, gloomy, high-ceilinged hall. In one corner, a naked, low-watt electric bulb cast a dingy arc of light, as pathetic and irrelevant as the widows. There was nothing devotional about either the room or the women. The atmosphere was heavy and depressing. S.L. Mishra, a local priest, said, 'These women have only death to look forward to.'

Their misery worsened in winter. Most of them owned only a threadbare shawl to protect themselves from the biting cold. Heads bowed and eyes shut, they punctuated their dejected chant with the clanging of small cymbals. 'Hare Krishna, Hare Krishna, Hare Hare,' they intoned endlessly. Sometimes their chant trailed off into an unintelligible murmur as some of them nodded off to sleep. Whenever the drone slowed down, the leader raised her voice—a cue to the sleepy, listless women to chant more enthusiastically. Those who had fallen asleep jolted out of their slumber and for a while the decibel level of the intonation rose, only to subside after a while. The monotonous routine was repeated for eight hours in a desolate rhythm of compulsion and boredom, compulsion and boredom. A woman sat near the entrance to make sure nobody sneaked out during the prayers.

Some of them did, not because they wanted to run away from the monotony of prayer, but to augment their meagre income by working as servants in homes nearby. But most were too old, ill or crippled to do any work. Yet, they too had to earn something over and above their niggardly stipend, which was not sufficient to meet their personal expenses that included rent. So they tried to raise more money by begging, selling some of their saris or even hawking part of their food rations, which was only fifty grams of dal and two hundred and fifty grams of rice to begin with. Some of the women summoned up the courage to agitate and even staged a demonstration asking for increased stipend. They were given an additional 25 paise a day! Grumbled M.P. Sharma, a clerk in the ashram, 'These women know only how to complain. If it hadn't been for us, they would have been dead long ago.'

The widows knew that, and most of them looked forward to death as a liberation from this life of loneliness and drudgery. Karuna, one of the widows of Vrindavan, was the epitome of misery. She was an ugly crone—wrinkled and bent almost double. She had no idea how old she was. She seemed at least eighty, but she might have been only fifty; poverty, misery and hardship age a person immeasurably. She said she had been in Vrindavan for something like 'twenty-five years, maybe thirty-five, maybe forty, who knows'. Somewhere along the line she had stopped counting.

Her story was typical. A native of Bengal, she was married at eleven and widowed at nineteen. At first, the members of her family took care of her, but after some years, they began to mistreat her. Penniless, she set off for

Vrindavan in the hope of getting some food, and 'perhaps the opportunity to pray'. She did not even have money for a train ticket. But when the ticket collector came around, she told him she was on her way to spend her final years in Vrindavan, and he left her alone.

I spent a day with Karuna and experienced the pathos of her existence. After morning prayer, she hobbled out of the hall with the aid of a crooked walking stick. On the way home, she stopped and bought half a cup of milk. 'Today I will give myself the luxury of a glass of tea,' she croaked in delighted anticipation. 'It's very cold.' From an earthen pot of curd, the corpulent shopkeeper scooped out a cupful of whey and poured it into her little, dented aluminium container. He did not charge her for that. She thanked him gratefully. The day was turning out to be very special. With the liquid, she could make a curry to flavour her midday gruel. Karuna then opened the tiny bundle of coins she had tied to the edge of her sari, paid the shopkeeper for the milk and shuffled down the narrow overcrowded lane to her tiny room. A thin, worn mattress, a clothes-line, a bundle of clothes and a few utensils—these were the sum total of her worldly possessions. 'I came here to die, but so many years have gone by,' she said. 'Death would be better than this miserable life.'

As I write this, almost ten years after my encounter with Karuna, the only comfort I can draw is that she must surely be dead by now.

SUFFER, LITTLE CHILDREN

'Daddy kutta, are you sleeping?' calls out my mother, Nancy, affectionately when she hears my father pouring a glass of buttermilk for himself in the dining room.

It's past midnight and my mother, Zubin and I are lying on the broad, wooden family bed, gossiping in my bedroom in my parents' home in Kochi. My mother is sprawled like a queen in the middle, and we both are lying on either side. Three generations indulging in the favourite family pastime—catching up with scandal. My mother is an encyclopaedia of trivia. She knows how everyone is related to everyone all the way back in time to when we were all swinging from the trees—'You've met Valsa, she is the daughter of Thomasachayan, whose sister's husband's aunt is married to Thattarathatta Chackochen, whose wife's step-sister's grandfather's funeral you attended in 1984.'

My father, Simon, who thinks gossip is a frightful waste of time, never joins these sessions. My mother prefers to keep it that way because she likes to concentrate on gossip about his side of the family. She can be wickedly funny, and when egged on by Zubin and me, her tongue gets more acerbic. Our cackling gets louder as the night wears on, waking up my father. A man of methodical habits, he had gone to bed as usual at eleven, after watching Star News and taking his vitamins.

My mother calls him Daddy, the way he is addressed by my sister Sunita, Zubin and me. Now she adds 'kutta', a term of endearment in Malayalam, because she is in a fine mood.

My father ignores her silly question. Obviously he has woken up, he couldn't be in the dining room otherwise. But my mother trills again, coquettishly.

'Daddy kutta, say no, are you sleeping?' she coos, louder this time.

'Yes, I am sleeping. What do you want?' he growls, clearly not amused.

'Nothing, nothing at all, just calling you out of affection.'

'Hah, don't bore me,' he snaps querulously.

Zubin and I burst out laughing.

'Oh, Simon Saar is in a bad mood,' my mother says, grimacing in mock-seriousness. Then, turning to me she grumbles, 'Look at your father, he barks when I am being romantic. I might as well have married an Alsatian dog. It's impossible to flirt with him. I should have married someone else.'

'It's not too late yet,' says my father drily. 'At least I will get some peace of mind at this late stage in my life.'

'And I will get some excitement. Living for forty-six years with a man who looks three hundred years old and behaves as if he's six hundred is not much fun,' says my mother.

'Living with a woman who is sixty but behaves as if she's sixteen is not much fun either. You are so silly. If I had married a mature, efficient woman, I would have really gone places,' retorts my father.

'Like hell! You would have been stuck in Varapetty, wandering about bare-chested, chewing betel nut and fathering fourteen children while your efficient wife efficiently cleaned chicken shit from the verandas all day long. It's because of me that you became sophisticated and travelled around the world. Whatever you have achieved in life is because of me. Nancys have always brought luck to their husbands—look at Ronald Reagan, Henry Kissinger, Zubin Mehta. It is a fancy to marry Nancy,' she ends with a flourish.

'It is a pity to marry Nanjikutty,' retorts my father, using the Malayalam version of her name.

'Why do you call me Nanjikutty? Why can't you call me Nancy? You're just envious. See how modern my mother was, she gave me such a beautiful, posh name. And your mother named you after a simpleton in a silly nursery rhyme.'

'I was named after Christ's apostle, and you know it. What a burden you are. Christ had to carry his cross only for a few hours, but I have been carrying mine for forty-six years.'

'Then you will become a saint. St. Simon the Second,' teases my mother, bursting into a loud peal of laughter. 'Well, St. Simon is better than Simple Simon. Aren't you lucky? I bring prosperity to you on earth, and because of me you will even have a special place in heaven. What more can you ask for?'

Zubin and I are giggling away. We love these exchanges between my father and mother. There can't be two more dissimilar people in a marriage. My mother is emotional, he is rational; she is lazy, he is hardworking; she is impractical, he is pragmatic; she is soft, he is tough; she is chaotic, he is organized; she is earthy, he is urbane; she is timid, he is brave. But both invariably come to the same conclusions—he is guided by common sense, she by intuition. Both also have a robust sense of humour. They have been terrific parents to Suni and me. Thanks to their love and constant caring, we had a wonderfully secure, stable and happy childhood.

So very different from the childhood of the little boys and girls I have encountered in my professional life. Like the sixteen children in the north Indian village of Tilthi, who were sitting in three sheds weaving exquisite Persian-style carpets. Heads bent, they worked fast, deftly moving their fingers in and out of the large, tightly threaded looms. Small, dark and undernourished, they were between eight and fourteen years of age.

Twelve-year-old Pannu never aspired to be a weaver. He didn't want to leave home. But when he was eight years old, his father Raghuvir 'lent' Pannu and his elder brother to loom-owner Ramnath Yadav for Rs 2500. Raghuvir, an impoverished Dalit, needed the money to urgently repair his hut, which had collapsed in heavy rains.

In the beginning, Pannu missed his parents terribly. 'I felt like running away, but I never had the courage,' he said. Life was hard in his village in the most backward district of Palamau in Bihar. But he was with his parents, who were kind, even though they could not always afford to give him a meal. It was much better than the life he led with Yadav. Here Pannu and the other children lived in filth. Twice a day they ate a meal of coarse rice and tasteless curry that had as many stones as lentils. They ate in a kitchen that also served as a cowshed. At night, the children were herded into a small thatched hut to sleep on a bed of straw. Sometimes when orders piled up, they were allowed to sleep for only three hours a night. If they stopped or even slowed down due to fatigue, Yadav beat them.

All sixteen children were 'bonded labourers'— individuals or members of families who had borrowed money from landlords or moneylenders for a variety of essentials such as clothes or medicines, or to pay for a wedding. They repaid the debt by living a life of servitude that lasted years, decades, even generations. There are at least three million bonded workers in India, though some activists claim the figure is as high as five million.

Thirty-year-old farm-worker Chinta was bonded to the local landlord Dharamjit Tiwari, in a small village in Uttar Pradesh, twenty years ago. He was still struggling to work off an unknown sum of money borrowed by his great-grandfather decades ago. For his labour, Chinta, like his grandfather and father before him, was paid one and a half kilos of rice a day and nothing more. Obviously, to survive he had to borrow money. His landlord told him the family's cumulative debt now stood at nearly Rs 20,000, a massive sum for a landless farm worker. At this rate, even his great-grandchildren would be condemned to a life of servitude to work off the family's debt.

Government officials and NGOs are striving to change the rules. Labour activists scour the countryside in search of these hapless victims, especially children. They cooperate with the local magistrates and policemen to conduct raids to rescue them. I went along on one such raid that rescued Pannu and his group. After ordering the puzzled children into the afternoon sunshine, the chief of the raiding mission, Surendra Pandey, told them, 'You are free. We will take you home tonight.'

Pannu was thrilled, but some of the other children were afraid their parents would beat them for returning home. Going by past experience, these children would soon be back at work, if not at the looms—these days there is growing pressure on loom-owners to desist from employing children—then in nearby farms or highway dhabas.

Children in South Asia are exploited for reasons ranging from sex to sheer greed. In Sri Lanka, little boys are forced to satiate the hunger of German paedophiles. From Bangladesh, Pakistan and India, little boys are sent to the Persian Gulf to serve as jockeys in camel races to amuse the sheikhs.

The lid to this scandal blew open after an immigration inspector at New Delhi's Indira Gandhi International Airport, R.C. Ramchander, became suspicious when two little boys, headed for the Persian Gulf emirate of Abu Dhabi, stood before him for clearance. Their passports said they were ten years old, but they looked much younger, maybe five or six, at best. He detained them and their adult escorts and turned them over to the police.

Investigations revealed that Habib was five and Pandiya seven years old. Both were unsuspecting commodities in a thriving new business: the export of camel jockeys. Small children are smuggled out from the impoverished areas of South Asia to the oil-rich states of the Middle East, where the Bedouin pastime of camel racing has become the premier sport of sultans, emirs and sheikhs. To get the best speed, jockeys must weigh less than 25 kg. Who but children can weigh so little? Some of the child jockeys are only four or five years old. They are so small and frightened that they are often fastened to the camels' backs with Velcro! The terrified screams of the child goad the animal into running faster.

Some of the children are kidnapped from their homes by touts. But most are lured with the promise of jobs as domestic help in rich Arab homes. Greed, poverty and desperation force many parents to part with their little children. Once gone, in many cases, they have never been heard of again.

But not all parents part with their children. Most poor people have no choice but to keep their children with them, for the same reason: to earn money. Poverty robs these children of their innocence and leisure.

Five-year-old Hussain could not afford the luxury of play. He was born to a poverty-stricken ragpicker family in New Delhi. Every day, for eight hours, the family sifted through stinking garbage dumps, searching for bottles, papers and plastic, which they could sell to shops that recycled waste. The family earned thirty to sixty rupees a day. Hussain had to bid goodbye to childhood, education and playtime because he had to contribute to the family income. He was small and newly initiated to ragpicking, so his contribution to the family coffer was a meagre one rupee a day. But every penny was needed for the day-to-day survival of the family.

They lived in a tiny, shabby one-room hovel on the pavement. For a roof they had blue plastic sheets, and for a floor, they had the ground. Their daily income was sometimes insufficient for one square meal a day. Desperation often drove Hussain's father to steal. But he invariably got caught. The cops would arrive and give the whole family, including little Hussain, a sound warning and a sounder thrashing.

Hussain was small, but he had his ambitions. Actually two. One was short term—to acquire a pair of boots (he went barefoot as he did not own chappals), and the other was long-term—when he grew up, he wanted to become a policeman. He loved that baton. Right now, he and his family were at the receiving end. But he longed for the day when he could be at the giving end.

There was another Hussain who too spent a childhood devoid of play—in his case the problem was not poverty, but disease. He suffered from thalassaemia, a hereditary blood disorder caused by a defective gene. His body couldn't produce red blood cells. The disease is prevalent in India, but is almost an epidemic in the beautiful Indian Ocean archipelago of Maldives. One out of every 120 newborns there is thalassaemic. The disease surfaces when both parents are carriers, and a quarter of the children born to such parents are thalassaemic.

Both treatment and cure are extremely expensive, so the government is focusing heavily on prevention, which is simple enough. Couples intending to marry must have a blood test and, should both be thalassaemic carriers, they must rethink their decision or be fully aware of the danger that lurks ahead if they beget children. Blood tests are now done in schools, so that young boys and girls and their parents (who often arrange the marriage) know their status and can make wedding plans accordingly. So, while in other parts of the world parents ask for horoscopes or dating youngsters ask for each other's sun signs, in the Maldives they want to know each other's blood group.

One of the reasons for the high incidence of thalassaemia in the Maldives is that there were no blood tests done in the past, and the disease spread rapidly as the conservative Muslims tended to marry within their own community.

Four-year-old Hussain Fatheem lived in the capital city, Male. From the time he was born, he was not just pale and frail, but constantly sick, with fever, cough and cold. At eight months, a blood test confirmed the terrifying news that he was thalassaemic.

His parents brought him to the National Thalassaemic Centre for his monthly transfusion—a painful ordeal, but the only way to keep him alive. The sole cure for the disease was bone marrow transplant, which cost fifteen to sixteen lakh rupees. Most Maldivians could not afford this princely sum. Hussain dreaded the monthly visits. He had to be literally dragged to the centre. While he lay on the bed, awaiting the transfusion, he wailed and clutched his mother, tense as a coiled spring. Every time a nurse walked past his room, his terror rose. He screamed and clung tighter to his anguished mother.

Hussain was obsessed with death. He assailed his mother with questions—What happened to people when they died? Where did they go? Would she go with him when he died? How often could he see her if he died? Why did some people die young and some old? Would he have to continue with these blood transfusions even after he died? Endless questions that pierced her heart like rusty, serrated knives.

Hussain pleaded to go home. Then he asked his mother, 'If I don't take the blood, will I die?' Tears rolled down his mother's ravaged face. She averted her face and hugged her son tightly to her chest. Though only four years old, he was already trapped in the process of weighing his options. What was better, easier? Dying, or living a life of painful transfusions? Mothers around the world grumble when their children ask them questions like, can I have another cookie? Can I do my homework later? Can I buy that new toy? Can I play for an extra hour? They are lucky they don't have to answer the kind of life-and-death questions Hussain's agonized mother was faced with, day after day. Questions that would end only when he died on her.

Children can sometimes be the source of such sorrow to their parents. Harjot was a beautiful Sikh child. He was so adorable and healthy that he won two baby competitions. His first and second birthdays were celebrated as if they were once-in-a-lifetime family occasions. Every move, every step, was videotaped by his doting parents.

Sometime after his second birthday, Harjot came down with a none too serious infection. He was taken to a well-known hospital in New Delhi. He went in a plump, healthy child and came out a vegetable. His nurse had administered a wrong injection. The two-year-old went into cardiac arrest. By the time he was revived, he had suffered permanent brain damage. He could neither walk nor talk. He was still a beautiful child, but utterly helpless. His mother gave up her career to look after him, and his father fought legal battles. After four years, they won a court-decreed compensation from the hospital for fifteen lakh rupees. It was not even sufficient to meet Harjot's medical expenses.

Harjot was six years old when his father won the court case. He was still a heartbreakingly lovely child, but he could not walk or talk. He could be fed only liquid and semi-solid food. For no known reason, he cried—constantly, as if in pain. It drove his mother to distraction. She said, 'I feel so helpless. I don't know what he wants. I don't know if he needs something, if he is in pain. I can't distract him with a toy. How can I make him stop crying? I have tried everything. But he just cries. I don't know if I can cope with this much longer.'

There was no discernible pattern to Harjot's crying. It was not as though he cried when there was some change— if someone walked into the room, switched on the light or drew the curtains. He just lay in bed and rolled his eyes. Then, as if someone had suddenly stuck a pin into him or as if he had remembered something terribly painful, he let out a wail—loud and sharp. After a few moments, his sobs would subside to a piteous cry. It was almost as if the mere remembrance of a past hurt induced a fresh, sharp twist of physical pain.

This is not unusual in children. Six-year-old Ranjan also cried a lot, sometimes for two or three hours at a stretch. A year and a half ago, she had been raped by a middle-aged man. How can one even begin to imagine the trauma of a four-year-old child being sexually attacked? Her mother said she was bleeding profusely when she was discovered. The rapist had also slashed her all over the body.

Omwati's four-year-old daughter Anu was also raped. Omwati recalled, 'Anu said a man took her, tried to strangle her. He beat her up and threatened to kill her if she screamed.'

The two children responded differently to their trauma. Anu became stubborn and aggressive. She beat up other children and refused to listen to anyone. Ranjan turned into an introverted, frightened child, who had problems sleeping at night. She suffered from terrible nightmares and spent much of the day crying.

Both Anu and Ranjan live in New Delhi, where 300 children are raped every year. Some of them are as young as a year and a half. Many more are sexually abused, often by their uncles, cousins, brothers and even fathers. The crime draws a ten-year jail term, but shame and fear of public disgrace still prevent families from going to the police.

Trauma makes children cry in ways we cannot fully fathom. There was a one-year-old baby in a Sri Lankan war orphanage who cried incessantly. If anyone went near to comfort her, she would shriek louder. Her body language expressed sheer terror. She tightened herself into a ball like a frightened little armadillo, clenching her fists and shutting her eyes tightly, as if trying to squeeze out the image of the intruder. Only one woman attendant could pacify her. When lifted out of the cradle by this woman, the baby girl clutched her as if she would never let go. Slowly her sobs would subside. When she fell asleep exhausted, the attendant would lay her down gently in the baby cot, but the process, however slowly or gently executed, would wake her up, and she would start crying again. It was impossible for the woman to administer to this child alone, so she went on with her duties, leaving the baby to her tears. According to her, the child slept fitfully, often awakened by her own sobs. What trauma had this little baby seen that the face of any stranger filled her with such abject terror, that her every waking moment was spent crying?

More than 65,000 Sri Lankans have died in nearly two decades of a brutal civil war that has scarred and brutalized the nation. It is a land of war orphans. A few of them found refuge in an orphanage for war babies run by a Buddhist monk called Vajira Sri Thero on the outskirts of Colombo. He started the orphanage in 1983 and since then has provided home, shelter, comfort and education to 1400 war orphans. What is truly remarkable is that he has opened his heart and his orphanage to both Sinhalese and Tamil babies.

Kumari, a Sinhalese girl, grew up in this orphanage. A few years ago, she returned home from school to find her parents and two brothers shot dead by the LTTE. Vallinayakam, a Tamil girl, was her friend in the orphanage. Vallinayakam's entire family—parents, four brothers and a sister—were massacred by Tamil guerrillas because they had helped the Sinhalese. Jagan, a young Tamil boy, was returning home from play one afternoon when he heard his mother scream—'Run, the soldiers are firing.' He did, and survived, but his parents and sister were killed in the shoot-out between Sri Lankan soldiers and Tamil rebels.

The orphanage survived on donations, but it was a constant struggle to make ends meet. There were about 400 Tamil and Sinhalese children of varying ages. They spent ten to fifteen years in the orphanage and left when they secured jobs or got married.

The orphans smiled, played and studied with the innocence of youth, but teachers said most of them had psychological disorders that surfaced in the lonesome terrors of the night. Bed-wetting was common, and they suffered nightmares. Sinhalese children cried out in terror that the Tigers were upon them, while Tamil children screamed that the soldiers were attacking them. They cried out often for their dead mothers.

Conflict, poverty and perversion make life hell for millions of children. Yet, the absence of this is also no guarantee for a stress-free life. Jobs are few, driving parents, especially in India, to force their children to study all the time and get good grades. For these children, there are no picnics, no music lessons, no chasing chickens in the farmyard. Asked to identify the high point of his childhood, fifteen-year-old Ashish retorted: 'What childhood? I don't know what that means. All I can remember is that even when mummy would take me for a walk to the market, she would be reciting the 14-times table with me.' By the time they finish school, these children have carried books that weigh as much as one truck on their backs.

The first thing children learn is failure. And increasingly they lack the emotional strength, the safety valves and the shock absorbers in the form of hobbies and a supportive network of relatives and friends to cope with failure. So they react radically—some even take the extreme step of attempting suicide for failing an exam.

Then there are children who prefer death to the terror of facing an exam. Jonathan Williams was fourteen years old when he preferred to avoid taking an exam by jumping off the fourth floor of his school. He didn't die. He twisted his pelvis, broke five vertebrae and nine teeth.

But education is an absolute necessity in India, where opportunities are limited even for the educated. Increasingly, poor parents are beginning to see education as the only way out of poverty. There are millions of parents and children who voluntarily opt for a life of back-breaking hard work in search of that magic dream of a good education.

Abdul Majid was a very poor Kashmiri and his only hope lay in educating his son, Mohammad Yasin, at any cost.

But he had not expected the price to be so high.

There was no proper school in his village, so thirteen-year-old Yasin had to move to Jammu to enrol in a decent school. But this meant coping with a burst of expenditure—room rent, school fees, textbooks. So Majid arranged to have his son help with domestic work at his landlord's house. Said Yasin, 'I agreed to work in Niaz's house because I wanted to lighten my father's burden.'

But his own burden increased to unendurable limits. He had to get up early in the morning to wash all the dishes, make tea and breakfast for everyone in the landlord's home before he could run to school. When he returned, he had to wash clothes, clean the house, prepare dinner. All this left him with little time to do his homework.

One day, the landlord ordered him to whitewash the house, all eight rooms. It would save him a lot of money. But it cost Yasin his leg. He had to balance himself on the ledge of the second-floor window to paint the outer wall. He slipped and fell. It hurt, but there was no outward injury. So the family ordered him to carry on with his household chores. His leg began to hurt and swell. They told him not to fuss. No doctor was brought in, and septicaemia set in. When they eventually took him to the hospital a fortnight later, it was too late.

Yasin's leg had to be amputated.

His spirit was broken, his leg was gone, but Yasin was at least able to pursue his dream. But there are many in Kashmir who have no means of leaving their insurgency-stricken valley. A whole decade has gone by, with children yearning in vain to do the normal thing of going to school. They cannot learn their alphabet because schools are closed for weeks on end, shut down by endless curfews, bomb explosions and general strikes. Closeted in their dingy homes, they grow up learning the Alphabet of Life in a battle zone: A for Army, B for Bomb, C for Curfew, D for Death...

EPILOGUE

Sometimes I wonder if there is anything I haven't seen in my professional life: children with legs blown off, mangled bodies, severed heads, burning flesh, machetes dripping with human blood. I have seen countless dead bodies—carts full of them while covering riots in the remote Indian countryside, hospitals full of them after earthquakes, villages full of them in the aftermath of cyclones.

All through, I maintained my calm, always the determined Ms Professional, journeying to inaccessible areas, reporting, taking notes, dredging details and information that no one else could, faithfully telling the world what I'd seen and heard, competing to be the first to break the news, seeking to be fair and present all points of view, but above all striving to humanize the conflict so that my readers and viewers would *feel* and not merely intellectualize the experience of wars and catastrophes.

While reporting these tragic events, there were times when I felt faint, felt ill. But succumbing would have meant missing the deadline. After the deadline had been met, sometimes sickness would take its toll, like the trembling that refused to stop for three days after the July 1983 assignment to Sri Lanka, or the 103° fever that raged for a full fortnight after the Kandy trip when I saw the 'necklaced' young men, their skin charred, their blood staining their homeland red.

Constant exposure to extraordinary events has its side-effects. Along the way, I accumulated sediments that became my personal baggage, developing an irrational but nonetheless deep-seated aversion to harmless things like white flowers and yellow eyes. Sometimes, for no reason, I would be startled by a gleam or a smile.

Yet, I survived, maintaining my sanity, perhaps even my innocence, by learning to celebrate the ordinary. Governments fell, wars were fought, airplanes collided in mid-air, nuclear bombs exploded, scams wiped out middle-class savings, political leaders were assassinated, cyclones devastated coastal villages, earthquakes ravaged cities, but in my personal life I stuck to the straight and simple path, keeping my head on my shoulders by enjoying the ordinary pleasures of life: reading bed-time stories to Zubin, going out for picnics, walking in the woods, holidaying with family, listening to music, cracking jokes, philosophizing and solving India's unsolvable problems with friends...till the next bomb exploded.

I learned to appreciate and enjoy the ordinary pleasures that the world takes for granted, which in fact often bore and frustrate most people. But I have always been grateful for these. They recharge my spirit, they give meaning to my life, they help me respond to new situations with curiosity and delight.

Like the joy I experienced when I saw my first snowfall. I marvelled at the cosmic dance of the little white flakes as they floated down, ever so gracefully, ever so gently, ever so silently. I was forty-one.

I had reported from both sides of the highest battleground in the world, from 18,000 feet on Siachen Glacier in the Himalayas where Indian and Pakistani armies have been waging war since 1984, but I had never seen snowfall. In tropical Kerala, the only things that fall from the sky are rain and coconuts.

I learned to value ordinary pleasures because every

assignment helped me to realize how treacherous life can be, how unpredictable and vulnerable, how devastating.

Like when bombs exploded in a shopping area in Delhi in May 1996. I was watching a film in a theatre after a gap of ten years. Suddenly my cellphone started ringing. I went out and one of my informants told me a bomb had just exploded in Lajpat Nagar, in central Delhi.

End of movie.

I drove at breakneck speed to the bomb site. It was a ghastly scene: tongues of flames leaping out of buildings like evil dragons; twisted steel and mortar; mutilated human beings—some dead, some dying—screaming in torment. Disembodied but terrified voices of victims trapped under the debris, pleading for help. Police and firemen yelling instructions, ordering bystanders to keep away.

You wanted to shut off your senses—block your nostrils to keep out the acrid smell of burning human flesh, seal your ears to the screams of agony, close your eyes to the scene of pain and destruction. But even when smoke stung your eyes, you struggled to keep them open, the journalist in you absorbing and reporting live, the sights and sounds of tragedy.

'Oh God, why did we come out shopping today? I should have listened to you and come tomorrow. Then you would be alive. Oh, how can I live after this, Pinky,' sobbed a middle-aged woman in Hindi, beating her chest in an agony of sorrow and guilt.

Her daughter was a mangled mess of flesh and bone. Charred shopping bags lay nearby. Minutes earlier, she had been a beautiful bride-to-be: fair, long-haired, wide-eyed and rosy-cheeked, on the threshold of womanhood. Her mother had been in a hurry to finish shopping for her trousseau.

You wonder, how *can* she lead a normal life again? How

can her trauma ever heal?

And you experience a burning sense of shame, shame at your worries, your vexations and preoccupations. So silly, so trivial, so meaningless. How annoyed I'd been to have my movie expedition cut short so abruptly. 'Can't I enjoy a movie at least once in a decade?' I had raged to my friend after receiving the phone call. 'Am I not entitled to even one evening of peace? Can't I enjoy one of the simplest pleasures of life that everyone around me enjoys every other day? Why, why why?' I had ranted in grief.

Grief! What right did I have to use the word when here I was watching the sorrow of a mother holding up bits and pieces of what had once been her daughter? I could so easily have been that girl staring sightlessly at my mother's distress. I could so easily have been the distraught mother holding a mangled Zubin. And for all my so-called toughness, I don't think I would be able to handle such grief. I watched the woman and marvelled at her ability to stay alive in the throes of such anguish. And I thanked God for sparing me such agony.

I have to thank journalism for putting my life into perspective, for making me treasure the ordinariness of my personal life. I am glad I am alive and so are my loved ones—that's good enough for me. Most people realize the value of their relationships only after they are over. By then it's too late. They repent, and they mourn, but they don't have it any more and in all likelihood will never have it again.

That's Life. But it needn't be, if you realize how brutal and sudden and all-changing Death can be. It needn't be, if you realize how precious the gift of Life is; how important it is to safeguard it, to nurture, value and enjoy the giving and the receiving of it.

Like treasuring the moment when your child is born.